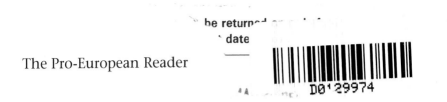

be returned ⌐ ⌐ ⌐ ⌐
date

The Pro-European Reader

D0129974

# The Pro-European Reader

Edited by

Dick Leonard

and

Mark Leonard

in association with the Foreign Policy Centre

First published 2002 by
PALGRAVE
Houndmills, Basingstoke, Hampshire RG21 6XS and
175 Fifth Avenue, New York, N.Y. 10010
Companies and representatives throughout the world

PALGRAVE is the new global academic imprint of
St Martin's Press LLC Scholarly and Reference Division and
Palgrave Publishers Ltd (formerly Macmillan Press Ltd).

ISBN 0–333–77889–8 hardback
ISBN 0–333–97721–1 paperback

This book is printed on paper suitable for recycling and made from fully managed and sustained forest sources.

A catalogue record for this book is available from the British Library.

Library of Congress Cataloging-in-Publication Data
The pro-European reader / edited by Dick Leonard and Mark Leonard.
    p. cm.
  Includes bibliographical references and index.
  ISBN 0–333–77889–8
  1. European federation. 2. European Union. I. Leonard, R. L.
(Richard Lawrence) II. Leonard, Mark, 1974–

JN15 .P73 2001
341.24'2—dc21
                                                        2001036894

10   9   8   7   6   5   4   3   2   1
11   10  09  08  07  06  05  04  03  02

Printed and bound in Great Britain by
Antony Rowe Ltd, Chippenham, Wiltshire

*For Irène and Miriam*

# Contents

**Part IV    Beyond Politics: The Everyday Case for Europe**

# Notes on Contributors and Editors

**Yasmin Alibhai-Brown**: Senior Researcher at the Foreign Policy Centre. She has a weekly column in the *Independent*, and also writes for the *Guardian*, the *Observer* and many other newspapers and also broadcasts regularly on Radio 4 and the World Service. Her most recent book is *Who Do We Think We Are? Imagining the New Britain*. Her previous books include *The Colour of Love, True Colours* and her autobiography *No Place Like Home*.

**Tony Blair**: British Prime Minister since 1997. A barrister, educated at Oxford, he has been Labour MP for Sedgefield since 1983. Was a member of the Shadow Cabinet between 1988 and 1997, and Leader of the Opposition between 1994 and 1997. Awarded the Charlemagne Prize, previously held by both Heath and Jenkins, in 1999.

**Winston Churchill** (1874–1965): Former British Prime Minister (1940–45, 1951–55), Cabinet Minister (including Chancellor, Home Secretary, First Lord of the Admiralty and War Secretary), and Leader of the Opposition, 1945–51. Took the lead in forming the European Movement after the Second World War. Knighted in 1953. Nobel Laureate for Literature in 1953; author of 43 works including *The Second World War* and *A History of the English-Speaking Peoples*.

**Linda Colley**: Professor of History at the European Institute, London School of Economics. Formerly Richard M. Colgate Professor of History at Yale University and the first female lecturer and Fellow at Christ's College, Cambridge. Also the first woman to deliver the Trevelyan Lectures at Cambridge. Her published works include *Britons: Forging the Nation 1707–1837, In Defence of Oligarchy* and *Namier*.

**Robert Cooper**: Deputy Secretary of the Defence and Overseas Secretariat in the British Cabinet Office. Author of the Foreign Policy Centre and Demos pamphlet *The Postmodern State and the World Order*.

**Anthony Crosland** (1918–77): Leading Socialist intellectual in post-war Britain and author of the vastly influential *The Future of Socialism* (1956). MP for South Gloucestershire, 1950–55 and Grimsby, 1959–77. Held senior Cabinet posts in the Wilson and Callaghan governments, including

Education Secretary, President of the Board of Trade, Environment Secretary, and finally, Foreign Secretary before his early death.

**Jacques Delors**: President of European Commission (1985–95). Formerly involved in banking and state planning, then French economics and finance minister (1981–83) and economics, finance, and budget minister (1983–84). His achievements at the Commission included the adoption of the Single European Act (1986), which laid the groundwork for the creation of a single EC market in 1993, the preparation for Economic and Monetary Union with a single currency and putting the budget of the European Union on a proper long-term basis by the adoption of five- or seven-yearly financial perspectives.

**Philip Dodd**: Director of the Institute of Contemporary Arts (ICA). Formerly a university academic in literature, Deputy Editor of *New Statesman*, and Editor of *Sight and Sound*, he also has extensive broadcasting experience. His publications include *Englishness: Politics and Culture 1880–1920* (1986) and, more recently, *The Battle Over Britain*, and numerous catalogues for art and photography shows. He co-curated *Spellbound: Art and Film* at the Hayward Gallery, 1995.

**Anthony Giddens**: Director of the London School of Economics and Political Science since 1977, previously Professor of Sociology and a Fellow of King's College, Cambridge. Author of 34 books published in over 30 languages, and numerous articles and reviews. His textbook *Sociology* has sold over 600 000 copies and is the standard introductory text in universities and colleges in many different countries. His 1999 Reith Lectures were subsequently published under the title *Runaway World*. He has also been at the forefront of developing ideas in left-of-centre politics and has helped to popularize the idea of the 'third way'.

**Mikhail Gorbachev**: Soviet political leader, and last president of the USSR (1988–91). Elected to the Communist Party's central committee in 1971 and became a full member of the Politburo in 1980. Succeeded Chernenko as general secretary of the Communist Party in 1985; was elected President of the USSR in 1988 and to a new, more powerful presidency in 1989. Introduced policies whose guiding principles *glasnost* [openness] and *perestroika* [restructuring] were intended to liberalize and revitalize Soviet socialism and society. Awarded the Nobel Peace Prize in 1990. In 1993 he became head of the International Green Cross.

**Charles Grant**: Director of the Centre for European Reform, which he helped to set up in 1996. Formerly a journalist on *Euromoney* and *The*

*Economist*, for which he was Brussels correspondent and later Defence Editor. Author, with David Goodhart, of the Fabian pamphlet, 'Making the City work'. He is the author of *Delors: The House that Jacques built*, and of several CER publications including 'Strength in Numbers: European Foreign and Defence Policy', 'Can Britain Lead in Europe?' and 'Europe 2010: an Optimistic Sketch of the Future'.

**Peter Hall**: Sir Peter Hall is Professor of Planning at the Bartlett School of Architecture and Planning, University College London. From 1991 to 1994 he was Special Adviser on Strategic Planning to the Secretary of State for the Environment and was also a member of the Deputy Prime Minister's Urban Task Force (1998–99). He has received the Founder's Medal of the Royal Geographical Society for distinction in research, and is an honorary member of the Royal Town Planning Institute. He is a Fellow of the British Academy. He was a founder member of the Regional Studies Association and first editor of its journal *Regional Studies*. He was Chairman of the Town and Country Planning Association (1995–99). Sir Peter Hall is author or editor of nearly thirty books on urban and regional planning and related topics, including *London 2000* and *The World Cities*.

**Roy Hattersley**: Labour MP for Birmingham Sparkbrook 1964–97, when he became a life peer. Deputy Leader of the Labour Party, 1983–92, he was a Cabinet minister in the Callaghan government from 1976 to 1979, and previously served as a junior minister in the employment and defence ministries and in the Foreign Office. A strongly committed European, he is a prolific writer, contributing to many newspapers and is a columnist for the *Guardian*. He also writes both fiction and non-fiction, and has written and presented television programmes for the BBC and GMTV.

**Václav Havel**: Czech playwright, President of Czechoslovakia (1989–92) and the Czech Republic (1993–). His experimental, absurdist plays attacking totalitarianism became popular in Prague and abroad but were suppressed after the Soviet invasion in 1968. Havel became a prominent dissident and was arrested several times and imprisoned twice. He was the principal spokesman for the Civic Forum, an opposition group, when it succeeded in forcing (1989) the Communist Party to share power, and he became interim president of Czechoslovakia before the separation of 1992.

**Edward Heath**: British Prime Minister from 1970 to 1974 and Leader of the Conservative Party from 1965 to 1975. Studied PPE at Oxford and fought in the Second World War. Worked in the Civil Service, banking and journalism before becoming MP for Bexley in 1950. In 1959 he became Minister of Labour and in 1960 Lord Privy Seal, speaking for the government on foreign affairs. He was in charge of Britain's first application to join the European Community and received the Charlemagne Prize for encouraging international co-operation. In 1963 he was appointed Secretary of State for Industry, Trade and Development and President of the Board of Trade. Became the first elected Leader of the Conservative Party while in Opposition in 1965, and Prime Minister in 1970. In 1971, he signed the Treaty of Accession to the European Community, having successfully negotiated the terms of entry in the previous year. In 1974 he was successfully challenged for the Conservative Party leadership by Margaret Thatcher following Tory defeats in the two general elections of that year, but continued to sit in the House of Commons, becoming 'Father of the House' in 1997, and completing 50 years' membership in 2000. Was knighted in 1992.

**Michael Heseltine**: British politician. Studied law at Oxford and worked in publishing before entering the House of Commons as a Conservative in 1966. Held junior posts in the Heath government and under Margaret Thatcher, served as Secretary for the Environment (1979–83) and then Secretary for Defence in 1983, resigning in protest over his treatment in the 1986 Westland helicopter affair. Initiated a challenge to Thatcher's leadership in 1990, after which he became Environment Secretary again under John Major. In 1992 he became President of the Board of Trade and Secretary for Trade and Industry. From 1995 to 1997 he was Deputy Prime Minister. He did not contest the 2001 parliamentary election, but remains a leading figure in the Britain in Europe movement.

**Geoffrey Howe**: Former Conservative Deputy Prime Minister under Margaret Thatcher between 1989 and 1990. Worked as a barrister before serving in the House of Commons between 1964 and 1966, and 1970 and 1992. Was Solicitor General (1970–72) and Minister of State for Trade and Commercial Affairs (1972–74). Later became Chancellor of the Exchequer (1979–83) and Foreign Secretary (1983–89). His resignation in 1990 triggered the challenge to Margaret Thatcher, which resulted in her replacement by John Major. Became a life peer, as Lord Howe of Aberavon, in 1997.

**Roy Jenkins**: With Edward Heath, has been the outstanding British exponent of membership of the European Union. First elected as a Labour MP in 1948, he became a close supporter of Labour leader Hugh Gaitskell, but dramatically opposed him at the 1962 Labour conference when he rejected the terms of Britain's first application to join the EEC. In the first Wilson government of 1964–70, he was Minister of Aviation, Home

Secretary and Chancellor of the Exchequer, and was elected as Labour's deputy leader after the 1970 election. In 1971 he led 69 Labour MPs to vote against the party whip in favour of the EEC membership terms negotiated by Heath. He was subsequently again Home Secretary in 1974–76, when he became President of the European Commission, leaving in 1981 to co-found the Social Democratic Party, of which he became the first leader and MP for Glasgow Hillhead from 1982 to 1987, when he became a life peer as Lord Jenkins of Hillhead. He subsequently became Chancellor of Oxford University, leader of the Liberal Democrat peers and chairman of the Independent Commission on the Voting System. His many books include highly regarded biographies of Sir Charles Dilke, Asquith and Gladstone.

**Charles Kennedy**: Leader of the Liberal Democrat Party. Kennedy worked as a journalist and broadcaster with BBC Highland in Inverness and was then awarded a Fulbright Scholarship to attend Indiana University in the United States where he taught public speaking and carried out graduate research in speech communication, political rhetoric and British politics. Was elected SDP MP for Ross, Cromarty & Skye in 1983. He served as a spokesman on a range of welfare state issues and after the merger with the Liberals was elected UK Party President, and re-elected for a second term in 1992. He has also served as the party spokesman on European affairs and was elected to succeed Paddy Ashdown as Liberal Democrat leader in August 1999.

**John F. Kennedy**: President of the United States from January 1961 to November 1963.

**Neil Kinnock**: Deputy President of the European Commission and Commissioner for Administrative Reform. Joined the Commission in 1995 and served as Commissioner for Transport between 1995 and 1999. Previously MP for Islwyn (1970–94), and leader of the British Labour Party (1983–92). Originally an opponent of British membership of the EEC, he gradually shifted his position, and eased the party back into a more co-operative stance during his years as party leader. Neil Kinnock is also the current Vice-President of Socialist International.

**Milan Kundera**: Celebrated Czech writer. His first novel, *The Joke*, is about a student whose joking reference to Trotsky earns him a sentence of hard labour. It brought Kundera into official disfavour in Prague and resulted in the loss of his citizenship. He moved to France and became a French citizen in 1980. He has also written poems, plays, short stories, and other novels, including *The Book of Laughter and Forgetting*, *The Unbearable Lightness of Being* and *Immortality*.

**Simon Kuper**: Uganda-born and Oxford-educated Dutch sports journalist for the *Observer* and the *Financial Times*. Author of *Football Against the Enemy*, he is a regular columnist who also edits the football compilation *Perfect Pitch*.

**John Mackintosh**: A Labour MP for Berwick and East Lothian from 1966 to 1978, apart from a short break between the general elections of February and October 1974. Was probably the most effective speaker on the pro-European side among the Labour backbenchers. He was Professor of Politics at both the University of Strathclyde and the University of Edinburgh, a renowned international lecturer, and the author of many books and other written works. As an early exponent of devolution, John Mackintosh was also a leading voice for many years in the campaign for a Scottish Parliament.

**Harold Macmillan** (1894–1986): British Prime Minister between 1957 and 1963. First elected to Parliament in 1924 as Conservative MP for Stockton. In the 1930s was a leading Tory rebel, advocating left-centre policies at home and opposing the appeasement policy of Neville Chamberlain. Was Minister for Housing (1951–54), Defence (1954–55), Foreign Secretary in 1955, and Chancellor of the Exchequer (1955–57). Became Prime Minister after the Suez fiasco, in which he had been a leading actor, and launched the first British application to join the EEC in 1961, which was vetoed by Presdient Charles de Gaulle in January 1963. He retired from the premiership in October 1963, and much later – in 1984 – was created Earl of Stockton.

**John Major**: British Prime Minister, 1990–97. Formerly a banking executive with Standard Chartered Bank and a local councillor before being elected as the Conservative MP for Huntingdon in 1979. Joined the Cabinet in 1985 where his posts included Chief Secretary to the Treasury, Foreign Secretary and Chancellor of the Exchequer. As Prime Minister signed the Treaty of Maastricht in December 1991, having negotiated two important opt-outs for Britain, but the remainder of his premiership was dogged by constant sniping from Eurosceptics in his own party which drove him into an increasingly anti-European stance and largely contributed to the overwhelming Tory defeat in the 1997 general election.

**Jean Monnet** (1888–1979): Father figure of the movement for European integration, Monnet was the author of the Schuman Plan, which led to the establishment in 1952 of the European Coal and Steel Community. Started life as a brandy salesman, but came to prominence as the co-ordinator of British and French munitions supplies during the First World War, a role he repeated in the Second World War, when he was the main originator of Churchill's dramatic appeal for Anglo-French union in 1940. Deputy Secretary General of the League of Nations in 1919–23, he subsequently became a banker. In post-war France he was the Director of the National Plan for economic revival and was responsible for French participation in the Marshall Plan. He was the first President of the ECSC in 1952–55, and subsequently devoted himself to campaigning for ever closer European unity.

**George Orwell** (1903–50): British novelist, journalist and satirist, born Eric Arthur Blair in 1903. Achieved prominence in the late 1940s as the author of two brilliant satires attacking totalitarianism. After an Eton education, Orwell joined the Indian Imperial Police in Burma in 1922. His first book, *Down and Out in Paris and London*, was published in 1933. Other major works followed including *The Road to Wigan Pier*, *Homage to Catalonia*, *Animal Farm* and *Nineteen Eighty-Four*. He also fought in the Spanish Civil War and worked for the BBC during the Second World War. Orwell was also famous as an essayist, 'Politics and the English Language' (1950) being the most important of many journalistic pieces he wrote.

**Romano Prodi**: Current President of the European Commission. Romano Prodi is an industrial economist and university professor who only became a full-time politician in 1995, having formerly been Professor of Economics at Bologna University. He was Italian Prime Minister between 1996 and 1998: Italy's second-longest serving government since the Second World War, and notable for the progress it made on reducing Italy's debts and trade deficit in order to enable entry into the single currency.

**David Puttnam**: Director of Enigma Productions. Lord Puttnam has produced many films including *Chariots of Fire, Local Hero, The Killing Fields* and *Midnight Express*. His productions have won Academy Awards, Emmy Awards and Golden Globes. Lord Puttnam began in advertising before co-founding the VPS/Goodtimes Production Company. Other interests have involved being Chairman of Britain's National Film and Television School, and a director of the National Film Finance Corporation. Lord Puttnam is a Visiting Professor at Bristol University where he lectures on film and television, and is a trustee of the National Energy Foundation and the National Aids Trust. In 1982 the British Academy presented him with its prestigious Michael Balcon Award for his outstanding contribution to the British Film Industry and later that year he was made a Commander of the British Empire. From 1985 until 1992, Puttnam was President of the Council for the Protection of Rural England and, during that same period, a Trustee of the Tate Gallery.

**Helmut Schmidt**: Chancellor of the Federal Republic of Germany between 1974 and 1982. Schmidt started out in local administration in the State of Hamburg before becoming a Bundestag Member in 1953. He served as Chairman of the Social Democratic Party (SPD) faction there between 1967 and 1969, and was Vice-Chairman of the SPD between 1968 and 1984. Ministerial posts included: Senator (Minister) for Domestic Affairs in Hamburg (1961–65), Minister of Defence (1969–72), and Minister for Finance (1972–74). Since October 1985, he has served as Publisher of *Die Zeit*.

**Robert Schuman** (1886–1963): French statesman. Finance minister (1946, 1947), Prime Minister (1947–48), and Foreign Minister (1948–53) in the Fourth Republic. The Schuman Plan led to the formation in 1952 of the European Coal and Steel Community, the first step in the creation of the European Union.

**Robert Skidelsky**: Professor Lord Robert Skidelsky is an economic historian and much acclaimed biographer of John Maynard Keynes. He has written and lectured extensively on post-collectivization, Thatcherism and the welfare state, and Eastern Europe. He is Professor of Political Economy at Warwick University, Chairman of the Social Market Foundation, an economic think-tank, and was formerly an Opposition spokesman on the Treasury. Lord Skidelsky's books include *Keynes* and *The World After Communism,* also published as *The Road From Serfdom*.

**Margaret Thatcher**: Baroness Thatcher of Kesteven was the first female British Prime Minister, holding office between 1979 and 1990, the longest serving Prime Minister in the twentieth century. She was educated at Oxford and worked as a research chemist and barrister before becoming Conservative MP for Finchley in 1953. She served as Education Minister between 1970 and 1974, when she successfully challenged Edward Heath for the party leadership and became leader of the Opposition until the general election of 1979. Thatcher supported British membership of the EEC, and as Prime Minister played a leading role in developing closer European integration, particularly the passage of the European Single Act in 1985. She subsequently became more critical, and, particularly after she ceased to be Prime Minister, adopted an increasingly Eurosceptical approach.

**Simone Veil**: First President of the European Parliament (1979–82) and Vice-President thereafter. Also past President of the European Parliament Judicial Commission. Survivor of Auschwitz and Bergen-Belsen, a former lawyer and French Minister of Health. Appointed French Minister of Housing, Urban and Social Affairs in 1993.

**Harold Wilson (1916–95)**: British Prime Minister between 1964 and 1970, and between 1974 and 1976. Studied as an economist and was a civil servant during the Second World War. He entered Parliament in 1945 and became President of the Board of Trade (1947–51). Resigning, with Aneurin Bevan in 1951, in protest against charges in the National Health Service, he became Labour Party leader and Opposition leader in 1963 and Prime Minister in 1964. He lost the 1970 election to Heath, but won again in 1974. He resigned in 1976 and was knighted. He became a life peer in 1983. Wilson's attitude to Europe was highly inconsistent; he was hostile to the first British membership application in 1961–63, but launched the second application in 1967 and set up the third try in 1970 before his election defeat. Under strong party pressure, he subsequently opposed the terms negotiated by Heath, but was instrumental in carrying through the 1975 referendum, which ensured that there would be no British withdrawal.

**Hugo Young**: Political columnist for the *Guardian* and the *Observer*. Director of the *Guardian*. Formerly at the *Sunday Times*. His books include *The Crossman Affair, One of Us: A Biography of Margaret Thatcher* and *This Blessed Plot: Britain and Europe from Churchill to Blair*. He wrote and presented the noted television series *The Last Europeans* on Channel Four.

**Jan Zielonka:** Professor of Social and Political Science at the European University Institute in Florence. Studied Law at the University of Wroclaw, and a doctorate in political science at the University of Warsaw. Associate Professor at Leiden University since 1983. He was Fellow of the Netherlands Institute for Advanced Studies in the Human and Social Sciences (NIAS, Wassenaar) in 1983/84 and 1989/90, research associate at the International Institute for Strategic Studies, London (1990/91) and Senior Associate Member at St Antony's College, Oxford (1994/95). Author of many books and articles on the politics of Eastern Europe and on Western policies towards this region, his latest book is *Explaining Euro-paralysis: Why Europe is Unable to Act in International Politics.*

## The editors

**Dick Leonard**: Labour MP for Romford 1970–74, and was one of 69 Labour MPs who voted against the party whip in favour of British membership of the European Community in 1971. Parliamentary Private Secretary to Anthony Crosland, and a former Chairman of the Fabian Society. A political writer and journalist, he has worked in Brussels since 1980, initially for *The Economist*, of which he was Assistant Editor 1974–85, and subsequently for the *Observer*, *Europe* magazine and *European Voice*. Formerly Senior Adviser to the Centre for European Policy Studies. Author or part-author of some 20 books, including *Elections in Britain*, *The Economist Guide to the European Union* (now in its seventh edition), *Eminent Europeans* and *Crosland and New Labour*.

**Mark Leonard**: Director of the Foreign Policy Centre, an independent think-tank launched by the British Prime Minister Tony Blair (Patron) and the former Foreign Secretary Robin Cook (President). Mark's reports on European legitimacy have influenced several European governments, while his report *Britain™* sparked an international debate on 'Rebranding Britain'. He writes and broadcasts extensively on British, European and International politics, for publications including the *Guardian*, *Financial Times*, the *Express*, *New Statesman*, *Management Today* and *Newsweek*, and has presented the BBC's *Analysis* programme. Mark previously worked as Senior Researcher at the think-tank Demos and as a journalist at *The Economist*. His recent publications include: *Winning the Euro Referendum* (co-editor with Tom Arbuthnott), *The Future Shape of Europe* (editor), *Going Public: Diplomacy for the Information Society*; *Network Europe: The New Case for Europe*; *Modernising the Monarchy*; *Rediscovering Europe*; *Britain™: Renewing Our Identity*; and *Politics Without Frontiers: The Role of Political Parties in Europe's Future*.

# Acknowledgements

The editors and publishers would like to thank the following for their kind permission to include copyright material:

The Council of Europe for the extracts from the speeches of Mikhail Gorbachev and Václav Havel; the European Parliament for those by Anthony Crosland, Simone Veil and Romano Prodi; the Cabinet Office (Crown Copyright) for ministerial speeches by Harold Macmillan, Harold Wilson, Margaret Thatcher and Tony Blair and parliamentary speeches by Roy Hattersley, Edward Heath and Sir Geoffrey Howe; the Labour Party for conference speeches by Roy Jenkins, John Mackintosh and Helmut Schmidt; the Trades Union Congress for that by Jacques Delors; Neil Kinnock for his speech in Berlin; Britain in Europe for the speeches by Michael Heseltine and Charles Kennedy and for reprinting the 'Yes' document from the 1975 referendum; the Centre for European Reform for the contributions by Charles Grant and Philip Dodd; the Foreign Policy Centre for those by Mark Leonard, Anthony Giddens and Jan Zielonka; Demos for that by Robert Cooper, and Hugo Young for reprinting his article which originally appeared in the *Guardian*.

Thanks are also due to the Churchill Estate, and Curtis Brown, for permission to reprint the extract from the speech by Winston Churchill; Lord Skidelsky and the Macmillan Publishing Co. for his contribution, which originally appeared in his book, *Interests and Obsessions: Selected Essays* published in 1993; Librarie Arthéme Fayard and HarperCollins for the extract from Jean Monnet's *Memoirs*, published in 1978 and Milan Kundera and Faber & Faber for his speech reprinted from *The Art of the Novel*, published in 1988. The essay by George Orwell, 'Toward European Unity' was taken from *The Collected Essays, Journalism and Letters of George Orwell, Volume 4* (Copyright © George Orwell, 1947) and appears with the permission of Bill Hamilton as the Literary Executor of the Estate of the Late Sonia Brownell Orwell, Martin Secker & Warburg Ltd and of Harcourt Brace Jovanovich Inc.

The original idea for this book came from Tim Farmiloe of Palgrave, and thanks are due to him and Alison Howson, the commissioning editor, for their warm and consistent support, and to Claire Sands who has been largely responsible for the launch. This publication would not have been possible without the help of a number of interns at the Foreign Policy Centre, notably Vidhya Alakeson, David Graham, James Smither and Ben Elton, who also compiled the index.

# Introduction:
# The Whole Case for Europe

Europe is the most explosive issue in British politics. It has divided parties, demanded enormous personal and political sacrifice, made and destroyed reputations, and dominated the front pages and news bulletins for over 40 years. This period has effectively spanned the active lives, so far, of the two editors of this volume, who are father and son, and who have each played their own modest role in the developing controversy: Dick as a founding member of the Labour Committee for Europe in the 1950s and 60s, as a Labour MP voting in favour of the EEC in defiance of a three-line whip with 68 other rebel Labour MPs in the 1970s, and as European Editor of *The Economist* and the *Observer* in the 1980s and 1990s; Mark picked up the baton in the 1990s and has tried to reframe the European legitimacy debate through his publications as head of the Europe programme at the Demos think-tank, Director of the Foreign Policy Centre, and as a member of the Executive Council of the cross-party pro-European coalition, Britain in Europe. It has to be admitted, however, that the debate so far has produced more heat than light, done more to confuse than illuminate the public, and signally failed to engage anyone beyond a small and passionately committed elite. This *Pro-European Reader* is published at a time when the political stakes in the European debate have never been higher and when the country is at a clear junction in the painful debate about its identity.

It also comes at a time when, for most people, Europe has ceased to be a cause – it has become an everyday reality that we can't imagine being without whether as citizens, consumers, tourists, businesses, or employees. Our cuisine, travelling habits, politics and culture have been transformed by our increased contact with our European neighbours – and very few people want to turn the clock back whether by dismantling the channel tunnel, cancelling package tours to Spain and Greece, ethnically cleansing our supermarket shelves, losing the 3 million jobs which depend on the Single Market, or leaving the European Union. Today Euroscepticism *is* a cause – one which incites real passions and galvanizes people into action. In some ways this is an advantage for those who believe that Britain should be an enthusiastic member of the European Union, because the increasingly shrill arguments of Eurosceptics will not appeal to the unideological and pragmatic instincts of a British public which is instinctively conservative and so unlikely to be swayed by arguments for withdrawal. But it is also a danger for pro-Europeans who have become complacent. This is what Tony Blair was attacking when he said that 'Once every generation the case for Europe needs to be made from first principles.' But the problem is not just that pro-Europeans have lost the will to fight, it is that their traditional arguments don't hit home any more.

This volume is intended as a rallying cry for pro-Europeans and brings together the most eloquent, elegant and extensive body of arguments that make the case for Europe. But as well as collecting the best expressions of the case for Europe in the past, it is intended to overcome the limitations of that debate and chart out the new territory on which the debate will be won in the future. Though we support the traditional arguments about peace, prosperity and democracy – we believe that the new agenda will be fought on different ground. If the EU is ever going to be able to lead or inspire it will be because Europe has entered our everyday lives – and we see the advantages it will bring to our futures.

The book is divided into four parts looking at the traditional political case in different periods of the debate; mapping out the future shape of Europe; and examining the positive and powerful impact of Europe on our everyday lives. Parts I and II, which consist mainly of reprinted extracts from speeches, set out the traditional political case for Europe. The general thrust remains consistent, but the emphasis gradually shifts between the three main arguments in favour of European unity: from Orwell and Churchill's visions of peace in the early post-war years, through Schuman, Monnet, Wilson and Heath's arguments for prosperity between about 1960 to 1980, to Gorbachev, Havel and Kinnock's pleas for democracy in the final two decades when the European Union increasingly became a magnet for countries formerly ruled by dictators – Greece, Spain, Portugal and subsequently the former Communist states of central and eastern Europe. The final speeches in Part Two by Blair and Prodi also show how these arguments about democracy are now focused on the EU's own structures rather than just on the countries that make it up.

Part III consists of a series of essays, mostly written specifically for this volume, carrying the political debate forward into the future and discussing what the shape of Europe should be in the twenty-first century. Part IV, which also consists mainly of original contributions, sets out the everyday case for Europe in a series of essays by distinguished writers who highlight cultural and sociological rather than political or economic factors.

## Reluctant Europeans

The speeches in Parts I and II are at times magical, hypnotic, capable of stirring hearts and minds, articulating hope and inciting actions. They are as fine as any set of speeches on any subject. But they also represent an elite debate on Europe which has failed to build a popular constituency for European integration. Collectively they suffer from key failings which have held the British debate back.

First, they reflect the fact that EU membership was not a positive decision, more a negative realization that all the practical alternatives for Britain had disappeared one after another. The first great shock to British complacency was the disastrous Suez intervention in November 1956. With both the United States and the bulk of the Commonwealth strongly opposed, the action ended in humiliating failure, and demonstrated that Britain no longer had the capacity to act as a world power, even in partnership with France, the other formerly great colonial power. The French were rather quicker to draw the consequences from this devastating setback, signing the Treaty of Rome four months later, and subsequently the Franco-German Treaty in January 1963. In Britain, Harold Macmillan – whose inglorious role in the Suez affair led to him being characterized as 'first in, first out' – responded by promoting the European Free Trade Association (EFTA), essentially as a spoiling tactic, and it was only when it became apparent that this would not do the trick that he became convinced that Britain should seek full membership of the EEC. His 1961 speech in this volume marks the turning point. This approach of dithering on the sidelines and signing up at the last minute became characteristic of British involvement. The price of missed chances and foot-dragging has been high as several contributors to this volume, including Roy Jenkins, John Mackintosh and Edward Heath, at different stages in the process, have emphasized. Because we have never been in at the beginning, we have never been able to draw up the rules – whether of the EU's budget, the Common Agricultural Policy, the European Monetary System, the Exchange Rate Mechanism, or even the euro. This history of half-hearted engagement has also stopped pro-Europeans from making their case on its merits.[1] They are often tempted to cite a list of missed opportunities from Messina to Schengen as a reason for participating in the future (we missed out then and we will again unless we sign up now). But unless they set out a positive case for each individual step they will lose the argument – because the public are more likely to be swayed by fear of the unknown than by fear of missing out.

## Political football

Secondly, these speeches reflect the way that the European issue was never decided on its merits – it became a ping-pong both *between* the two major political parties and *within* them as different groups seized on the issue to support their campaigns to maximize their power and influence.

Macmillan created a precedent for political bickering by making the first British application to the European Community a party-political issue.[2] It is possible that Gaitskell, who was believed at the time to be 'privately a cautious supporter of entry'[3] might not have responded to an approach by Macmillan for bipartisanship, but at the very least he would have been much less likely to have come down so passionately against at the end of the day.

Europe became a totemic issue within the two parties because it pitted important parts of their traditions against each other – threatening to destroy the bargains that had held these two broad churches together. The Tory Party had always been based on an uneasy coalition between preserving the nation(tradition) and promoting the interests of capital (big business). The European issue ripped these two traditions apart. Support for Europe was promoted by Macmillan, Edward Heath and Margaret Thatcher on economic grounds. The speeches of the first two (included in this volume) at different stages in British applications to join are powerful, but it is worth remembering that it was not until she lost the premiership that Margaret Thatcher became viscerally opposed to the EU. She played an important part in the Yes campaign in the 1975 referendum, presided over the most important phase of European integration with the signature of the Single European Act, and made powerful speeches in favour of the EU. Her famous Bruges speech became the standard for Eurosceptics because of some short passages attacking the European Commission, but the rest of the speech remains one of the most powerful, emotive and passionate expressions of Britain's European destiny. It is for that reason that we have reclaimed it for the pro-European cause and included an extract from it in this volume. Margaret Thatcher's personal schizophrenia on the European issue is a powerful metaphor for her party's deep divisions on it. The stridently nationalistic rhetoric of her various conflicts with her European partners struck a chord among the Conservative rank-and-file and among many Tory MPs as well as provoking Geoffrey Howe's powerful attempt to turn the tide (reproduced on pages 108–12) which triggered the Iron Lady's final downfall. John Major failed to make real his pledge in his speech in this volume to put Britain 'at the heart of Europe', because of the 'protracted agony', to which he was submitted by the growing number of Eurosceptics in his party.[4] It is unlikely that the two wings of Toryism will be brought back together before an irrevocable decision about British membership of the single currency has been made.

The Labour Party has been equally divided. Gaitskell's stand against the EU led respectability to forces particularly on the left-wing who were opposed to the EU. The party had always been an alliance between European-style social democrats and quasi-Marxist opponents of capitalism. The European issue played up this split and meant that the majority was hostile to the European Community for most of the time between 1962 and the mid-1980s, when Neil Kinnock, a former anti-marketeer coaxed the party into accepting a more positive stance. It wasn't until the mainstream of the Labour Party had unequivocally made its peace with capitalism (deciding to tame it rather than defeat it); and that the EU under the leadership of Jacques Delors committed itself to social protection, that this conflict was resolved. His now famous speech to the TUC Conference in 1988 (included in this volume) showed that European integration could be part of a progressive political programme. This was followed by Kinnock's brave speech in 1989 which cleared the way for growing enthusiasm under his successor John Smith and a real expression of commitment by Tony Blair whose speech in this volume promises to end British ambivalence towards Europe. So in both major parties, though at different times, pro-Europeans have been brave but isolated voices crying out in the wilderness.

## Insularity

The speeches in this volume show how the debate we have had in Britain has been disconnected from the one which took place everywhere else. It was the differential experience of Britain and the other West European countries in the Second World War which led to the lukewarm or hostile British reaction to post-war moves towards European integration. All the Continental countries involved had been defeated and occupied during or after the War, and the inadequacy of the nation state standing alone to ensure the peace and security of its citizens had been starkly demonstrated. Britain, however, despite its wartime losses, emerged as a victorious power – undefeated and unoccupied. The British people and their leaders retained the illusion that the days of their imperial glory were not yet at an end. Insofar as the realization existed that Britain could not stand alone in the world, it was primarily to the United States and secondarily to the Commonwealth that mainstream British opinion looked for mutual support. So when six countries decided in 1950/51 to pool their sovereignty so far as the then basic industries – coal and steel – were concerned very few Britons challenged the decision of the Attlee government to remain aloof. Nor was this decision questioned by the incoming Conservative government in October 1951, led by Winston Churchill, whose speech in this volume shows him to be one of the 'prophets' of a United Europe.

It is true that there has never been a truly 'European' European debate, because our countries have experienced our shared history in very different ways. The European bargain arose from a coincidence of different national interests and priorities in the immediate post-war period. Germany's need to return gradually to respectability through deferential co-operation and being 'tied in' to Europe coincided with the French desire to achieve security and exercise a share of power beyond her material means. And the national origins of European integration are still reflected in debates about European reform where each country sees its own political system as a model of political legitimacy and would like to see it writ large. The Germans, motivated by the success of their own 'constitutional Patriotism', see a constitution as an answer to the EU's legitimacy problems. The French who are suspicious of parliamentary power would like to see the European Parliament supplemented by a second chamber of national parliamentarians based on their senate. And the Italians and Belgians are so suspicious of their own national systems that they will support whichever blueprint bears the least resemblance to the polities they love to hate.

But although the debate in France, Germany, Belgium and Italy has also been nationally driven, no country apart from the UK has consistently seen the EU as a threat to its national identity. And this understanding of British exceptionalism, which runs through so many contributions to the European debate, is a recent creation – as Linda Colley, Robert Skidelsky and Margaret Thatcher so eloquently point out in their contributions to this volume. To turn the European debate around in the future, we will have to start with a renewed understanding of how similar we are to everyone else and how much our fate depends on their fates. That is why we have included key speeches by other European leaders such as Schmidt, Havel and Gorbachev. Connecting our debate with the debates in other countries will allow us to return to our European past when British figures were leading moves for closer European integration.

A hundred years ago both Keir Hardie, the first leader of the Labour Party, and Conservative Prime Minister Arthur Balfour were both advocates of a federal or confederal union of European states, as was Lord Salisbury, Balfour's uncle and predecessor.[5]

## The future shape of Europe

Part III tries to move on from the European debate in the past, and outline a bold vision for the future. This is an attempt to end the fatalism of the British European debate which has often seen Europe as something developed outside which we could choose to take or leave – and try and remove the most obnoxious bits. For powerful engrained reasons there has never been a British vision of the future shape of Europe.

First, Britain has always seen itself as a *status quo* power: the knee-jerk reaction of British Governments has been to believe that change will inexorably harm British national interests. Grim-faced British ministers have historically said 'No' to as much of European policy as they can get away with. But this approach has proved wrong-headed. The reality is that we should view ourselves as a *reform power*. Britain can only gain from constructive and considered European reform. At the moment the Common Agricultural Policy is stacked against British interests. Britain, as a country that takes defence seriously, should be at the forefront of the debate over a common defence policy. Economic reform is also a high priority, and serious efforts to confront and rectify the democratic deficit are imperative.

The second factor that impeded British involvement was the ongoing belief that British interventions would be counterproductive. This was certainly true until the 1990s. Britain's reputation as a European player was so damaged by the Thatcher years that any initiative originating in London was inevitably seen as a wrecking tactic. John Major's championing of the hard ECU and the enlargement process were interpreted as attempts to scupper EMU, and were rejected accordingly.

But Part III shows that the European political landscape is barely recognizable today. Anthony Giddens shows how, in an age of globalization, talk of a Franco-German axis looks increasingly anachronistic. He shows how the star of federalism waned when a generation of politicians shaped by war, whose lifetime political project was 'ever closer union' left the stage. Jan Zielonka looks at the fields of security and border policy to show why Europe can never be a state, and why Europe's baby-boomer leaders share a more practical vision of the EU and have a different understanding of its strengths. Charles Grant shows that Britain can take advantage of an increasingly assertive European Council which has redefined its relationship with the Commission, and is determined to set the strategic agenda. The chapter 'Network Europe', sets out an alternative model to federalism and free trade areas and makes a number of recommendations – including a strengthened European Council with annual work plans, reforming the European Presidency, and Europe-wide referendums allowing citizens to overturn legislation – which entered the mainstream political debate as a result of Mark Leonard's pamphlet of the same title.

Pro-European visions of Europe's future which are critical both of the way Europe works now and of the traditional pro-European remedies are today in the political ascendancy. There is no doubt that this is what citizens across Europe want and demand – and the Eurobarometer poll evidence of their lack of connection to the European institutions shows why reform must be an urgent priority for those who believe in the pro-European project. We need a Europe which has the capacity to act where only Europe-wide action can be effective and the legitimacy and trust to take its citizens with it.

## The everyday case for Europe

The final part of the volume is meant to show that the Europe debate needn't be arcane and disconnected from ordinary peoples' lives. An all-star cast assess the important and positive impact that Europe has had in areas as diverse as sport, culture and the fabric of our cities. Simon Kuper claims that football has transformed the parameters of European debate by putting us into contact with positive role models from other countries; Sir Peter Hall examines the relationship between Europe's urban architecture and its politics and argues that the unique grammar of European cities is a powerful unifying force; and a magisterial contribution from Milan Kundera shows how the invention of the European novel was a critical milestone in our identity. Philip Dodd investigates the wider cultural sphere, Yasmin Alibhai-Brown writes on the experience of Europe's Muslims, Linda Colley lends a historical perspective, David Puttnam investigates Europe's film industries and Hugo Young looks at the thorny question of a European identity.

The lesson that emerges from this section is that if pro-Europeans today do not benefit from the pioneering spirit which they had in the past, they do have one significant advantage. Europe today is no longer some alien imposition – but a fact of our everyday lives. The values, lifestyles and politics of the British people have been transformed by three decades of exposure to a European market. Almost everybody has been on holiday to another European country. Half of British teenagers speak a second language well enough to have a conversation in it. The shelves of every supermarket in Britain laden with fresh pasta, French cheeses, Greek olives, or Danish bacon are an advertisement for European cuisine. And a large majority of people accept that it makes sense to co-operate with our European neighbours to solve shared problems on the environment, on drugs and organized crime, and on security and defence. They remain to be convinced that the current EU is effective – or concentrating on the right things – but the theoretical argument about sovereignty has been won by those in favour of pooling it. All opinion polls in recent years have shown that people are not averse in principle to trading sovereignty for economic benefits. In their everyday lives people have chosen, and chosen again, to be European. This means that Europe today is not an ideology – as it was for the pro-Europeans who had lived through the horror of the Second World War – it is a lived experience which most people never want to do without again.

But the pro-Europeans have not shifted the argument enough to take account of this. Pro-Europeans often seem to focus on making speeches at CBI and TUC conferences, placing articles in the broadsheet press, and holding conferences on the political benefits of European integration rather than building connections with ordinary people. But the everyday Europe of holidays, cheap wine and beer, tackling organized crime and protecting the environment, will always have more resonance than the European Parliament or European Treaties.

## The European dream

By looking to the future this book seeks to learn a lesson from the Czech President Václav Havel's contribution where he memorably says: 'Without dreaming of a better Europe we shall never build a better Europe.' We believe that this is something which we can learn from America which nurtures a dream that inspired successive generations to succeed, held together a mongrel country, and has always given Americans a clear sense of the future. This is of much more relevance to us than their constitution which we are so often urged to emulate. The various contributions to this volume contain the material for a European Dream.

It shows what is unique about European values, and how working together can allow us to develop a uniquely rich way of life. While Americans glory in the melting-pot culture that salutes the flag and sings the 'Star-Spangled Banner', Europe's greatest strength is its cultural diversity. It shows how a European vision of the good life will go beyond rampant consumerism to include the balances we want to strike in our lives, between work and family; between economic growth and environmental well-being. It shows that where the US extols the virtues of individualism, European countries do not accept the vast inequalities it can produce. Europe's unique achievement has been to marry economic dynamism *with* social cohesion. Finally, it demonstrates how a history of solidarity will allow the EU to show how nations and peoples can come together to deal with common threats: organizing a credible defence identity; developing common measures to tackle international crime and drugs; leading the search for international commitments to protect the planet.

The European Dream must build on the things that Europeans value, to offer them what *they* really want. By imagining the twenty-first-century Europe in which we want to live, work and play, we can show how Europe can bring us closer to that dream. We can also leave behind the European nightmares, not just of war and federal superstates, but of a continent too weak to act and deliver the things we want.

## Notes

1. No one has told this story better than Hugo Young in *This Blessed Plot* (London: Macmillan, 1998).
2. As Philip Williams, the biographer of Labour leader Hugh Gaitskell, put it: 'To some leaders such a great historic decision, about which alarm and enthusiasm both cut across party lines, might have seemed appropriate for an attempt at bipartisanship. Macmillan never made the smallest gesture in that direction, for he was planning a crusade to carry the great decision into history – and the Conservative Party back to power' (Philip M. Williams, *Hugh Gaitskell* (Oxford: Oxford University Press, 1982), p. 396).
3. Ibid., p. 391.
4. John Major, *The Autobiography* (London: HarperCollins, 1999), p. 600.
5. In a perceptive contribution to *Eminent Europeans*, entitled 'Pre-War Ideas of European Union', John Pinder argued forcefully that most of the intellectual underpinning of the movement towards European Union came from British academics and politicians, naming in particular Sir John Seeley, Lord Acton, Philip Kerr (later Lord Lothian), Lionel Curtis, Winston Churchill and Harold Laski. See Martin Bond, Julie Smith and William Wallace (eds), *Eminent Europeans* (London: Greycoat Press, 1996), pp. 1–21.

# Part I

# Peace: The Political Case for Europe 1945–73

# 1
# United States of Europe

*Winston Churchill*

## Extract from speech at the University of Zurich, 19 September 1946

*Churchill was undoubtedly one of the great inspirers of the post-war movement towards European integration. In 1940, he had proposed – in vain – an 'indissoluble union' between Britain and France, and his immense prestige as Britain's war leader, despite his rejection in the general election of 1945, gave his words enormous resonance throughout continental Europe. In a series of speeches, he appealed for reconciliation between Germany and her former enemies, and he electrified his audience at Zurich with his call for the creation of a United States of Europe. In Britain he set up the United Europe Movement, which was largely responsible for the founding of the Council of Europe in 1948. Churchill later disappointed his many European admirers when, on becoming Prime Minister again in 1951, he made no effort to bring Britain into the European Coal and Steel Industry which had been created six months earlier. In reality, though Churchill had grand romantic ideas about European unity, and was often carried away by his own exuberance in presenting them, a close reading of his speeches reveals that he did not envisage his own country playing more than a semi-detached role.*

I wish to speak to you today about the tragedy of Europe. This noble continent, comprising on the whole the fairest and the most cultivated regions of the earth, enjoying a temperate and equable climate, is the home of all the great parent races of the Western world. It is the fountain of Christian faith and Christian ethics. It is the origin of most of the culture, arts, philosophy and science both of ancient and modern times. If Europe were once united in the sharing of its common inheritance, there would be no limit to the happiness, to the prosperity and glory which its three or four hundred million people would enjoy. Yet it is from Europe that have sprung that series of frightful nationalistic quarrels, originated by the Teutonic nations, which we have seen even in this twentieth century and in our own lifetime, wreck the peace and mar the prospects of all mankind.

And what is the plight to which Europe has been reduced? Some of the smaller states have indeed made a good recovery, but over wide areas a vast quivering mass of tormented, hungry, care-worn and bewildered human beings gape at the ruins of their cities and homes, and scan the dark horizons for the approach of some new peril, tyranny or terror. Among the victors there is a babel of jarring voices; among the vanquished the sullen silence of despair. That is all that Europeans, grouped in so many ancient states and nations, that is all that the Germanic powers have got by tearing each other to pieces and spreading havoc far and wide. Indeed, but for the fact that the great Republic across the Atlantic Ocean has at length realized that the ruin or enslavement of Europe would involve their own fate as well, and has stretched out hands of succour and guidance, the Dark Ages would have returned in all their cruelty and squalor. They may still return.

Yet all the while there is a remedy which, if it were generally and spontaneously adopted, would as if by a miracle transform the whole scene, and would in a few years make all Europe, or the greater part of it, as free and as happy as Switzerland is today. What is this sovereign remedy? It is to re-create the European Family, or as much of it as we can, and provide it with a structure under which it can dwell in peace, in safety and in freedom. We must build a kind of United States of Europe. In this way only will hundreds of millions of toilers be able to regain the simple joys and hopes which make life worth living. The process is simple. All that is needed is the resolve of hundreds of millions of men and women to do right instead of wrong and gain as their reward blessing instead of cursing.

Much work has been done upon this task by the exertions of the Pan-European Union which owes so much to Count Coudenhove-Kalergi and which commanded the services of the famous French patriot and statesman, Aristide Briand. There is also that immense body of doctrine and procedure, which was brought into being amid high hopes after the First World War, as the League of Nations. The League of Nations did not fail because of its principles or conceptions. It failed because these principles were deserted by those states who had brought it into being. It failed because the governments of those days feared to face the facts, and act while time remained. This disaster must not be repeated. There is therefore much knowledge and material with which to build; and also bitter dear-bought experience.

I was very glad to read in the newspapers two days ago that my friend President Truman had expressed his interest and sympathy with this great design. There is no reason why a regional organization of Europe should in any way conflict with the world organization of the United Nations. On the contrary, I believe that the larger synthesis will only survive if it is founded upon coherent natural groupings. There is already a natural grouping in the Western Hemisphere. We British have our own Commonwealth of Nations. These do not weaken, on the contrary they strengthen, the world organization. They are in fact its main support. And why should there not be a European group which could give a sense of enlarged patriotism and common citizenship to the distracted peoples of this turbulent and mighty continent and why should it not take its rightful place with other great groupings in shaping the destinies of men? In order that this should be accomplished there must be an act of faith in which millions of families speaking many languages must consciously take part.

We all know that the two world wars through which we have passed arose out of the vain passion of a newly united Germany to play the dominating part in the world. In this last struggle crimes and massacres have been committed for which there is no parallel since the invasions of the Mongols in the fourteenth century and no equal at any time in human history. The guilty must be punished. Germany must be deprived of the power to rearm and make another aggressive war. But when all this has been done, as it will be done, as it is being done, there must be an end to retribution. There must be what Mr Gladstone many years ago called 'a blessed act of oblivion'. We must all turn our backs upon the horrors of the past. We must look to the future. We cannot afford to drag forward across the years that are to come the hatreds and revenges which have sprung from the injuries of the past. If Europe is to be saved from infinite misery, and indeed from final doom, there must be an act of faith in the European family and an act of oblivion against all the crimes and follies of the past.

Can the free peoples of Europe rise to the height of these resolves of the soul and instincts of the spirit of man? If they can, the wrongs and injuries which have been inflicted will have been washed away on all sides by the miseries which have been endured. Is there any need for further floods of agony? Is it the only lesson of history that mankind is unteachable? Let there be justice, mercy and freedom. The peoples have only to will it, and all will achieve their hearts' desire.

I am now going to say something that will astonish you. The first step in the re-creation of the European family must be a partnership between

France and Germany. In this way only can France recover the moral leadership of Europe. There can be no revival of Europe without a spiritually great France and a spiritually great Germany. The structure of the United States of Europe, if well and truly built, will be such as to make the material strength of a single state less important. Small nations will count as much as large ones and gain their honour by their contribution to the common cause. The ancient states and principalities of Germany, freely joined together for mutual convenience in a federal system, might each take their individual place among the United States of Europe. I shall not try to make a detailed programme for hundreds of millions of people who want to be happy and free, prosperous and safe, who wish to enjoy the four freedoms of which the great President Roosevelt spoke, and live in accordance with the principles embodied in the Atlantic Charter. If this is their wish they have only to say so, and means can certainly be found, and machinery erected, to carry that wish into full fruition.

But I must give you a warning. Time may be short. At present there is a breathing-space. The cannon have ceased firing. The fighting has stopped; but the dangers have not stopped. If we are to form the United States of Europe or whatever name or form it may take, we must begin now.

In these present days we dwell strangely and precariously under the shield and protection of the atomic bomb. The atomic bomb is still only in the hands of a State and nation which we know will never use it except in the cause of right and freedom. But it may well be that in a few years this awful agency of destruction will be widespread and the catastrophe following from its use by several warring nations will not only bring to an end all that we call civilization, but may possibly disintegrate the globe itself.

I must now sum up the propositions which are before you. Our constant aim must be to build and fortify the strength of UNO [United Nations Organization]. Under and within that world concept we must recreate the European family in a regional structure called, it may be, the United States of Europe. The first step is to form a Council of Europe. If at first all the States of Europe are not willing or able to join the Union, we must nevertheless proceed to assemble and combine those who will and those who can. The salvation of the common people of every race and of every land from war or servitude must be established on solid foundations and must be guarded by the readiness of all men and women to die rather than submit to tyranny. In all this urgent work, France and Germany must take the lead together. Great Britain, the British Commonwealth of Nations, mighty America, and I trust Soviet Russia – for then indeed all would be well – must be the friends and sponsors of the new Europe and must champion its right to live and shine.

# 2
# Toward European Unity

*George Orwell*

## Article from the *Partisan Review*, July–August 1947

*The name of George Orwell is not widely associated with the drive for European unity. He is better known for what he was against – totalitarianism in all its forms, the wilful distortion of truth, the evils of colonialism, the injustice of the class system and the tragic waste of avoidable poverty. After the Second World War, no doubt subconsciously influenced by his debilitating struggle against the tuberculosis which was to kill him at the age of 46, he went through a phase of deep pessimism which culminated in the writing of his most celebrated work,* Nineteen Eighty-Four. *Yet he was never the victim of total despair, believing that there was at least a fragile hope that mankind would avoid either nuclear destruction or the bleak future which he foretold in his final novel. That hope was that Europe, under democratic Socialist leadership, would succeed in coming together and create a decent society which would 'make life tolerable and even offer some hope of progress'. The prospects, as well as the difficulties of such a development, were spelled out in this little-known article, which appeared in the left-wing but anti-Communist American magazine,* Partisan Review.*

A Socialist today is in the position of a doctor treating an all but hopeless case. As a doctor, it is his duty to keep the patient alive, and therefore to assume that the patient has at least a chance of recovery. As a scientist, it is his duty to face the facts, and therefore to admit that the patient will probably die. Our activities as Socialists only have meaning if we assume that Socialism *can* be established, but if we stop to consider what probably *will* happen, then we must admit I think, that the chances are against us. If I were a bookmaker, simply calculating the probabilities and leaving my own wishes out of account, I would give odds against the survival of civilization within the next few hundred years. As far as I can see, there are three possibilities ahead of us:

1. That the Americans will decide to use the atomic bomb while they have it and the Russians haven't. This would solve nothing. It would do away with the particular danger that is now presented by the USSR, but would lead to the rise of new empires, fresh rivalries, more wars, more atomic bombs, etc. In any case this is, I think, the least likely outcome of the three, because a preventive war is not easily committed by a country that retains any traces of democracy.

2. That the present 'cold war' will continue until the USSR, and several other countries, have atomic bombs as well. Then there will only be a short breathing-space before whizz! go the rockets, wallop! go the bombs, and the industrial centres of the world are wiped out, probably beyond repair. Even if any one state, or group of states, emerges from such a war as technical victor, it will probably be unable to build up the machine civilization anew. The world, therefore, will once again be inhabited by a few million, or a few hundred million human beings living by subsistence agriculture, and probably, after a couple of generations, retaining no more of the culture of the past than a knowledge of how to smelt metals. Conceivably this is a desirable outcome, but obviously it has nothing to do with Socialism.

3. That the fear inspired by the atomic bomb and other weapons yet to come will be so great that everyone will refrain from using them. This seems to me the worst possibility of all. It would mean the division of the world among two or three vast super-states, unable to conquer one another and unable to be overthrown by any internal rebellion. In all probability their structure would be hierarchic, with a semi-divine caste at the top and outright slavery at the bottom, and the crushing out of liberty would exceed anything that the world has yet seen. Within each state the necessary psychological atmosphere would be kept up by complete severance from the outer world, and by a continuous phony war against rival states. Civilizations of this type might remain static for thousands of years.

Most of the dangers that I have outlined existed and were foreseeable long before the atomic bomb was invented. The only way of avoiding them that I can imagine is to present somewhere or other, on a large scale, the spectacle of a community where people are relatively free and happy and where the main motive in life is not the pursuit of money or power. In other words, democratic Socialism must be made to work throughout some large area. But the only area in which it could conceivably be made to work, in any near future, is Western Europe. Apart from Australia and New Zealand, the tradition of democratic Socialism can only be said to exist

– and even there it only exists precariously – in Scandinavia, Germany, Austria, Czechoslovakia, Switzerland, the Low Countries, France, Britain, Spain, and Italy. Only in those countries are there still large numbers of people to whom the word 'Socialism' has some appeal and for whom it is bound up with liberty, equality, and internationalism.

Elsewhere it either has no foothold or it means something different. In North America the masses are contented with capitalism, and one cannot tell what turn they will take when capitalism begins to collapse. In the USSR there prevails a sort of oligarchical collectivism which could only develop into democratic Socialism against the will of the ruling minority. Into Asia, even the word 'Socialism' has barely penetrated. The Asiatic nationalist movements are either Fascist in character, or look towards Moscow, or manage to combine both attitudes: and at present all movements among the coloured peoples are tinged by racial mysticism. In most of South America the position is essentially similar, so is it in Africa and the Middle East. Socialism does not exist anywhere, but even as an idea it is at present valid only in Europe. Of course, Socialism cannot properly be said to be established until it is world-wide, but the process must begin somewhere, and I cannot imagine it beginning except through the federation of the Western European states transformed into Socialist republics without colonial dependencies. Therefore a Socialist United States of Europe seems to me the only worthwhile political objective today. Such a federation would contain about 250 million people, including perhaps half the skilled industrial workers of the world. I do not need to be told that the difficulties of bringing any such thing into being are enormous and terrifying, and I will list some of them in a moment. But we ought not to feel that it is of its nature impossible, or that countries so different from one another would not voluntarily unite. A Western European union is in itself a less improbable concatenation than the Soviet Union or the British empire.

Now as to the difficulties. The greatest difficulty of all is the apathy and conservatism of people everywhere, their unawareness of danger, their inability to imagine anything new – in general, as Bertrand Russell put it recently, the unwillingness of the human race to acquiesce in its own survival. But there are also active malignant forces working against European unity, and there are existing economic relationships on which the European peoples depend for their standard of life and which are not compatible with true Socialism. I list what seem to me to be the four main obstacles, explaining each of them as shortly as I can manage:

1.  Russian hostility. The Russians cannot but be hostile to a European
    union not under their own control. The reasons, both the pretended
    and the real ones, are obvious. One has to count therefore, with the
    danger of a preventive war, with the systematic terrorizing of the
    smaller nations, and with the sabotage of the Communist Parties
    everywhere. Above all there is the danger that the European masses
    will continue to believe in the Russian myth. As long as they believe
    it, the idea of a Socialist Europe will not be sufficiently magnetic to
    call forth the necessary effort.
2.  American hostility. If the United States remains capitalist, and
    especially if it needs markets for exports, it cannot regard a Socialist
    Europe with a friendly eye. No doubt it is less likely than the USSR
    to intervene with brute force, but American pressure is an important
    factor because it can be exerted most easily on Britain, the one country
    in Europe which is outside the Russian orbit. Since 1940 Britain has
    kept its feet against the European dictators at the expense of becoming
    almost a dependency of the USA. Indeed, Britain can only get free of
    America by dropping the attempt to be an extra-European power. The
    English-speaking Dominions, colonial dependencies, except perhaps
    in Africa, and even Britain's supplies of oil, are all hostages in American
    hands. Therefore there is always the danger that the United States will
    break up any European coalition by drawing Britain out of it.
3.  Imperialism. The European peoples, and especially the British, have
    long owed their high standard of life to direct or indirect exploitation
    of the coloured peoples. This relationship has never been made clear
    by official Socialist propaganda, and the British worker, instead of being
    told that, by world standards, he is living above his income, has been
    taught to think of himself as an overworked, down-trodden slave. To
    the masses everywhere 'Socialism' means, or at least is associated
    with, higher wages, shorter hours, better houses, all-round social
    insurance, etc., etc. But it is by no means certain that we can afford
    these things if we throw away the advantages we derive from colonial
    exploitation. However evenly the national income is divided up, if
    the income as a whole falls, the working-class standard of living must
    fall with it. At best there is liable to be a long and uncomfortable
    reconstruction period for which public opinion has nowhere prepared.
    But at the same time the European nations must stop being exploiters
    abroad if they are to build true Socialism at home. The first step
    toward a European Socialist federation is for the British to get out of
    India. But this entails something else. If the United States of Europe
    is to be self-sufficient and able to hold its own against Russia and

America, it must include Africa and the Middle East. But that means that the position of the indigenous peoples in those countries must be changed out of recognition – that Morocco or Nigeria or Abyssinia must cease to be colonies or semi-colonies and become autonomous republics on a complete equality with the European peoples. This entails a vast change of outlook and a bitter, complex struggle which is not likely to be settled without bloodshed. When the pinch comes the forces of imperialism will turn out to be extremely strong, and the British worker, if he has been taught to think of Socialism in materialistic terms, may ultimately decide that it is better to remain an imperial power at the expense of playing second fiddle to America. In varying degrees all the European peoples, at any rate those who are to form part of the proposed union, will be faced with the same choice.

4.  The Catholic Church. As the struggle between East and West becomes more naked, there is danger that democratic Socialists and mere reactionaries will be driven into combining in a sort of Popular Front. The Church is the likeliest bridge between them. In any case the Church will make every effort to capture and sterilize any movement aiming at European unity. The dangerous thing about the Church is that it is not reactionary in the ordinary sense. It is not tied to laissez-faire capitalism or to the existing class system, and will not necessarily perish with them. It is perfectly capable of coming to terms with Socialism, or appearing to do so, provided that its own position is safeguarded. But if it is allowed to survive as a powerful organization, it will make the establishment of true Socialism impossible, because its influence is and always must be against freedom of thought and speech, against human equality, and against any form of society tending to promote earthly happiness.

When I think of these and other difficulties, when I think of the enormous mental readjustment that would have to be made, the appearance of a Socialist United States of Europe seems to me a very unlikely event. I don't mean that the bulk of the people are not prepared for it, in a passive way. I mean that I see no person or group of persons with the slightest chance of attaining power and at the same time with the imaginative grasp to see what is needed and to demand the necessary sacrifices from their followers. But I also can't at present see any other hopeful objective. At one time I believed that it might be possible to form the British empire into a federation of Socialist republics, but if that chance ever existed, we lost it by failing to liberate India, and by our attitude toward the coloured peoples generally. It may be that Europe is finished and that in the long run some better form of society will arise in India or China. But I believe that it is only in Europe, if anywhere, that democratic Socialism could be made a reality in short enough time to prevent the dropping of the atom bombs.

Of course, there are reasons, if not for optimism, at least for suspending judgement on certain points. One thing in our favour is that a major war is not likely to happen immediately. We could, I suppose, have the kind of war that consists in shooting rockets, but not a war involving the mobilization of tens of millions of men. At present any large army would simply melt away, and that may remain true for ten or even 20 years. Within that time some unexpected things might happen. For example, a powerful Socialist movement might for the first time arise in the United States. In England it is now the fashion to talk of the United States as 'capitalistic', with the implication that this is something unalterable, a sort of racial characteristic like the colour of eyes or hair. But in fact it cannot be unalterable, since capitalism itself has manifestly no future, and we cannot be sure in advance that the next change in the United States will not be a change for the better.

Then, again, we do not know what changes will take place in the USSR if war can be staved off for the next generation or so. In a society of that type, a radical change of outlook always seems unlikely, not only because there can be no open opposition but because the regime, with its complete hold over education, news, etc., deliberately aims at preventing the pendulum swing between generations which seems to occur naturally in liberal societies. But for all we know the tendency of one generation to reject the ideas of the last is an abiding human characteristic which even the NKVD will be unable to eradicate. In that case there may by 1960 be millions of young Russians who are bored by dictatorship and loyalty parades, eager for more freedom, and friendly in their attitude toward the West.

Or again, it is even possible that if the world falls apart into three unconquerable super-states, the liberal tradition will be strong enough within the Anglo-American section of the world to make life tolerable and even offer some hope of progress. But all this is speculation. The actual outlook, so far as I can calculate the probabilities, is very dark, and any serious thought should start out from that fact.

# 3
# The Schuman Plan

*Robert Schuman*

## Extract from Press conference by Robert Schuman, 9 May 1950

*The Schuman Plan, which led to the establishment of the European Coal and Steel Community (ECSC), was devised to resolve a deadlock between France and West Germany concerning the Saarland, and the French desire to prevent its powerful coal and steel industries being merged with the rest of Germany's production, which they feared would lead once more to German economic domination of Europe. The solution proposed was to transfer broad control over the two industries in both countries to a supranational authority, an arrangement which would be open on similar terms to other European countries. The actual author of the plan was Jean Monnet (see Chapter 8), who was to become the first President of the High Authority of the ECSC. The French Foreign Minister, Robert Schuman, of Alsatian descent and born in Luxembourg, immediately saw the proposal as a means of bringing peace to the troubled border regions between France and Germany after some 75 years of conflict. The British government declined to participate, but six member states – France, Germany, Italy, Luxembourg, Belgium and the Netherlands – all signed the Treaty of Paris on 18 April 1951, which set up the ECSC.*

World peace cannot be safeguarded without the making of constructive efforts proportionate to the dangers which threaten it. The contribution which an organized and living Europe can bring to civilization is indispensable to the maintenance of peaceful relations. In taking upon herself for more than 20 years the role of champion of a united Europe, France has always had as her essential aim the service of peace. A united Europe was not achieved, and we have war.

Europe will not be made all at once, or according to a single, general plan. It will be built through concrete achievements, which first create a *de facto* solidarity. The gathering of the nations of Europe requires the elimination of the age-old opposition of France and Germany. The first concern in any action undertaken must be these two countries.

With this aim in view, the French government proposes that action be taken immediately on one limited but decisive point. The French government proposes that the whole of Franco-German coal and steel production be placed under a common 'higher authority', within the framework of an organization open to participation by the other countries of Europe.

The pooling of coal and steel production will immediately provide for the setting-up of common bases for economic development as a first step in the federation of Europe, and will change the destinies of those regions which have long been devoted to the manufacture of munitions of war, of which they have been the most constant victims.

The solidarity in production thus established will make it plain that any war between France and Germany becomes, not merely unthinkable, but materially impossible. The setting up of this powerful production unit, open to all countries willing to take part, and eventually capable of providing all the member countries with the basic elements of industrial production on the same terms, will lay the real foundations for their economic unification.

This production will be offered to the world as a whole without distinction or exception, with the aim of contributing to the raising of living standards and the promotion of peaceful achievements. Europe, with new means at her disposal, will be able to pursue the realization of one of her essential tasks, the development of the African continent.

In this way there will be realized, simply and speedily, that fusion of interests which is indispensable to the establishment of a common economic system; and that will be the leaven from which may grow a wider and deeper community between countries long opposed to one another by sanguinary divisions.

By pooling basic production and by setting up a new higher authority, whose decisions will be binding on France, Germany and other member countries, these proposals will build the first concrete foundation of the European Federation which is indispensable to the preservation of peace.

In order to promote the realization of the objectives it has thus defined, the French Government is ready to open negotiations on the following basis.

The task with which this common 'higher authority' will be charged will be that of securing in the shortest possible time the modernization of production and the improvement of its quality; the supply of coal and steel on identical terms to the French and German markets, as well as to the markets of other member countries; the development in common of exports to other countries; and the equalization as well as improvement of the living conditions of the workers in these industries.

To achieve these objectives, starting from the very disparate conditions in which the productions of the member countries are at present situated, certain transitional measures will have to be instituted, such as a production and investment plan, compensating machinery for equalizing prices, and an amortization fund to facilitate the rationalization of production. The movement of coal and steel between member countries will immediately be freed of all Customs duties; it will not be permissible to apply differential transport rates to them. Conditions will gradually be created which will spontaneously ensure the most rational distribution of production at the highest level of productivity.

In contrast to international cartels, which aim at dividing up and exploiting the national markets by means of restrictive practices and the maintenance of high profits, the proposed organization will ensure the fusion of the markets and the expansion of production ...

The common High Authority entrusted with the working of the whole scheme will consist of independent persons chosen by the governments on a basis of equality; a president will be chosen by common agreement by the governments; its decisions will be mandatory in France, in Germany and in the other member countries. Appropriate provisions will ensure the necessary channels of appeal against the decisions of the High Authority. A representative of the United Nations accredited to this authority will be charged with making a public report twice a year to the United Nations Organization dealing with the working of the new organization, particularly with regard to the safeguarding of its peaceful objectives.

The institution of the High Authority does not in any way prejudice the system of ownership of firms. In undertaking its task, the common High Authority will take into account the powers conferred on the International Ruhr Authority and the obligations of all types imposed on Germany to the extent that these are still in force.

# 4
# The Common Market

## Extract from the Treaty of Rome, 25 March 1957

*The successful launch of the European Coal and Steel Community (ECSC) led
its members, under the continual prompting of Jean Monnet, to explore other
areas for supranational co-operation. A plan for a common European Army,
the European Defence Community (EDC) was eventually voted down by the
French National Assembly, after Britain had refused to participate. More success
attended the proposal, agreed at a meeting of the foreign ministers of the six
ECSC states at Messina in June 1955, to explore the possibility of establishing
a European Common Market. A committee chaired by the Belgian Foreign
Minister, Paul-Henri Spaak, produced a report which was the basis of the
Treaty of Rome, signed on 25 March 1957. This established the European
Economic Community (EEC), Britain again having declined to participate. A
separate treaty signed the same day by the same six signatories established
Euratom, the European Atomic Energy Community. The three communities were
combined as the European Community (EC) in July 1967, which became the
central element in the European Union (EU), under the Treaty of Maastricht,
signed on 7 February 1992. The Treaty of Rome is a bulky document comprising
248 articles and an additional 160 pages of annexes, protocols and conventions.
The first four articles, quoted here in their entirety, define the purposes of the
European Economic Community, and the principal institutions to be created
to ensure their achievement.*

Article 1. By this Treaty, the HIGH CONTRACTING PARTIES establish
among themselves a EUROPEAN ECONOMIC COMMUNITY.

Article 2. The Community shall have as its task, by establishing a common
market and progressively approximating the economic policies of Member
States, to promote throughout the Community a harmonious
development of economic activities, a continuous and balanced
expansion, an increase in stability, an accelerated raising of the standard
of living and closer relations between the States belonging to it.

Article 3. For the purposes set out in Article 2, the activities of the Community shall include, as provided in this Treaty and in accordance with the timetable set out therein:

(a) the elimination, as between Member States, of customs duties and of quantitative restrictions on the import and export of goods, and of all other measures having equivalent effect;
(b) the establishment of a common customs tariff and of a common commercial policy towards third countries;
(c) the abolition, as between Member States, of obstacles to freedom of movement for persons, services and capital;
(d) the adoption of a common policy in the sphere of agriculture;
(e) the adoption of a common policy in the sphere of transport;
(f) the institution of a system ensuring that competition in the common market is not distorted;
(g) the application of procedures by which the economic policies of Member States can be co-ordinated and disequilibria in their balances of payments remedied;
(h) the approximation of the laws of Member States to the extent required for the proper functioning of the common market;
(i) the creation of a European Social Fund in order to improve employment opportunities for workers and to contribute to the raising of their standard of living;
(j) the establishment of a European investment Bank to facilitate the economic expansion of the Community by opening up fresh resources;
(k) the association of the overseas countries and territories in order to increase trade and to promote jointly economic and social development.

Article 4.

1. The tasks entrusted to the Community shall be carried out by the following institutions:

- an ASSEMBLY
- a COUNCIL
- a COMMISSION
- a COURT OF JUSTICE

Each institution shall act within the limits of the powers conferred upon it by this Treaty.

2. The Council and the Commission shall be assisted by an Economic and Social Committee acting in an advisory capacity.

# 5
# Britain's Place and Purpose in the World

*Harold Macmillan*

## Extract from speech at Conservative Party conference, October 1961

*Within a year or two of Britain's self-exclusion from the Treaty of Rome, it began to dawn on governmental and civil service circles that a great mistake had been made, and that the country was threatened with increasing isolation. The attempt to form a counterpart to the EEC in the form of the European Free Trade Association (EFTA) had met with very limited success, and Prime Minister Harold Macmillan came to the conclusion that there was nothing for it but to go cap in hand to the six original members of the EEC to ask for admission. He announced his decision in an extraordinarily defensive statement in the House of Commons on 31 July 1961. Two months later he presented his case, in more positive terms, in his speech to the annual Conservative conference, linking it to the need for European solidarity in the face of the Soviet threat and arguing forcefully that British membership was also in the interests of the Commonwealth. Negotiations, led by Edward Heath, opened shortly afterwards, and appeared to be on the brink of a successful conclusion when, on 14 January 1963, they were abruptly terminated by President de Gaulle's veto.*

What is Britain's place and purpose in the modern world? What are our goals at home and abroad? What must we do to get there? What are the dangers? What are the prizes and what are the stakes? Nobody viewing the international scene today can fail to be concerned and saddened by the deterioration which has taken place during the past 18 months.

Faced with so many problems – not I am happy to think in our party – who would like Britain to retire into isolation and cease to play a major part in the world? We might perhaps make some minor contribution to some regional pact, or preferably contract out altogether – become 'sitters', not 'doers'. We should then, it is true, be less involved in the day-to-day struggle. Whether we should be any safer is another matter. All experience shows that you only stay neutral and safe if there are others who are prepared to defend you.

The world today is torn by one of its great doctrinal struggles, greater perhaps than any in the past. Nothing in our recent experience has ever approached the gulf between Communist ideology and our own. And not only between Communism and our own Christian philosophy but between Communism and any idealist philosophy based on a belief in God. Nothing can bridge that gap. What we can hope to do – and what we should continue to aim at doing – is so to contain the issue without abandoning our own positions that time is given a chance to do its healing work. In the fullness of time, if we believe our own faith, we must surely hope that what we regard as wicked and cynical doctrines will gradually change and lose their fervency and strength. Then Communist countries may begin to develop into more normal civilizations recovering a normal basis for their life.

Meanwhile we must accept the fact that this bleak ideological struggle may last for another generation; perhaps even longer. In this struggle we must have faith and a sense of purpose. In every civilized society there has been a conflict between the materialist and the idealist concept of life. Some of the noblest figures have devoted themselves entirely to the latter. These are the great lights that have shone through history. There have been many, too, who with pure cynicism and selfishness have followed only what they believe to be their immediate material interests. All the same, the great mass of us have been brought up to believe that practical day-to-day ambitions should be leavened by idealist inspiration. Now we are faced with vast communities and widespread doctrines which wholly reject any idea of this view of life. Materialism is all they think about. If this mood were to spread, either in the form of a positive acceptance of Marxist atheism or in the perhaps more dangerous form, the indolence of agnosticism, then I believe that Western society would be doomed.

Britain cannot retire from this contest, but we cannot wage it alone. We must bring to the help of our friends and allies such moral and material strength as we can create at home. And we must do more. We must look outside our island, wherever we have authority and influence. That is one of the purposes of our policy. We can bring our influence in the Commonwealth. We can play our part in Europe. We must bring a continual effort to strengthen the organizations and groupings of the Free World, for the Free World is not strong enough to hold out unless it works – as a team – together.

It has been with this in mind that we have approached the question of Europe and the Common Market. In recent years, the countries of

Western Europe have drawn closer together in matters of common defence. But in economic affairs there is still a potentially dangerous rift – the Six and the Seven – both of them in themselves sincere attempts at co-operation and greater unity. But if the gulf cannot be bridged; or if it seems to be permanent and unbridgeable, then I greatly fear the consequences will be grave. It will be, as I said in the United States six months ago, 'a canker gnawing at the very heart of the Western Alliance'. The Lord Privy Seal, Mr Heath, and the Commonwealth Secretary, have dealt in detail with our position in these negotiations and with the safeguards that we require for the Commonwealth, our home agriculture and our EFTA partners. I need not go into it here. I am convinced that a more united Europe could be and will be of the utmost benefit to our Commonwealth family.

The prizes of success would be great, but they are long-term and not short-term prizes. Nor must we delude ourselves. Even if we succeed in negotiating our entry on acceptable terms, that will not be any short cut to an effortless prosperity. It will not absolve us from the stark necessity of earning our way in the world in the teeth of fierce competition. It will be no less necessary than now to keep a close eye on costs and prices. Indeed, we must expect competition to intensify. It is a bracing cold shower we shall enter, not a relaxing Turkish bath.

But that must be our experience whether we join or not. In or out of the Common Market, Britain in this decade must be prepared to face changes in her industrial life and organization, some of them novel, many of them painful, but all of them in the long run salutary. We in the government felt that there is now a chance of giving a new meaning to the future relations of Britain, Europe and the Commonwealth, and that in the state of the world today this may make a difference. We cannot guarantee that we shall succeed in our purpose. But I am sure that we should have been wrong, after full reflection and earnest weighing of all these things, not to have made the attempt. If through indecision, timidity, or sheer political expediency, we had allowed this opportunity to slip from us, we should have failed to rise to the level of events. Your vote on Thursday [some 40 votes out of 4000 were cast against the decision to apply for membership] showed that our party is ready to face the reality of the world today. Of course, the Socialists once again are undecided. They, as a party, belong to the class which the Gallup Poll calls 'don't knows'. Mr Gaitskell is still hesitating. Let him beware lest, if I may recall a famous phrase, he sits so long on the fence that the iron enters into his soul.

# 6
# The US Welcomes European Unity

*John F. Kennedy*

## Speech at Washington, DC, 17 May 1962

*One theme periodically rehearsed by Eurosceptics is that Britain would be better off in an exclusive partnership with the United States rather than linking up with its European neighbours. The suggestion is made that this is something which Americans themselves would welcome, and that the US is inherently hostile to the European Union and its predecessors. Nothing could be further from the truth. Every US President from Dwight Eisenhower onwards has welcomed the rise of the European Community as a positive development, and has encouraged Britain to play a full role within it. No one argued this case more eloquently than President John F. Kennedy in this short extract from a speech he made at a trade conference in Washington in May 1962.*

I am confident that Atlantic unity represents the true course of history, that Europe and the United States have not joined forces for more than a decade to be divided now by limited visions and suspicions. The direction of our destiny is toward community and confidence, and the United States is determined to fulfil that destiny.

Far from resenting the rise of a united Europe, this country welcomes it – a new Europe of equals instead of rivals, instead of the old Europe, torn by national and personal animosities. We look forward to its increased role, as a full and equal partner, in both the burdens and the opportunities of aid, trade, finance, diplomacy and defence. We look forward to the strengthening of world peace that would result from a European Community in which no member could either dominate or endanger the others. And surely, may I add, each member would find in the fabric of European unity and Atlantic Partnership an opportunity for achievement, for grandeur and for a voice in its own destiny far greater than it would find in the more traditional and vulnerable fabrics of disunity and mutual mistrust.

The debate now raging in Europe echoes on a grand scale the debates which took place in this country between 1783 and 1789. Small states are sometimes fearful of big ones. Big states are suspicious for historical reasons of each other. Some statesmen cling to traditional forms, others clamour for new ones. And every eye is on the hostile powers who are never far away. All this reminds us of our own organic deliberations.

But whatever the final resolution of today's debates, Western unity is not an end in itself. Collective security and deterrence are not enough. The time and the opportunity that they afford us are not worth the risk and the effort they require if we do not use them for constructive ends. If there is to be a new Atlantic Partnership, it must be a partnership of strong, not weak economies, of growing, not declining societies. And the great attraction of trade expansion for the United States is not only its contribution to a grand design of Atlantic Partnership, but its practical benefits to our own economy as well.

# 7
# Let Us Go In with Hope and Confidence

*Roy Jenkins*

## Speech at Labour Party conference, October 1962

*The first British application to join the EEC was not greeted with enthusiasm by most members of the Labour Party. Vocal opponents lost little time in mobilizing support, largely on the basis that British entry would be damaging to the interests of Commonwealth countries. The Labour leader, Hugh Gaitskell started from an agnostic position, but was generally regarded as being mildly in favour. But he was suspicious of Macmillan's motives, and gradually became convinced by the Commonwealth argument. His closest associates in the party, nearly all of whom were strongly pro-European, were unprepared for the vehemence which he showed in coming down on the anti-Common Market side in the magisterial speech which he made to the 1962 Labour Party conference. This was received with rapturous applause and united the entire conference, apart from the relatively small number of committed pro-Europeans. Showing considerable courage, Roy Jenkins put their case in a short speech from the floor of the conference, which was received in stony silence by the majority of delegates. This speech marked Jenkins out as the most committed Labour supporter of the EEC, a position which probably eventually cost him the leadership of the Labour Party and the possibility of becoming Prime Minister.*

This document which we have before us this morning, hammered out by the collective wisdom of the Executive, is inevitably, to some extent, a compromise document. Parts of it I welcome very much indeed: the mention of the great and imaginative concept of the European Community, the re-statement that the best thing is to go in on good terms. I think that those who are bitterly hostile to the EEC cannot like those bits.

But I am not going to pretend that there are not those of us who believe – and I am still as convinced as ever of this – that Britain's destiny lies with Europe and that unless we go in we shall be both poorer and weaker than we need be. Mr Gaitskell makes some very powerful criticism of the Prime Minister's handling of this issue. I do not think anyone in this hall would not have a great deal to say in attack of what the government have done, and we who have throughout been persistent Europeans can add a special attack of our own. It would have been much better to have gone in earlier. There is no doubt at all that the failure to go to Messina and join in framing the Treaty of Rome from the beginning is, from the point of view of anybody who wants to be in Europe, on any terms, one of the great missed opportunities of this century. Our influence would have been greater had we done that.

But do not let us underestimate the influence we can exercise now within the European Community. I cannot understand the defeatism of those who think that once in we should he in a perpetual minority of one. What is the position? The Italians have made it clear that they are longing for us to go in and to work with us; so have the Dutch and the Belgians. And so would half, at least, of the German nation. And we should have coming in with us the Norwegians and the Danes. I think it is the French, General de Gaulle, who may be in danger of being in a minority of one, and not ourselves, in those circumstances.

Now increasingly within the party the controversy has come in terms of the Commonwealth issue. It is quite right, perhaps, that that should be so, and there are certainly great Commonwealth interests to be safeguarded. I myself am more concerned about the new Commonwealth, about India, with its vast problems in particular, than I am about the old Commonwealth which I think apart from New Zealand, can stand fairly well on its own feet.

But let me say two words of warning about the Commonwealth issue. First, let us guard ourselves against the danger that by taking up too rigid an attitude now we might in a few months' time find ourselves more pro-Commonwealth interests than the Commonwealth itself. There are certain indications that this may be happening. Two Socialist Prime Ministers – of small countries, admittedly, but they count too – in the Commonwealth are fairly satisfied already. Mr Nehru, Mr Holyoake, Mr Menzies and President Ayub Khan of Pakistan, have all made noticeably more moderate speeches since leaving London, and Mr Diefenbaker's position in his own country – and none of us here should deplore this – seems to weaken every day.

Therefore, let us fight hard for legitimate Commonwealth interests – and I agree there is a good deal more to be done in Brussels – but do not let us be left in occupation of a position which most Commonwealth leaders have themselves evacuated.

I want to any a word about Imperial Preference. Do not let us treat it as the heart and centre of the Commonwealth. After all, it is only a 30-year-old trading device, and there is nothing about its origin to make it particularly sacred to Socialists. It is, in fact, a Chamberlain family invention, thought up by Joseph Chamberlain, propagandized by Austen Chamberlain, introduced by Neville Chamberlain at Ottawa in 1932 and opposed by the Labour Party at that time. And, of course, when the old Commonwealth came to our help at Gallipoli and Vimy Ridge, it did it without Imperial Preference. The Commonwealth, I believe, is something more important and of far tougher fibre than Imperial Preference.

There are certainly problems to be solved before we go into Europe, but do not let us forget the problems that would he created if at this stage we were to recoil from Europe, and, still more, if we were to undo a treaty once it had been made. A period of all-round recrimination would follow. Some of the Six would blame us, some might blame themselves, some of us would blame the Commonwealth. More of us would probably blame the Europeans, and the Americans would certainly add their fair share, both of handing out and of receiving blame. The only result could be a decade of bickering and weakness for the West as a whole.

My last word is this. If we go in, let us try to do it as a Labour Movement, with enthusiasm, Let us remember that every single Socialist Party in the Six – and this goes for the many Socialists in Italy, too – has grown more enthusiastic for the work of the Community as time has gone by and as they have seen it working. Let us go in to help them, to work with them, to achieve something for ourselves but also to contribute something to the common pool. Let us go in with hope and confidence and not with constant backward-looking, nagging suspicion.

*Editors' note: Nehru was Prime Minister of India in 1962, Holyoake of New Zealand, Menzies of Australia and Diefenbaker of Canada. Gallipoli and Vimy Ridge were First World War battle zones, referred to by Gaitskell in his speech, where Commonwealth soldiers fought alongside British troops*

# 8
# Europe Needs Britain

*Jean Monnet*

## Extract from Jean Monnet, *Memoirs* (London: Collins, 1978)

*If one man could be identified as the original architect of the European Union it was Jean Monnet (1888–1979). Starting out as a brandy salesman for his father's Cognac-based firm, he had an extraordinary career, becoming responsible in the First World War for co-ordinating French and British military supplies and playing a comparable role in the Second World War between Britain and the United States. In 1940 he was the main instigator of Churchill's dramatic offer to France of a union between the two countries. After the war he was put in charge of the French national plan, and in 1950 was the author of the Schuman Plan which led to the establishment of the European Coal and Steel Community, of whose High Authority he was the first President. Subsequently, he was a tireless advocate of further European integration, and played a crucial behind the scenes role in persuading British leaders that their destiny lay in Europe and the leaders of the Six that they should welcome the British as members. In this extract, he recalls the situation on the eve of the first British application for membership in 1961, and the advice that he gave, which was unfortunately not heeded, to prevent the negotiations being bogged down over details which he believed could more appropriately be dealt subsequently in the normal bargaining processes within the EEC.*

The civilization of the West needs Britain; and Europe, to continue her unique contribution to that civilisation, needs the qualities that reside in the British people. I first went to London in 1905, and since then I have usually been back several times a year. I spent the dark hours of two world wars there. I remember the great days of the City when it was an unrivalled world power. I had admired the stability of the Empire, and I admired the orderly process of decolonization. Over two generations I have seen the role of Great Britain diminish; but I have not witnessed any decline. If I am asked: 'What remains of that astonishing country today?' my answer is: 'The British people.' They have not suddenly stepped aside from history. Passing difficulties may eclipse their contribution; but once the British have surmounted them, the world will see that creative faculties bred over the centuries do not disappear so fast.

Of all the contributions that the British have made to civilization, two seem to me essential: respect for freedom, and the working of democratic institutions. Where would our society be without habeas corpus and without Parliaments to counterbalance executive power? It is not simply that the British invented the principle and that we have followed them. It has to be applied in daily life. Here, Britain and the countries of continental Europe have much to learn from each other's democratic practice. The British have a better understanding than the Continentals of institutions and how to use them. Continentals tend to believe that problems are solved by men. Undoubtedly, men are important; but without institutions they reach no great and enduring decisions. This the British have long understood. That is why, unlike many people, I had no fear that their accession would upset the working of the Community.

'They want things to work,' I explained; 'and when they see that Europe only works by means of institutions, the British will become the foremost champions of those institutions, and especially of their parliamentary aspect. Continental Europeans have Parliaments too, of course; but no one can say how deeply rooted they are. There was an old man I knew in America who used to say: "You think you understand this in your head, but you will only really understand it when you feel it in your bones." I think the British feel the necessity of parliamentary action: they feel it in their bones.'

I had no illusions about how long this evolution might take, and I would not have ventured to work out a timetable for the necessary process of adjustment. What mattered was to make a start: for nothing would happen so long as the British lacked a view from within. Looking on from outside, they lulled themselves with illusions of grandeur. They had not known the trauma of wartime occupation; they had not been conquered; their system seemed intact. In reality they suffered – paradoxically – from not having had their pride broken and their factories destroyed. The continental Europeans had: at one time or another all of them had been conquered, and they had been obliged to draw up a balance-sheet of their losses, psychological and material, in order to rebuild and to seek a new role. More and more of Britain's leaders were becoming aware of how much her victory had cost her, and they realized that by herself the country would not accept the necessity for change. They had heard Dean Acheson's verdict: 'Britain has lost an Empire and not yet found a role.' They could conclude that the United States was not prepared to offer them a share in its own role: they would find it only by catching up with the Europe that was on the move. By doing so, they would transform Britain's own situation and that of Europe, to which she would bring her resources, her inventiveness, her world-wide view, and her understanding of government. That was a great deal. It was certainly enough to justify a little disturbance in the delicate balance that the Six had established among themselves during the past ten years.

The British are reputed to be difficult partners, and so they are when they negotiate on their own account, in their own way. But they are loyal colleagues when they sit with you on the same side of the table. Then, you can count on them to make things work. That is why it was essential that in joining the Community they should accept all the rules that the Six observed among themselves. Naturally, this stipulation would not prevent Britain's particular problems being dealt with, as had those of Germany and France. Likewise, the method followed to give the British their place would be very important; and on this I made the same very simple proposal that I had tried to have adopted since the beginning of the Schuman Plan: to agree on the objective and negotiate afterwards. To diplomats, this seemed paradoxical: to me it was a matter of logic. An overall settlement is unlikely to be reached by haggling over details. On the contrary, details fall into place, and specific problems are more easily solved, when they are looked at in the framework of a general agreement. The technical questions posed by British accession should be solved within the Common Market, using Common Market procedures: that was the approach that seemed to me reasonable. It placed its trust in the wisdom and strength of the existing institutions. And trust was the whole point. In 1950, the British had not trusted either the objective or the method we proposed to them. Would they this time negotiate right to the end with their own weapons, at the risk of never succeeding? Or would they agree to discuss their problems as common problems, using the machinery of the Community, which had been devised for that very purpose? I hoped that they would have learned from experience, and have been convinced by the example which the Brussels institutions had made clear.

On 30 July 1961, I received a messenger from Edward Heath, then Britain's Lord Privy Seal, bringing me news that the United Kingdom was about to announce its request to join the Community. The message read:

We are sure our decision will be welcome to him. It has of course been a difficult one for the United Kingdom Government. We are very grateful for the efforts which Monsieur Monnet has made to smooth our path and are confident that we can count on his help in overcoming the many difficulties which remain to be solved.

In the answer which I gave the messenger I said:

> I assure you, as you already well know, that I will do all on my part to smooth the way towards Great Britain joining in the efforts, both economic and political, to create the unity of Europe, and particularly to help solving the difficulties in connection with the Common Market.

# 9
# We Mean Business

*Harold Wilson*

## Extract from speech to the Council of Europe, Strasbourg, 23 January 1967

*Less than four years after de Gaulle's veto of the first British application, a second attempt was launched to enter the Common Market. This time it was made by a Labour government, led by Harold Wilson, who had firmly opposed the earlier approach. Yet in the intervening period, official and public opinion in Britain had moved strongly in favour, though opinion polls continued to reveal a large number of 'don't knows'. Wilson and a majority, though by no means all, of his cabinet colleagues seem to have concluded from their experience in office that their problems would be sensibly reduced if they were able to obtain access to the EEC. With mounting enthusiasm, accompanied by his Foreign Secretary, George Brown, Wilson conducted a 'probe', visiting the six capitals of the member states and talking in the Assembly of the Council of Europe, where this speech was delivered. Everywhere he received a warm welcome, except in Paris, where de Gaulle was reserved but not openly hostile. Fortified by a House of Commons vote of 488 in favour, and only 62 against, the government formally lodged its application in May 1967, only to see it rebuffed, even before negotiations had begun, by a second veto pronounced by de Gaulle on 27 November 1967.*

We who are citizens of this great continent have the right to take pride in the part we have played in history, not least in the creation of great – and themselves diverse – nations beyond the seas. And if in a rapidly shrinking world a great challenge we now face is that of coming to terms with the thrusting urgency of new populous, hungry nations, on a basis no longer so much of what we can take from them as of what we can give to them, there is nothing inward looking nor complacent in drawing on the richness of our own past here in Europe. And we can put forth, in all the massive strength of which we are capable, the effort we should make, and must make, on behalf of the new nations in Asia and Africa and Latin America – an effort that will call for really massive strength – if our Europe itself is united and strong.

Nor, again, can those nations here represented, with all the unexampled contribution we have it in our power to make to the achievement of peace, make that contribution unless we can achieve a greater unity of purpose. A unity of purpose which must be directed not only to the solution of our own problems in Europe – that wider Europe whose true boundaries transcend the man-made divisions deepened by two world wars – but which must be directed equally to the solution of the wider world problems which year by year constitute the pattern of international discussion at the United Nations ...

This effort can never achieve its full purpose, whether in terms of development or of peace, unless we learn the way to build up, through a more real unity, our common economy and our mutual political strength.

For economic strength and political unity must develop together. And, just as we are all dedicated to the proposition that economic strength should be developed in an outward-looking sense, so every one of us is resolved that the political objective is not only to end the series of conflicts which have torn Europe apart twice in this century but to create first a dialogue and then a real and living peace with our neighbours to the east, and, still more widely, to strengthen the voice of each one of us in the councils of the world ...

Ten weeks ago I announced in Parliament ... that the government had decided that a new high-level approach must now be made to see whether the conditions existed – or did not exist – for fruitful negotiations, and the basis on which such negotiations could take place. And I said to the House of Commons:

> I want the House, the country, and our friends abroad to know that the Government are approaching the discussions I have foreshadowed with the clear intention and determination to enter the European Economic Community if, as we hope, our essential British and Commonwealth interests can be safeguarded. We mean business.

That, Mr President, is our position. We mean business. And I am going to say why we mean business.

We mean business because we believe that British entry and the involvement of other EFTA countries, whether by entry or association, will of themselves contribute massively to the economic unity and strength of Europe. What is today a market of about 180 millions becomes a potential market of nearly 280 millions, the biggest among all the industrially advanced countries, west or east.

Not only consumers, but producers, too. The adherence of most or all of the EFTA [European Free Trade Association] countries would bring to the existing communities not only a wider market but also the skill, the expertise, the science and technology of millions of workers and thousands upon thousands trained in the highest refinements of modern technology.

We mean business again because the interests of Europe as a whole – wider Europe no less than those of western, northern and southern Europe – will be served, as equally our own separate interests will be served, by creating a greater and more powerful economic community. I have always made clear that, in my view, the concept of a powerful Atlantic partnership can be realized only when Europe is able to put forth her full economic strength so that we can in industrial affairs speak from strength to our Atlantic partners.

Let no one here doubt Britain's loyalty to NATO and the Atlantic Alliance. But I have also always said that that loyalty must never mean subservience. Still less must it mean an industrial helotry under which we in Europe produce only the conventional apparatus of a modern economy while becoming increasingly dependent on American business for the sophisticated apparatus which will call the industrial tune in the 1970s and 1980s.

We mean business in a political sense because over the next year, the next ten years, the next 20 years, the unity of Europe is going to be forged, and geography, history, interest and sentiment alike demand that we play our part in forging it – and working it.

There may be those who believe that to widen the Community will be to weaken it or to dilute its existing sense of purpose and its institutions. Change there will be, as there has been throughout these ten years. For he who rejects change is the architect of decay. The only human institution which rejects progress is the cemetery. We within Europe will play our full part in generating change, whatever that means for vested interests or for the protectionist-minded, in Britain or elsewhere. It will be not on stagnation but on movement, continual movement, that the momentum created in post-war Europe can continue, indeed accelerate. Widening therefore, based on change, will mean not weakening, but strengthening.

I have said that Britain will gain if the right conditions can be established for a decisive and urgent move forward. But equally let no one here underestimate what Britain can also contribute.

We shall be bringing, not only to the council chamber but to the power house of Europe, a new, more determined Britain, a Britain whose answer to the sick jibes of some commentators is being given not in words but in deeds ...

Besides an economy growing in strength we bring all that British technology has to offer. Let us not be defeatist about Europe's technological contribution compared with that of the United States. Each European country can speak for itself. But what would the American industrial economy look like today without jet aircraft, directly based on a British invention freely made available as part of our war effort; antibiotics similarly made over; the electronic revolution based on the British development of radar; indeed, the entire nuclear superstructure which could never have been created except on the basic research of Rutherford and other British scientists. If this is our decision, I hope the negotiations will be on a minimum number of broad issues and not on an infinity of details.

Many of the details, many of the consequential decisions – important though they be – can best be settled on a continuing basis from within the Community ...

But I should be less than frank if I did not at least refer to the problems created particularly by the financial aspects of the Community's agricultural policy, by arrangements made and appropriately, to secure fairness and equity between the agricultural interests of the six countries concerned; but arrangements which do not reflect – clearly they could not reflect – the problem created by the entry of a major food importing nation such as Britain.

For they would mean a financial contribution which would fundamentally affect not only the balance so painfully worked out two years ago but also the balance of equity, as well as the balance of payments, between Britain – and other countries who would seek to join – and the existing Six.

To outline this question, and to be aware of others, is not designed to evoke any spirit of depression, still less defeatism. These problems are there to be overcome. I believe they can be overcome, given the same spirit of constructive ingenuity, tolerance and understanding, give and take, which have animated the relations of the six members in their dealings with one another from the outset . . .

In the last century the creation of the nation states of Europe called on the citizens of those nations to sacrifice their lives. In this century the future of Europe, and of the world has twice required a generation of men to give their lives in the defence of freedom. The Europe of today, the Europe it is in our power to fashion, with all that this means for a wider world, calls for no such heroic sacrifices – the sacrifices which are asked of this generation are sacrifices only of supposed short-term interests, of short-term prejudices and stereotyped modes of thought. I believe that this generation has decided on its answer.

# 10
# The Choice for Europe

*Robert Skidelsky*

**Extract from Robert Skidelsky, *Interests and Obsessions: Selected Essays* (London: Macmillan, 1993)**

*Robert Skidelsky, Professor of Political Economy at the University of Warwick, is the author of highly regarded biographies of John Maynard Keynes and Sir Oswald Mosley. He is also a Conservative life peer, of a markedly independent disposition. On the eve of the launching of the third British application for membership of the EEC, in 1970, he argued in this essay that for too long Britain had avoided a full commitment to Europe, even though its key interests pointed indisputably in that direction. To continue to stand aside would, he asserted, be 'the real betrayal of England's past and the real guarantee that it would have no future'.*

> We warmly desire to improve the co-operation between European countries for the promotion of their common interests and will help to bring it about. We cannot, however, help to create any political or economic group which could in any way be regarded as hostile to the American or any other continent, or which would weaken our political co-operation with the other members of the British Commonwealth.

Are these the words of Mr Michael Stewart, Sir Alec Douglas-Home, or any other British Foreign Secretary over the last 15 years? Not at all. This was the official Foreign Office response to the Briand Plan for the union of Europe put forward in 1930. To recall this and other pronouncements by British spokesmen in almost identical terms down to the present day is to understand something of the strength of the opposition to the European commitment which has existed, and continues to exist, at all levels of British society.

At the grass roots this expresses itself as fear of increased food prices and dislike of foreigners. Among economists of the Anglo-American orientation, there is a profound mistrust of customs union derived from a commitment to free trade and a belief in a one-world economy. (The anti-European bias of one or two eminent *émigré* economists, who having escaped from Central Europe are determined never to go back there, reinforces this.) In Foreign Office circles, there still lingers the conviction that Britain's future lies in a wider grouping, or in overlapping groupings – for example, Mr Stewart's recent denial of any incompatibility between European integration with Britain taking part, and a Commonwealth 'growing in cooperation through its own unique nexus of consultative institutions' *(The Times, 20 February 1970)*.

What is the common thread running through all these responses? Surely it is the fear of being boxed into a Continental system. Every major power seeks as far as possible to secure a world compatible with its own interests and needs: it universalizes its own aspirations. For modern Britain the 'ideal' world was one in which commercial connections were maximized (free trade), in which there was permanent peace (the corollary of the first) and in which power was divided up into large numbers of units (thus enabling Britain to exert a political leverage out of all proportion to its physical resources). This was, if you like, the liberal vision projected onto the world stage. It was unequivocally anti-integrationist, for integration implied not just a cession of sovereignty (which any country which seeks to join another has to face) but for Britain the abandonment of a unique posture: of being both independent *and* universal, of being committed to none, and yet having a hand (or at least a finger) in the shaping of all. What other country has had as much impact on the world in the last 200 years? What continent exists which has not felt the profound influence of English ideas, language, commerce and institutions? The great European powers have seemed almost parochial by comparison and it is easy to understand the British feeling that to enter a purely European concern would be to betray the past and to cramp the future.

Yet such a choice is dictated, not just by present needs, but by past experience. Despite its far-flung possessions, its world-wide interests. England is, has been, and always will be, primarily a European power, for the simple reason that what happens just across the Channel is bound to be more important to it than what happens several thousand miles away. This has been the single, consistent theme of British history, with the possible exception of the brief period of 'splendid isolation' in the middle of the nineteenth century, which also coincided with the triumph of the Cobdenite, universal, ideal. But already by the end of the nineteenth century this thinking was completely obsolete, and at no point has this been more dramatically illustrated than by England's involvement in the two major European wars of this century.

For what happened in 1939? Hitler, in effect, offered England the alternatives of falling back on the undisturbed enjoyment of empire and embarking on a European war in which defeat was a real possibility: the choice between Commonwealth and Europe. England chose the latter, because in that moment of decision it realized that what might happen in India, Australia or Africa in the end mattered not a jot compared with what might happen in Paris, Rome, Prague, Berlin or Moscow. Churchill's quixotic offer of union with France in 1940 spelt out the same message. At that moment of supreme danger it was France that had to be preserved, not the empire. Though it was not obvious at the time, England's participation from the start in both World Wars, in effect, foreclosed the imperial option, and signified its commitment to a European destiny.

The lesson was ignored in the immediate post-war era. England emerged from the war bound firmly to America and the Commonwealth.

Its 'solution' to the European problem was to dissolve West Europe in a developing complex of Atlanticist institutions like NATO, OEEC, IMF, GATT, etc., which it and America jointly controlled. The British response to the growth of the European movement was therefore schizophrenic. On the one hand, it welcomed it, as a step towards transcending age-old European rivalries. On the other hand, it could not but reflect that its own traditional 'divide and rule' policy had depended precisely on the existence and perpetuation of these rivalries. The concentration of European power, the creation of a European economic bloc, even the minor resurgence of European nationalism (this time French, not German), therefore posed the same sort of challenge in the new context as did the efforts of Napoleon and Hitler earlier on: they threatened, not so much England's security, as its influence in the world. America might prefer to deal direct with a united Europe, bypassing the 'special relationship'; Britain would no longer be able to hold the balance of power in Western Europe; finally, all the Commonwealth preferences in the world would not compensate for exclusion from a growing European market. No wonder, as Macmillan told Washington in 1959, that Britain was 'deeply concerned at the political implications of a new independent power on the Continent'.

Britain's response to these developments might best be described as selective sabotage. The basic purpose of European policy was to encourage the movement towards European free trade (from which the sluggish British economy would presumably benefit) while seeking to weaken the political impetus which lay at the heart of the European movement. At the same time it firmly resisted the notion that there might be any conflict of interests between Europe and the United States. The stages of this policy may be briefly described. In 1948 Britain tried to stop the discussion of tariffs and quotas on a regional, European basis. In the early 1950s it opposed EDC or the idea of a *European* (as opposed to a NATO) defence community. In 1955 it warned the Messina Powers not to proceed with the project for a Common Market. In 1956 it tried to fob them off with the European Free Trade Area Proposals. Common to all these schemes was an attempt to dilute the impulse to unity, to dissolve the European venture into some much wider and more nebulous grouping which would lack any political meaning: hence the repeated British injunction to Europe that it should be more 'outward-looking'.

It is at least arguable that the 1961 application to join the EEC was a continuation of the same policy by other means: since Britain could no longer stop the thrust to unity from the outside, it would try from the inside. Even such a strong supporter of entry as *The Economist* could not fail to notice that 'the swing of British policy coincided, within a few weeks in the summer of 1960 with General de Gaulle's proposal to the other common market members that they should form a political union' (14 July 1962). By this time, too, America, alarmed at the turn in French foreign policy, was anxious for Britain to get inside to prevent de Gaulle, with the aged Adenauer in tow, from running away with the European movement. If Britain was to be America's Trojan Horse in Europe, Holland was Britain's. The Dutch insisted that de Gaulle's Fouchet Plan for confederation be held up till Britain joined and finally killed it in the autumn of 1962 and, together with Macmillan's Nassau Agreement with President Kennedy, this led directly to the French veto. This is all now old history. The point is that it is still an open question whether Britain in 1962 was trying to get onto the European bus with the intention of going on a real journey, or merely to drive it off to the nearest scrap heap.

The significance of the story of Britain's post-war relations with Europe lies in the revelation of how continually and intimately concerned the British were with everything going on in Western Europe. In our opposition to the projects of the Continental powers, we were showing ourselves to be just as European as they were; in their desire to have Britain in, they acknowledged the simple fact that without Britain their efforts would be incomplete. The whole struggle was an entirely European affair. Once the Six had overcome Britain's efforts to thwart the impetus towards integration, then Britain, as a European power, had no real alternative but to align itself with it.

Surely this lesson has now been learnt? An encouraging sign is that British officials are now starting to think and talk much more seriously about a shared European future – as witness the interest in a European monetary union, the switch to a European defence policy and the support for stronger Community institutions. On the other hand, the opinion polls have turned decisively hostile to the idea of Britain's entry, and with the (temporary) recovery of economic well-being has come a regrettable recovery of delusions of grandeur. Having successfully gone it alone for just over twelve months, some people now think that there's no reason why we shouldn't go it alone, equally successfully, for ever.[1] Mr Wilson's firm commitment has become Mr Shore's 'option'. The White Paper spells out a gloomy tale of additional costs.

It is therefore worth emphasizing and restating at every opportunity the incontrovertible political argument. Britain has always been a European power. What happens on the other side of the Channel has, by the simple facts of geography and history, always mattered more to Britain than what happens elsewhere in the world. This remains as true today as it ever did. Today the European powers are coming together in political union. Britain can no longer stop it. To stand outside would be to cut itself off for the first time from the Continent of which it has always been a part. That would be the real betrayal of England's past, and the real guarantee that it would have no future.

## Note

1. A reference to the floating of the pound in 1970.

# 11
# We Must Break Down the Barriers

*John Mackintosh*

## Speech at Labour Party special conference, July 1971

*The resignation of President de Gaulle in July 1969, followed by his death the following year, opened the way for yet another British bid for membership, and the Wilson government prepared the ground to make a formal application in late June 1970. Yet its unexpected defeat in the general election on 11 June, meant that it was a Conservative government, led by Edward Heath, that was responsible for conducting the negotiations. In opposition, the Labour Party was badly split on the issue, but as the anti-marketeers, predominantly on the left of the party, appeared to be gaining the upper hand, Wilson performed an about-turn, declaring that the terms negotiated by Heath were unsatisfactory, despite the confident claim by his own former minister, George Thomson, who would have been Labour's chief negotiator, that they would have been acceptable to the Labour government. At a special Labour Party Conference on Europe held in London in July 1971, the unrepentant pro-Europeans in the party made it clear that they would stand firm by their commitment. Perhaps the most effective contribution was made by a leading backbench MP, John Mackintosh, who – speaking from the balcony of the hall – electrified the audience by the force and passion of his delivery.*

We have now heard two eloquent anti-Marketeers, Eric Heffer and Peter Shore. I want to begin by saying Peter Shore's case rests on the argument that something very new has happened. Eric repeated this in the whole terms of the relationship that we will join if we enter Europe.

Let us be clear about this. Every one of the major aspects of the Common Market which Shore referred to in his speech was there in 1967 when the Labour Cabinet made its application to join. Let us be clear on a further point. Let us be absolutely honest about this, that not only was it there in 1967, but the one change which he referred to – the organization of payment for the common budget – was fixed in December 1969, and the Labour Cabinet reapplied to join in May 1970.

Now this was not a frivolous application. This was not a piece of child's play. This was serious, and when our Leader said 'We mean business. We will not take no for an answer', it was because we seriously wanted to join in the Common Market principles as elaborated by the beginning of May last year. And I cannot believe there have been such fundamental changes between May of last year and now as to merit the kind of dreadful picture that Shore and Eric Heffer are now painting.

What worries me is the introduction of such terms as deceit and hypocrisy into this argument, to suggest that those of us who believe we would get more growth in Europe are somehow hypocritical. If that is true, it must include the majority of the last Labour Cabinet who supported this application.

I would like to suggest further on this question of internationalism. Do not imagine representatives of marginal seats like myself, a member of the Labour Party all my life, people like myself, do not feel we need to defend the British working class. I understand that deep feeling that we want our own Socialism in our own country, and we want to construct it ourselves.

What bothers me is when I look back at the experience of the last Labour government over six years. Peter Shore was Minister of Economic Affairs. [*Applause*] Does he remember – I wonder if he has been living in the same world as I have. Does he remember having to explain how we were blown off course? Does he remember a forced devaluation? Does he remember the cuts and the deflation which we had to explain all round the country? What is so desperately negative and insular about this situation is that we have to go back to that sort of situation with the next Labour Government. [*Applause*]

If there is another answer, it is no good producing slogans and talking about Socialism. Our Labour Cabinet – did it not include Socialists? Were not they trying within the limits? We are not going to turn on our own Movement. We are going to have the same sort of leadership again. We cannot turn on our own Movement and say, 'Let us destroy it', or 'Let us turn it down!' If we had had one year of the growth which all the Common Market countries have had, we would still have been in power today, Comrades. [*Applause*]

I turn to this argument about our Socialist colleagues in Europe. Let us be clear about this one. The fears we have heard today in this Conference – every one of these fears was felt by our Socialist comrades in Europe in 1957 and 1958 before they formed the Market. There is not one thing that has been said here that was not said in the German Socialist Party, by Italian trade unionists, by Frenchmen worried about forming the

Market. What is the situation today? Not one of these fears has been realized – not one.

If I heard one of our foreign Socialist friends come and say, 'We were right. Stay out. We will not join a regional policy', it would be different. But do they say that? On the contrary, they have been able to do that effectively, as they wanted. If they come and tell us they could not raise their standard of living, I would believe them. They cannot say that.

The most eloquent testimony of the lot, that I heard was two weeks ago in Rome when I was speaking to one of the leaders of the Italian Communist Party – one of the most progressive and best organized Communist parties. He said that in the near future they hoped to support a coalition in Italy. I said, 'How can you possibly do that when you believe that the EEC is a capitalist bloc?' He shrugged his shoulders and simply said, 'That is what we used to think, but it has simply done too much for the Italian working class for us to turn against them now!'

Comrades, I end with two points. Internationalism we have heard a lot about. I distrust people who are world-wide internationalists who do not risk their lives. The brotherhood of man begins with believing in, and co-operating with, the man sitting next to you. We must break down the barriers. We must build a new approach in this country. We must break the class system and carry our policies through to a conclusion. I believe that this is inside Europe. [*Applause*]

# 12
# Voting for Europe

*Roy Hattersley*

## Extract from House of Commons speech, 27 October 1971

*The dispute in the Labour Party over the terms on which the Conservative government had negotiated British membership of the EEC continued through the summer and autumn of 1971, culminating in decisive votes against at the Labour Party conference and in the Parliamentary Labour Party. Nevertheless, a substantial minority of Labour MPs, led by Roy Jenkins, then the deputy leader of the party, was determined to vote in favour in the crucial House of Commons debate despite the strong pressure which was put on them and the denial by the Labour leadership of the 'free vote' which they had earlier been promised. In the event, in the face of a three-line whip, 69 Labour MPs (including, incidentally, one of the editors of this book) voted in favour, and another 20 abstained. Their action meant that the motion approving British entry was carried, as their votes outweighed the 40 or so Tory MPs who, taking advantage of the free vote allowed by their party, voted against. Many of the Labour dissidents explained their reasons during the five-day debate, most of them claiming that they could not in good conscience reject terms which they believed would have been acceptable to a Labour government. The speech made by Roy Hattersley, then an up-and-coming member of the Opposition front bench, was a good example.*

**Mr Roy Hattersley (Birmingham, Sparkbrook):** I wish to make my judgement on the government's terms very plain. I do not regard them as ideal. I believe that had they been negotiated by a Labour government they might have been marginally better because they would have reflected more the social and economic priorities which my right hon. and hon. Friends and I share. But the real comparison which the House must make before it decides how it votes tomorrow is not between the terms negotiated by the government and the terms which might be or might have been negotiated by some regrettably hypothetical Labour government, but today's package of terms and the sort of terms we might obtain were we to abandon our application now and make it again in the future. That is the choice for those of us who believe in the principle of entry.

It is my judgement that anyone who finds today's terms unacceptable would certainly discover that any terms negotiated after the withdrawal of our application and a re-negotiation were a great deal less acceptable than the terms we have before us today. That is one reason why I believe that there is an imperative necessity for those of us who are supporters of the ideal of Europe to demonstrate our support tomorrow. I intend to do that.

The implication of what I have said – that the terms become more difficult and the price higher the longer the Community changes without us – is a frank and obvious acceptance that a price must be paid for our entry. No sensible person denies that. But, in my judgement, the potential benefits of European membership incomparably outweigh the price. Principal among those potential benefits is the prospect of economic growth.

That growth is potentially possible not simply because of the huge benefits of the large market – although they are important in themselves – but because of the nature of the Community. It is not simply a giant free trade area. It is, as it calls itself, an economic community which endeavours to stimulate trade and to promote commerce, and by its conscious attempts at promotion and stimulation it is likely to produce an investment situation which this country has not been able to achieve in the last ten years.

I regard the prospect of economic growth as the primary object or the principal prize of Europe for reasons which in some ways are materialistic but about which I am in no way ashamed. When I look at the record of the government of which I was proud to be a member for six years and I see our very considerable achievements between 1964 and 1970, I have no doubt that we would have done a great deal better had we achieved the right level of economic growth during that time. The housing targets would have been achieved; the school leaving age would have been raised; the National Health Service would have been financed differently; our overseas aid targets would have been met. I express no apology for making the political point that I became a member of the Labour Party to achieve that sort of goal. I wish to achieve it not only because the Labour Party should be concerned with the rising level of material prosperity but because the housing, hospital and school building programmes are a central element in its drive towards a more equal society. Those things can and will come from economic growth.

I would vote for Europe if that were the only prospect that it offered – but it is not, particularly at a time of crucially high unemployment. I represent part of a city which is facing high unemployment for the first time in the memory of many, indeed most, working people. Birmingham is now afflicted by some of the problems which have faced the rest of the country on and off for the last 40 years. I am told that it is the calculated assessment of all those who advise Birmingham and Midland companies that their prospects for growth, investment and expansion would be appreciably better if Britain were a member of the Community.

Having said that, it is hardly necessary for me to say that the Europe I support and want to join is not the Europe of right. Hon. and hon. Members opposite. Our prospect now is entering Europe on what some of my hon. Friends crudely call Tory terms but of using the fruits of those Tory terms according to Socialist principles. That is what I believe can and should be done. Anyone who wants to compare the difference between their Europe and ours need do no more than read their White Paper.

**Mr Dick Leonard (Romford):** Is it not true that the Socialists in Germany, France, Belgium, Luxembourg and the Netherlands thought that they were joining Europe on Christian Democrat terms and are now fully in favour of membership because they see this as the best proposition for Socialists?

**Mr Hattersley:** The conversion from opposition to support among the other Social Democratic countries of the EEC will, I hope be emulated by the British Labour Party.

It has become fashionable and, perhaps, almost obligatory for those of us who support British membership to say a word about our personal attitude to our party obligations and constituents. I say straightaway that I do not argue with the hon. Gentleman below the Gangway who reminded many of us earlier that we were in the House because we were candidates of our party rather than for our personal qualifications. Like him, I am fortunate enough to serve in the House of Commons because my ballot paper in the last election and propaganda in previous elections described me as the Labour candidate. The propaganda in the previous elections and in the last election made it very clear that not only was I the Labour candidate but I was a candidate committed in definite and strong terms to fighting for Britain's entry into the European Economic Community.

Yesterday evening the management committee of my Labour Party, when the attitudes of the Parliamentary Labour Party and their Members of Parliament were considered, reminded me that at my selection conference in 1962 – when the Labour Party was committed against British entry – I told the delegates to that meeting that I was for Europe and, in the foreseeable future, would remain for Europe. I have taken that stand virtually all my public life for reasons which I can only describe not simply as consistent with my view of social democracy but essential to that view. In those terms there is no choice for me tomorrow evening. My choice is breaking my word to my constituents and breaking my compact with my constituency party: but also, much more important, denying my judgement and beliefs. That would not be in the interests of the House. With some trepidation I say that it would not be in the interests of my party.

There are some of us – I do not know how many – who have publicly taken a view which may be wrong but which in all conscience they hold. We may be insignificant members of the Parliamentary Labour Party, but the country as a whole will not admire a party which has a group of men in its midst who, having said constantly that something they believe is still in the national interest, did not have the courage to carry that view into the Division Lobby.

My right hon. Friend the Member for Bristol, South-East [Mr Benn], who is not here at present, referred to what he described as the 'divine right' of some Members of Parliament. It is not a matter of divine right. I have never done anything in my life about which I was absolutely certain. But I am as certain as I have been about anything that my vote should go for Europe tomorrow. A previous Member for Bristol did not talk about a Member of Parliament's divine right but about a Member of Parliament's divine duty. That duty, as Burke saw it, was to use his judgement and then courageously apply that judgement. I propose to do that tomorrow night not by voting for the Conservative Party but by voting for Europe.

# 13
# A Historic Decision

*Edward Heath*

## Speech to the House of Commons, 28 October 1971

*When Edward Heath stood up to reply to the five-day debate on the terms negotiated for British membership of the EEC it was the culmination of a lifetime commitment. The seeds lay in his pre-war visits as a student to the Continent, including Nazi Germany and the Republican side in the Spanish Civil War. His wartime experience in the British army, and later in the British occupation zone in Germany led him to conclude that only a democratically united Europe could prevent a repetition of the disastrous conflicts which had devastated the Continent during the previous 75 years. On his election to Parliament in 1950, his maiden speech included a plea for Britain to enter the European Coal and Steel Community. Subsequently, he was appointed by Macmillan as the chief negotiator during the first British entry bid to the EEC in 1961–63. As Prime Minister since June 1970 he had given top priority to bringing the new talks to a successful conclusion. Together with President Georges Pompidou of France, he was responsible for breaking the log-jam in the negotiations in a remarkable two-man summit in Paris in May 1971. By the time of the October debate, all but a few details had been settled, and this represented the crucial moment of decision for Britain. In his speech, the greater part of which, reprinted from* Hansard, *is included here, he addressed himself mainly to the objections raised by James Callaghan, Labour's Foreign Affairs spokesman, who had just wound up the debate for the Opposition. The vote was taken immediately after Heath's speech, and thanks to the votes and abstentions of 89 pro-European Labour MPs, showed a large majority in favour of approving the terms for British entry.*

**The Prime Minister (Mr Edward Heath):** I do not think that any Prime Minister has stood at this Box in time of peace and asked the House to take a positive decision of such importance as I am asking it to take tonight. I am well aware of the responsibility which rests on my shoulders for so doing. After ten years of negotiation, after many years of discussion in this House and after ten years of debate, the moment of decision for

Parliament has come. I cannot over-emphasise tonight the importance of the vote which is being taken, the importance of the issue, the scale and quality of the decision and the impact that it will have equally inside and outside Britain. On one thing I agree very much with the right hon. Member for Cardiff, South-East [Mr Callaghan]. He finished by saying that he wished to set this against a world canvas. It has been said that this is a historic decision; it is being taken in what many would describe as a historic week.

Earlier, the world was watching New York. They were waiting to see whether China was going to become a member of the Security Council and of the General Assembly. Tonight, the world is similarly watching Westminster, waiting to see whether we are going to decide that Western Europe should now move along the path to real unity – or whether the British Parliament, now given the choice, not for the first time but probably for the last time for many years to come, will reject the chance of creating a united Europe.

There can be absolutely no doubt of the world interest in this matter – of those physically watching and those waiting for the outcome. Nor can there be any doubt of the reasons why. It is natural that we in this House, in this long debate, have been largely concerned with the impact on our own country, but our decision tonight will vitally affect the balance of forces in the modern world for many years to come.

The system of international trade and finance is disintegrating, and unsatisfied demands are there for a new system somehow to replace it. So much has been taken for granted over the last 25 years and so much of that no longer exists.

This is the position facing the Western world today, and if many of us have pursued the course of European unity for so many years with some persistence and, I suspect the right hon. Gentleman thinks, with some boredom, then the reason is perhaps that we have foreseen in part that some of these changes were bound to come about; and, by some strange permutation of history, in this very short span all these changes have come together. The right hon. Gentleman described the pursuit of a united Europe as an ideal which he respected. It inspired the founders of the European Communities after the war. At that time we in Britain held back, conscious of our ties with the Commonwealth and of our relationship with the United States, both of which had been so strongly reinforced in war. We did not then see how we could fit that into the framework of European unity. The Commonwealth has, since then, developed into an association of independent countries with now only a few island dependencies remaining. It is a unique association which we value, but the idea that it would become an effective economic or political, let alone military, bloc has never materialized. It has never become a reality. Our relationship with the United States is close, friendly and natural, but it is not unique. It is not fundamentally different from that of many other countries of Western Europe, except, again, for our natural ties of language and common law, tradition and history. The United States is now inevitably and increasingly concerned with its relationships with the other superpowers. This applies also in the economic field, because in the situation which I have described the United States is bound to find itself involved more and more with the large economic powers, Japan and the European Community. This is a time of profound change. It is a time in which United States policy towards Soviet Russia and Soviet China, and in the trade and monetary field, is changing. It is a time when we must see how these problems can best be handled by Britain. The post-war international monetary system, after which I think the right hon. Gentleman hankers, and its trade system is no longer the basis for international relations and, as a consequence the risks to liberal trading policies on which we ourselves so much depend are now immense.

We as a country are dangerously vulnerable to protectionist pressure if such a satisfactory outcome of a new financial and trading system is not achieved. But in Europe we can share and reinforce the strength and experience of the Community. We can work with partners whose interests are the same as ours.

In this time of change the Community, too, has developed. It has been not only working in the constitutional framework of the Treaty of Rome; it has been acting pragmatically and ancient and historic States have developed the habit of working more and more closely together.

Neither do I accept the strictures of the right hon. Member for Cardiff, South East about the situation in the Community at present. May I suggest that if he looks back over the history of the past 12 years he will find that there have been occasions when there have been differences between the members of the Community, but on each occasion this has led to a solution which has then reinforced the Community in its strength and in its purpose. So in the Community, old institutions have been adapted and new ones have been invented to meet the realities of the new situation.

In the debates of the last six days, the economic arguments have figured very prominently. They are important. Again, I do not accept the argument of the right hon. Member for Cardiff, South-East that merely to have a reduction of a 7½ per cent average tariff is not of great consequence. We know that it is not entirely the average tariff which matters; it is the very high level of some individual tariffs which are important to us and to our industries.

The questions of larger firms, technology, capital investment and rate of growth are of immense importance. I agree with those who say that there can be no final proof of this. It must be a matter of qualitative judgement. I accept that, and we have offered our judgement to the House. If one needed any indication of the difficulties, it has already been said that the economists have lined up in two columns in *The Times* I notice that one was one-quarter of an inch shorter than the other. On what basis can one make an economic judgement of one-quarter of an inch of a column in *The Times*?

But what is important is the question of being in the best possible position to influence economic decisions which are determining our future. That seems to be the real crux of the economic argument. Over these next few years, in which new patterns will be formed and new decisions will be taken, they will affect the livelihood of everyone in this country and they will be taken in practice by those who have the greatest economic power. We may not like it, and we may wish it otherwise, but we have to recognize these facts as they exist.

But this is coming about just at the moment when we have the opportunity of joining the Community and of influencing one of the major economic powers. In those circumstances, I believe that a Prime Minister who came to this Box and recommended that we should reject the opportunity now before us of taking an active part, a share in these decisions, would be taking a terrible gamble with the livelihood of the British people for many years to come. That Prime Minister would be saying to the House, in effect, that he was prepared to accept the situation in which vital decisions affecting all of us were taken in circumstances over which we had no control and little influence. This is a gamble which I, as Prime Minister, am not prepared to advise this House to take. Nor can these matters of trade and finance ever be separated entirely – as we are seeing today in the news which comes from the United States – from the security of our country or of the Community.

The right hon. Gentleman raised some matters about the terms. The government have made their recommendation on this. They have been discussed in great detail in the House. I was not proposing at this stage of the debate to go over them again. They are better than anyone thought possible when the negotiations began. This is widely recognized in Europe by the friends of this country. It is widely recognised by the friends of the Labour Party who had great influence in securing those terms. It has been widely recognized right across the Commonwealth and the world.

As to whether Britain is European, I fail entirely to understand the argument which the right hon. Gentleman was trying to advance about cutting all our links with the outside world, when the members of the Community itself are the great trading countries of the world; when the Community itself is the greatest trading bloc in the world: when, as the Leader of the Liberal Party pointed out this evening, the enlarged Community is created, it will have arrangements with 80 countries. Twenty-nine of the Commonwealth countries and 19 dependencies will be associated with the Community. What on earth does the right hon. Gentleman mean by our cutting off our links with the outside world? To sum up, the outcome of the right hon. Gentleman's analysis was, quite simply, that he wished to stipulate terms on which we would enter the Community which everybody who has observed events for the last 12 years knows from the beginning would not even have allowed negotiations to start and which, if the Community had been prepared to accept them, would have meant the break-up of the Community. That is the plain fact about the remarks which the right hon. Gentleman has made about the terms for going into negotiations. I have sometimes felt that among those who have been in this debate seeking to balance up the advantages and disadvantages there was a desire for a degree of certainty which is never obtainable in human affairs. Hon. Members will not ask for it in their lives, in their own businesses. As a nation we have never hitherto asked for it in a trading agreement or in international affairs, either economic or political. Anyone who studies the length of our trading agreements outside will accept that that is the case. It may be that it is showing a lack of confidence in ourselves, but I suggest that, whatever the explanation, we are worrying about the wrong question. Surely the right question to ask ourselves is this: has the Community the necessary and appropriate means for dealing with the problems of its members, whether they arise out of these present negotiations in which we have taken part or whether they arise from any other cause in the life of the Community? That surely is the question one has to put about a living, changing, developing organization such as the Community. That is what matters.

The answer to that question is undeniably – yes, it has got those means and, what is more they have been and are being used successfully. They are proven means for dealing with the problems inside the Community – through the Treaty, through the Commission, through the Council of Ministers these matters are being handled the whole time.

It is understandable after ten years of negotiation and frustration that many in debate and many in the country outside have fought and talked in terms of 'we' and 'they'. Some, I think, have been overwhelmed by a fear that this country in an organisation such as the Community must always be dominated by 'they'. That is certainly not how the rest of the Community sees it. But we are approaching the point where, if this House so decides tonight, it will become just as much our Community as their Community. We shall be partners, we shall be co-operating, and we shall be trying to find common solutions to common problems of all the members of an enlarged Community.

We have confidence that we can benefit as well as contribute, that we can further our own interests and the interests of the Community at one and the same time. After all, the leaders of all three parties in this House accept the principle of entry into the European Community, as the right hon. Gentleman reaffirmed this afternoon. The Community is not governed by any particular party ideology. How can it be, with a Socialist government in the Federal Republic, with a right-wing government in France, with a coalition in Italy containing Socialists? Of course not. What is more, all the opposition parties in the member countries of the Community support membership of the Community just as much as the governing parties.

It is right that there should have been so much discussion of sovereignty. I would put it very simply. If sovereignty exists to be used and to be of value, it must be effective. We have to make a judgement whether this is the most advantageous way of using our country's sovereignty. Sovereignty belongs to all of us, and to make that judgement we must look at the way in which the Community has actually worked during these last 12 years. In joining we are making a commitment which involves our sovereignty, but we are also gaining an opportunity. We are making a commitment to the Community as it exists tonight, if the House so decides. We are gaining an opportunity to influence its decisions in the future.

The right hon. Gentleman asked me questions as to how we saw this. The Community in future months will be discussing future policy in an enlarged community. No one is committed to this at the moment – no member country, nor we as a country, nor this House. What we shall have is an opportunity, which we do not possess and will not possess unless we join, of working out schemes for the future of the major part of Europe. I put this point in a practical form to the House. It is well known that the President of France, supported by the Chancellor of Germany, has proposed a summit meeting of heads of government in the course of next year and probably in the spring. This meeting, will, I believe, settle the European approach to the problems that we have been discussing of monetary arrangements, trading arrangements, and future political development.

If by any chance the House rejected this Motion tonight, that meeting would still go on and it would still take its decisions which will affect the greater part of Western Europe and affect us in our daily lives. But we would not be there to take a share in those decisions. That really would not be a sensible way to go about protecting our interests or our influence in Europe and the world. But to be there as a member of the Community, in my view, would be an effective use of our contribution of sovereignty.

Surely we must consider the consequences of staying out. We cannot delude ourselves that an early chance would be given us to take the decision again. We should be denying ourselves and succeeding generations the opportunities which are available to us in so many spheres; opportunities which we ourselves in this country have to seize. We should be leaving so many aspects of matters affecting our daily lives to be settled outside our own influence. That cannot be acceptable to us. We surely should be denying to Europe, also – let us look outside these shores for a moment – its full potential, its opportunities of developing economically and politically, maintaining its security, and securing for all its people a higher standard of prosperity.

All the consequences of that for many millions of people in Europe must be recognized tonight in the decision the House is taking. In addition, many projects for the future of Europe have been long delayed. There has been great uncertainty, and tonight all that can be removed.

The right hon. Gentleman the Member for Cardiff, South-East was very kind in the personal remarks he made about myself. Throughout my political career, if I may add one personal remark, it is well known that I have had the vision of a Britain in a united Europe; a Britain which would be united economically to Europe and which would be able to influence decisions affecting our own future, and which would enjoy a better standard of life and a fuller life. I have worked for a Europe which will play an increasing part in meeting the needs of those parts of the world which still lie in the shadow of want. I always understood that the right hon. Gentleman wanted that. I want Britain as a member of a Europe which is united politically, and which will enjoy lasting peace and the greater security which would ensue. Nor do I believe that the vision of Europe – and the right hon. Gentleman raised this specific point – is an unworthy vision, or an ignoble vision or an unworthy cause for which to have worked. I have always made it absolutely plain to the British people that consent to this course would be given by Parliament. Parliament is the Parliament of all the people. When we came to the end of the negotiations in 1963, after the veto had been imposed, the negotiator on behalf of India said: 'When you left India some people wept. And when you leave Europe tonight some will weep. And there is no other people in the world of whom these things could be said.' That was a tribute from the Indian to the British. But tonight when this House endorses this Motion many millions of people right across the world will rejoice that we have taken our rightful place in a truly United Europe.

*Question put:* The House divided Ayes 356, Noes 244.

# Part II

# From Prosperity to Democracy: The Political Case for Europe 1974–2000

# 14
## We Need the British

*Helmut Schmidt*

*The Labour Party fought the two general elections of 1974 on a pledge to seek a renegotiation of the terms of British membership, and then put them to the British people either in a referendum or in a further general election. This was despite the fact that a majority of Labour Party members would probably have preferred outright withdrawal. In the event, the other member states went out of their way to make it easy for Harold Wilson, who became Prime Minister for the second time in February 1974, to claim that the new terms, which James Callaghan as Foreign Secretary negotiated, were a marked improvement on those obtained three years earlier by Edward Heath, even if the changes proved to be largely cosmetic. A more difficult task for Wilson, who was now eager to retain British membership, was to persuade the Labour Party that this was a worthwhile objective. To help him in this task, he enrolled Helmut Schmidt, the German Chancellor, who, in a well directed and good humoured speech, made a favourable impression at the 1974 Labour Party conference.*

It is a pleasure and a privilege to speak to you today as a fraternal delegate. Thank you for your cordial invitation.

As already hinted by some English newspapers, and as some papers of my own country have beforehand insisted, I do have a certain reputation for being blunt. Some even call me names. But I think we have all got used to being misunderstood or indeed misrepresented. One has to accept that as a fact of life and live with it; and I think for you in the end, as ever, the proof of the pudding is in the eating.

When I spoke the first time to a Labour Party Conference in 1969 in Brighton my party was just about for the first time to form a government under Social Democratic leadership. This time you have again formed a Labour government after a very close election campaign and the first thing I want to say is therefore, on behalf of the Social Democratic Party of Germany, congratulations to you all on the political victory that put Labour back at the helm of this great country or yours. [*Applause*] The

German Social Democrats and I wish you all the success which you are working for.

Second, my party, the SPD, wants our fraternal solidarity to be continued for the benefit of our two nations and our two parties. It is solidarity we need especially at a moment of time when many people think we are on the brink of another grave world economic depression. It is in that spirit of solidarity, from which so often in the past both our parties have mutually benefited, that I have come here ...

For a number of years, I have had the opportunity as a fellow Minister to work closely together with the Labour government in London, especially with my old friend Denis Healey, who at that time was your Defence Secretary. I have known Harold and quite a few other leaders of the Labour Party for 20 years now. I myself was born and educated in the merchant and shipping city of Hamburg. That is a city which sometimes behaves as if it were even more British than the British themselves. [*Laughter*] I have always been an admirer of the glorious traditions and virtues of your democratic institutions, and in addition to that, in practising international relations I have come to admire the down-to-earth attitude and pragmatic ability of British leaders to solve complicated problems. This has proven itself true again within the Commission and Council of the European community, and I am not exaggerating in saying that already the beneficial influence of your attitude in handling affairs has made itself benevolently felt. I thank you for that ...

Let me also say a word on the European Community. Not because that was being predicted by almost all British newspapers, but because I would not serve the interests and expectations of my authority and country if I suppress the desire of your German comrades to have you British comrades on our side within the Community.

You know, being a European politician is not all that difficult, because all you have to do is satisfy the farmers, satisfy the trade unions, satisfy a few other groups and still get elected! [*Applause*]

We are, of course, aware that your decision is pending, and that it will depend on the outcome of the renegotiation efforts made by Harold Wilson and Jim Callaghan, and on a few other things also. [*Laughter*] I am not going to interfere with your decision. and of course I am not going to shoot from the hip, as someone has suggested! [*Applause*] But, Comrades, with regard to your vote of yesterday, I cannot totally avoid putting myself in the position of a nun who, in front of ladies and gentlemen belonging to the Salvation Army, tries to convince them of the advantages of drinking. [*Laughter and applause*]

All I really want to say – even at the risk of a walk-out, is that your comrades on the Continent want you to stay, and you will please have to weigh this. If you talk of solidarity, you have to weigh it. [*Applause*] Your comrades on the Continent believe that it is in their interests as well as in yours, too.

More than often, of course, we ourselves do have our own misgivings about the European Commission and its decisions. I think, for instance of its agricultural policies. I have no doubt that constantly advancing prices of meat are capable of dividing the people into two classes: those with large incomes on the one hand and vegetarians on the other! [*Laughter and applause*]

But let me also add a sober word on CAP. As in the past, European agricultural production must be oriented to meet the Community's food requirements, whilst making allowance for commercial obligations towards third countries, in particular the developing countries. We cannot afford costly surpluses, the sales of which we have, in addition, to subsidize from public funds. Nor should we hamper free world trade because of our Common Agricultural Policy.

I hope that the agricultural stock-taking exercise – I am not sure whether this is the right English word, but it is an understandable English word, I found it in my dictionary – by the EEC Commission in Brussels will bring to light the mistakes of the past regarding CAP and enable us to correct them.

Of course, Europe is not merely an agricultural affair. We have to concentrate on industrial growth and on industrial co-operation.

My Party feels that the advantages of the EEC so far do have greater weight than the stresses and burdens. After all, it is an organization whose pace and direction can only be decided by the agreement of all its members. We feel that it provides us with the necessary means for co-operation which we do need to solve the problems of the present-day crisis of the world economic structure.

Of course, we must not over-emphasise that crisis. It is a recession, so far, of the world economy. A recession is a period in which you tighten your belt. If it came to a depression, one might not any longer have a belt to tighten, and, or course, if you have no pants to hold up, then it is going to be a panic. But there really is no reason at all for panic. Instead, I think co-operation, if we bring it about, will produce confidence.

Let me conclude by remembering the long history of social democracy in Britain and other countries, in many phases of which my Party has learned from yours. We will not forget either the historic origins of Labour unions and co-operatives, or the intellectual contributions of the

Fabian Society or, immediately after the Second World War, of Clement Attlee, Ernest Bevin and Nye Bevan. [*Applause*]

I hope that there have also been a few contributions from the German Social Democrats which you might not want to miss. [*Applause*]

Let me end, Comrades, by quoting from Shakespeare's *Julius Caesar*:

> There is a tide in the affairs of men,
> Which taken at the flood, leads on to fortune;
> Omitted, all the voyage of their life
> Is bound in shallows and in miseries.
> On such a full tide are we now afloat,
> And we must take the current when it serves,
> Or lose our ventures.

I am, of course, not going to argue with William Shakespeare here. Thank you very much. [*Prolonged applause*]

# 15
## Why You Should Vote Yes

**Pamphlet by the pro-EEC group Britain in Europe, distributed to voters in the 1975 referendum**

*The referendum on whether Britain should stay in the European Economic Community was an unprecedented and unpredictable event. First proposed by Tony Benn, who hoped it would lead to Britain's withdrawal from the EEC, in the event it produced a two-to-one majority in favour of staying in. Its prime appeal to Prime Minister Harold Wilson was that it provided a means of holding the Labour Party together, despite its fierce internal divisions. This was achieved by suspending collective responsibility for Cabinet ministers, so that they could campaign on either side – 16 ministers supported the pro-EEC and seven the anti-EEC case. The campaigns were conducted not by the political parties themselves, but by two cross-party umbrella organizations. The pro-EEC group, known as Britain in Europe, was led by Home Secretary Roy Jenkins, supported by Edward Heath and Jo Grimond, former leader of the Liberal Party. Each side was allowed to send out to each voter, at public expense, a pamphlet setting out its case. The government also sent out a third pamphlet, commending the result of its re-negotiation and also recommending a yes vote. The Britain in Europe pamphlet, which bears unmistakable signs of Jenkins's style, is reproduced here in full. The decisive result was expected to settle the question of British membership for good, but within five years it was again being questioned, first in the Labour and, later, in the Conservative Party.*

**Why we should stay in the European Community**. On Wednesday, 9 April 1975, the House of Commons approved, by 396 votes to 170, the government's recommendation that we should stay in the European Community. For years we argued: should Britain join or not? At last we did. The question now is whether, after years of striving to get in, under both Conservative and Labour governments, we should go through the agony of pulling out. This tearing apart would be a major upheaval. The main brunt of it would fall on Britain, but it would also damage the whole of the West, at a dangerous time in a dangerous world. So the arguments against coming out are even stronger than were those for going in; that's why many people say 'Yes' now who were doubtful in 1971. And hardly anyone has moved the other way. Our case is not just a negative one – stay where we are for fear of something worse. It is based on the real advantages for Britain and Britain's friends of our staying in.

It makes good sense for our jobs and prosperity. It makes good sense for world peace. It makes good sense for the Commonwealth. It makes good sense for our children's future. Being in does not in itself solve our problems. No one pretends it could. It doesn't guarantee us a prosperous future. Only our own efforts will do that. But it offers the best framework for success, the best protection for our standard of living, the best foundation for greater prosperity. All the original six members have found that. They have done well – much better than we have – over the past 15 years.

> I believe that both the security and the prosperity of the country depend upon a Yes vote. Not to have gone into Europe would have been a misfortune. But to come out would be on an altogether greater scale of self-inflicted injury. It would be a catastrophe. It would leave us weak and unregarded, both economically and politically. (Roy Jenkins, 26 March 1975)

Our friends want us to stay in. If we left we would not go back to the world as it was when we joined, still less to the old world of Britain's imperial heyday. The world has been changing fast. And the changes have made things more difficult and more dangerous for this country. It is a time when we need friends. What do our friends think? The old Commonwealth wants us to stay in. Australia does, Canada does. New Zealand does. The new Commonwealth wants us to stay in. Not a single one of their 34 governments wants us to leave. The United States wants us to stay in. They want a close Atlantic relationship (upon which our whole security depends) with a Europe of which we are part; but not with us alone. The other members of the European Community want us to stay in. That is why they have been flexible in the recent re-negotiations and so made possible the improved terms which have converted many former doubters. Outside, we should be alone in a harsh, cold world, with none of our friends offering to revive old partnerships.

> I do not want to give any impression that the present Australian Government sees any advantage for Australia, for Europe or for the world in Britain leaving the Community – we regard European economic and political integration as one of the great historic forward movements

of this century. (Gough Whitlam, Prime Minister of Australia, 18 December 1974)

Our government recognizes the emerging fact (of Europe) and we applaud. We applauded last week in Brussels just as we applauded two years ago on the occasion of the entry into the Community of Britain, Ireland and Denmark. (Pierre Trudeau, Prime Minister of Canada, 13 November 1974)

Question 'Would you agree that if Britain does decide to withdraw from the Common Market it would be very much in the long-term interests of New Zealand?' Answer 'No.' Question 'Why do you say that?' Answer 'I think that New Zealand's interest must in the long-term be in the strongest possible Europe and the strongest possible U.K.' (Wallace Rowling, Prime Minister of New Zealand, answering questions on 22 February 1975)

Why can't we go it alone? To some this sounds attractive. Mind our own business. Make our own decisions. Pull up the drawbridge. In the modern world it just is not practicable. It wasn't so even 40 or 60 years ago. The world's troubles, the world's wars inevitably dragged us in. Much better to work together to prevent them happening. Today we are even more dependent on what happens outside. Our trade, our jobs, our food, our defence cannot be wholly within our own control. That is why so much of the argument about sovereignty is a false one. It's not a matter of dry legal theory. The real test is how we can protect our own interests and exercise British influence in the world. The best way is to work with our friends and neighbours. If we came out, the Community would go on taking decisions which affect us vitally – but we should have no say in them. We would be clinging to the shadow of British sovereignty while its substance flies out of the window. The European Community does not pretend that each member nation is not different. It strikes a balance between the wish to express our own national personalities and the need for common action. All decisions of any importance must be agreed by every member.

Our traditions are safe. We can work together and still stay British. The Community does not mean dull uniformity. It hasn't made the French eat German food or the Dutch drink Italian beer. Nor will it damage our British traditions and way of life. The position of the Queen is not affected. She will remain Sovereign of the United Kingdom and Head of the Commonwealth. Four of the other Community countries have monarchies of their own.

English Common Law is not affected. For a few commercial and industrial purposes there is need for Community Law. But our criminal law, trial by jury, presumption of innocence remain unaltered. So do our civil rights. Scotland, after 250 years of much closer union with England, still keeps its own legal system.

> I am proud to have been a member of the Cabinet that took Britain into Europe. At that time there were those who did not want us to join. I believe that many of them today have changed and now consider that once we are in, it would be catastrophic to withdraw. (William Whitelaw, 26 March 1975)

Staying in protects our jobs; jobs depend upon our industries investing more and being able to sell in the world. If we came out, our industry would be based on the smallest home market of any major exporting country in the world, instead of on the Community market of 250 million people. It is very doubtful if we could then negotiate a free trade agreement with the Community. Even if we could it would have damaging limitations and we would have to accept many Community rules without having the say we now have in their making. So we could lose free access not only to the Community market itself but to the 60 or more other countries with which the Community has trade agreements. The immediate effect on trade, on industrial confidence, on investment prospects, and hence on jobs, could well be disastrous.

> If we were to come out of Europe this summer I can see no other result except even fiercer inflation and even higher unemployment. (Jo Grimond, 26 March 1975)

Scotland, Wales, Northern Ireland and the less prosperous English regions will benefit if we stay in. We shall pursue our own national development area policies and continue to receive aid from the Community's Regional Fund.

Secure food at fair prices. Before we joined the Community everyone feared that membership would mean paying more for our food than if we were outside. This fear has proved wrong. If anything, the Community has saved us money on food in the past two years. Why? Not just by accident, but because stronger world demand has meant that the days when there were big surpluses of cheap food to be bought around the world have gone, and almost certainly gone for good. Sometimes Community prices may be a little above world prices, sometimes a little below. But Britain, as a country which cannot feed itself, will be safer in the Community which is almost self-sufficient in food. Otherwise we may find ourselves standing at the end of a world food queue. It also makes sense to grow more of our food. That we can do in the Community, and it's one reason why most British farmers want to stay in.

If we left the European Community tomorrow, we could not expect any reduction in the overall cost of our food as a result. (Shirley Williams, 27 March 1975)

**Britain's choice: the alternatives**. The Community is not perfect. Far from it. It makes mistakes and needs improvement. But that's no reason for contracting out. What are the alternatives? Those who want us to come out are deeply divided. Some want an isolationist Britain with a 'siege economy' – controls and rationing. Some want a Communist Britain – part of the Soviet bloc. Some want us even closer to the United States than to Europe – but America itself doesn't want that. Some want us to fall back on the Commonwealth – but the Commonwealth itself doesn't want that. Some want us to be half linked to Europe, as part of a free trade area – but the European Community itself doesn't want that. So when people say we should leave, ask them what positive way ahead they propose for Britain. You will get some very confusing answers. There are also differences amongst those of us who say 'stay in'. Some of us are Labour, some are Conservative, some are Liberal, some are non-party. But we all agree on the fundamental question before us. The safety and prosperity of this country demand that we stay in the European Community. So do our duty to the world and our hope for the new greatness of Britain. We believe in Britain – in Britain in Europe. For your own and your children's future it makes good sense to stay in.

Are we going to stay on the centre of the stage where we belong, or are we going to shuffle off into the dusty wings of history? (Edward Heath, 5 April 1975)

# 16
# We Are Now Inextricably Involved

*Anthony Crosland*

## Extract from speech to the European Parliament, 12 January 1977

*With the clear-cut referendum result, Britain was able effectively to take its place as a 'normal' member of the EEC, with no continuing question mark against its commitment. This was symbolized in January 1977 by Roy Jenkins becoming the President of the Commission in the same month when, for the first time, the British assumed the rotating presidency of the Council of Ministers. The presidency was introduced to the European Parliament in a wide-ranging and highly positive speech by the Foreign Secretary, Anthony Crosland, which was enthusiastically received. The extract included here dealt mainly with the long-term economic objectives of the Community, foreshadowing several of the issues, such as economic and monetary union, which became highly relevant and, in Britain at least, deeply controversial 20 years or so later. This was the last significant speech which Crosland made: he died just a month later from a stroke, possibly brought on, in part, by the strain of presiding over an all-night session of the Council of Ministers.*

I start, Mr President, with a word about the British relationship with Europe. Looking back over a long span of history, we see that there have been two main strands with our relations with the outside world. At times we have been deeply involved on the European continent – after all, it was 270 years ago that the great ancestor of Sir Winston Churchill marched an army south, passing not very far from where we are seated now. Then, more recently, owing largely to the preoccupations of empire, we pursued what has been described, as the 'blue-water' school of diplomacy. But one strand has never been completely exclusive of the other. It is now natural that with the change in the relationship with our former imperial territories, there should be a change in our relationship with our neighbours in Europe. What we have learnt from our 'blue-water' school will, of course, continue to influence us and colour our contribution to Europe. But it is with Europe that, by will of people and government, we are now inextricably involved ...

I therefore now turn to the central economic question of internal integration within the Community. There was always in the past, whether in the context of Economic and Monetary Union by 1980, or the more modest proposals in the Tindemans Report, a widespread hope and expectation that economic and financial policy-making would steadily pass from the hands of member states into those of the Community. And thus would the Community be gradually transformed from a mere Customs union into a fully integrated Economic union, complete with its own central bank, a single fixed exchange rate, and a growing harmonization of taxation.

But this has not occurred; nor are we even moving in that direction. Perhaps it would never have occurred; on this there was always a cleavage of opinion. At any rate the necessary condition was, at a minimum, a growing convergence of standards of living and of inflation, and a pattern of trade which did not produce persistent surpluses or deficits. For measures of integration are readily possible only between economies where living standards and economic performance are broadly similar. Only on such a basis could a common monetary and exchange rate policy rest. But that basis was drastically undermined by the cataclysmic effects of 1973 and the subsequent years – the oil price rise, followed by an inflation and recession, both unprecedented in the post-war years.

Member states reacted differently to these untoward events. As a result, economic performance grew more, not less, divergent; and the imbalance is the more serious because it is between the four largest and most important economies in the Community. The OECD, in its most recent *Economic Outlook* dated only a month ago, expects the imbalance to persist for some time ahead. Indeed, so alarmed is it by the divergent trends of inflation and the balance of payments, that it actually urges a deliberate desynchronization of policies in respect of home demand and economic growth. This will involve even wider disparities in standards of living. The essential basis for economic integration is therefore wholly lacking.

So we face a dual problem of baffling complexity. First, and most important in welfare terms, the level of unemployment in most of our countries is intolerably high; and while it remains so, public opinion at least in the United Kingdom finds it hard to perceive the benefits of Community membership. In addition, our economies, while all performing at an excessive level of unemployment, are diverging in other ways to an extent that in practice rules out major measures of integration. And a cure to the first of these problems is, in my view, a condition of solving the second.

Now what should the Community do in this situation? There is no slick, no simple answer to this question, which no doubt explains why there is so much wailing and gnashing of teeth, yet a marked absence of practical proposals. And indeed this is natural, for decisive action on unemployment and economic recovery must come primarily from nation states many of which, like the United States and Japan, are outside the Community.

Within the Community it is now clear that detailed measures of harmonization will not of themselves bring economic integration. In the same way, more direct attempts to achieve economic union have foundered because the degree of divergence which they sought to correct was beyond their power to correct. This was conspicuously true of attempts to attain a total or even a limited uniformity of exchange rate policy. The Regional and Social Funds, valuable as they are, have not had a significant impact in reducing the disparities in wealth and growth rates between different regions of the Community. And the efforts to achieve better sectoral policies, notably in the case of fisheries, have met a more stubborn resistance because of recession and unemployment. We cannot hope to achieve a better convergence or more integration until all our economies are once again on the path of full employment and healthy growth.

That must be our priority for the next few months. But we must look even further ahead and start to devise new policies that will help us, once we have left recession behind, to counteract the uneven growth in the economies of member states. We should explore ways in which the Community could help further to promote investment in those countries and regions where economic performance is below average. We should explore, as finance ministers are already doing, what contribution the Community can make to greater exchange rate stability. We should examine successor arrangements to the Regional and Social Funds which would permit a far more effective transfer of resources than hitherto, from richer to poorer regions. The more the Community can succeed in putting building blocks of this kind into place, the greater the chances of getting its internal economic development on the road again.

I turn from the internal economic to the internal political development of the Community. We all recognize the need for a greater sense of political purpose within the Community. But at the same time we recognize that the debate between federalists and confederalists is now irrelevant and unreal. We do not know what shape the Community will finally take; and to seek to define it now will get us nowhere. This was the insight which illumined the Tindemans Report.

This is not just a matter of putting aside unrealistic goals. It is a question of understanding the Community as it really is. In the first ten years of its life, the Community's history was foreseen and defined by the Treaty of Rome. At that time, it was vital for its initial progress and consolidation that it should have a number of clear and attainable goals at which it could aim. It was relatively easy for the Community to hit its original targets. But it has now entered a new and far more difficult stage of development. It is no longer the tolerably simple and unsophisticated institution of the first decade, acting (in Andrew Shonfield's phrase) 'in a kind of illusion of privacy within the international system'. It is a highly complex mechanism which has acquired a life of its own and numerous external ramifications.

The Community is now a unique political institution combining elements of domestic, as well as external, policy and with a built-in dynamism which has no parallel in other international organizations. This is due partly to the way in which the Treaty of Rome was originally framed; and partly to the way in which the Community has subsequently shown itself able to develop its practices and institutions to meet events. The Community is thus the creature partly of a written constitution, a feature which it shares with Latin and Napoleonic Europe as well as with the United States; and partly, and perhaps increasingly, of a developing and almost instinctive constitutional process, not dissimilar in principle from that which has characterized British history. The dynamic motor of these developments is the dialectic between the national interest as represented by the member states, and the collective interest, as represented by the Community's institutions, and particularly the Commission. This dialectic is inherent in the Treaty of Rome. But we find it also in the organic development of the Community's institutions, especially in the changing role of the Presidency and the growing vitality of the European Parliament.

Mr President, these developments are perhaps as important a landmark in European history as the emergence of the secular nation state at the end of the Middle Ages. Just as European man at that time could not possibly predict where Renaissance Europe would lead, so we are equally ill-placed to say how the process put in motion by the Treaty of Rome will culminate. While we must know where we are going in the medium and short term and set our priorities accordingly, a simplistic and abstract goal-setting for the long term is even less viable than before. What we *can* do immediately – and in our presidency we shall do our best – is to make the Community work as effectively as possible, thereby demonstrating that it exists politically as well as economically, even if the emergence of a new political structure is for tomorrow, and not for today.

# 17
# Our Parliament Must Be a Motive Force

*Simone Veil*

## Extract from speech on her election as President of the European Parliament, 18 July 1979

*The Assembly of the EEC, as originally constituted, was an entirely nominated body, made up of members of national parliaments who spent a few pleasant weeks each year in Strasbourg, where their role, except on budgetary matters, was almost entirely an advisory one. The Assembly's situation was transformed in 1979, when direct elections were held for a greatly enlarged assembly, which promptly renamed itself the European Parliament. The added legitimacy which the election gave, and the arrival of a large body of full-time European politicians, created an irresistible demand for an increase in the Parliament's powers. These were boosted by the provisions of the European Single Act (1986) and the Treaties of Maastricht (1992) and Amsterdam (1997). Although the Council of Ministers remains the main legislative body, the Parliament now has powers of 'co-decision' over the greater part of EU legislation. The new Parliament in 1979 elected Simone Veil, a former minister in France under President Giscard D'Estaing and a wartime survivor of a Nazi concentration camp, as its first President. In her inaugural speech, she set out her ambitions for an enhanced role for the Parliament.*

In its work ever since the first European Community, the Coal and Steel Community, was set up, and particularly since the establishment of the single Assembly of the Communities in 1958, the European Parliament has played a major and increasingly important part in the building of Europe. However new a departure its election by direct universal suffrage provides, our Assembly is first and foremost the heir to the parliamentary assemblies which have gone before it. It follows on in the path traced by those who have sat in this House from the time when, a generation ago, the European and the democratic ideal were brought together.

Its beginnings were modest and discreet, in keeping with the limited powers conferred on it by the Treaty of Rome, but through the growing political influence it has gradually acquired, the European Parliament has consolidated its role among the institutions and in the building of the Community. It was this growing influence which led to the signing of the Treaties of 21 April 1970 and 22 July 1975 which strengthened the Assembly's budgetary powers. Furthermore, through a number of practical arrangements, the part played by the Assembly in the exercise of the Community's responsibilities has been given sharper form and wider scope.

We in the new Parliament will not lose sight of these achievements of our predecessors. None of us will forget their contribution to the attainment of the hopes of the founding fathers of the Community for an ever-closer union between the peoples of Europe.

While we cannot forget the substantial achievements of the Assemblies which preceded us, I must now lay full emphasis on the fundamentally new departure that has been made by the European Communities in having their Parliament elected for the first time by direct universal suffrage.

For this is the first time in history – a history in which we have so frequently been divided, pitted one against the other, bent on mutual destruction – that the people of Europe have together elected their delegates to a common assembly representing, in this Chamber today, more than 260 million people. Let there be no doubt, these elections form a milestone on the path of Europe, the most important since the signing of the Treaties.

Because it has been elected by universal suffrage and will derive a new authority from that election, this Parliament will have a special role to play in enabling the European Community to attain [its] objectives and so prove equal to the challenges facing it. The historic election of June 1979 has raised hopes – tremendous hopes – in Europe. Our electors would not forgive us if we failed to take up this heavy but infinitely rewarding responsibility.

The European Parliament must exercise this responsibility in all its deliberations. I should, however, like to stress the extent to which, in my view, this new authority will prompt Parliament to intensify its action on two fronts: first, by performing its function of control more democratically, and secondly, by acting as a more effective motive force in European integration.

The directly elected European Parliament will be able fully to perform its function of democratic control, which is the prime function of any elected Assembly.

In particular, given the powers conferred upon it by the Treaties, the European Parliament has the task of authorizing the budget on behalf of the citizens of the Community. Henceforth in the Community, as in all the member states, it is the Assembly elected by the people that adopts the budget. The budget is the most important act over which this Parliament has specific powers, being able to amend it or reject it in its entirety.

I want to stress the importance of the budgetary dialogue at its various stages, from the drawing up of the draft budget right through to its final adoption. This is a complex and lengthy procedure, involving deadlines and a 'shuttle' between the Council and the Assembly, but this complexity and two-way traffic are counterbalanced by the opportunity to make our voice heard.

However, this can only hold good if certain conditions are met: the first is our presence throughout this process, as our presence is essential. Secondly, our strength will clearly be all the greater if we are in agreement among ourselves and take care not to indulge in demagoguery but keep our feet firmly on the ground.

In a more general appraisal of the exercise of the budgetary powers of the directly elected Parliament, it seems to me that one point deserves emphasis. A responsible Parliament should not confine itself, when drawing up the budget, to the adoption of a given volume of expenditure, but must also examine the collection of revenue. This is perfectly consistent with the democratic calling of this Parliament. History teaches us that the world's first parliaments stemmed from the authorization to levy taxes.

The urgency of this consideration is heightened by the fact that, during the life of this Parliament, the European Community budget will reach the ceiling of 1 per cent of VAT revenue laid down in the Treaties, for the collection of own resources. In the years to come, the problem of revenue must thus remain in the forefront of our minds, and this Parliament, representing as it does all the citizens and thus all the taxpayers of the Community, will necessarily be called upon to make a leading contribution to the solution of this problem.

Parliament must also be an organ of control of general policy within the Community. Let us not be deluded into believing that the strictly institutional limitations on its powers can prevent a Parliament such as ours from speaking out at all times, and in every field of Community action, with the political authority conferred on it by its election.

Our Parliament must also be a motive force in European integration. This is particularly true at a time when, as I already have mentioned,

Europe's prime need is a further measure of solidarity. This new Parliament will make it possible for the views of all Community citizens to be voiced at European level, and will at the same time more effectively impress upon every sector of society the need for a solidarity transcending immediate concerns, however legitimate, which must never be allowed to mask the fundamental interests of the Community.

We are, of course, aware of the existing allocation of powers in the Community, which confers autonomy on each institution. The Treaties attribute the right of initiative to the Commission and legislative power to the Council. The autonomy of each of the institutions, which is so necessary to the proper functioning of the Communities, does not prevent these institutions from essentially working together with one another and it is within the context of this co-operation that the fresh impetus provided by the newly acquired legitimacy of this Assembly must be turned into an effective driving force.

Our Parliament will therefore play its part in promoting European progress most effectively by strengthening co-operation with the other institutions. It should do so not only when its advice is sought – and here there are no limits that apply – but also under the new conciliation procedure, which should enable Parliament to participate effectively in the legislative decisions of the Communities.

The voice of our Assembly, confident in its newly acquired legitimacy, will be heard by all the Community authorities and, more especially, at the highest level of political decision-making. Here I am thinking in particular of the European Council.

As is only natural and normal in a democratic assembly such as ours, we differ on the programmes which we wish to implement, on the ideas which we wish to advocate and even on the very role we are to play.

Let us, however, avoid the error of turning our Assembly into a forum for rivalry and dissent. Too often in the past, public opinion in our countries has gained the impression that the European Communities are hamstrung institutions, incapable of reaching decisions within the necessary time-limits.

Our Parliament will entirely fulfil the hopes which it has raised if, far from being the sounding-board for the internal divisions of Europe, it succeeds in articulating and bringing home to the Community the spirit of solidarity that is so necessary today.

As far as I am concerned, I intend to devote my entire time and energies to the task before us. I am not unaware of the fact that, although we are the offspring of a common civilization and are fashioned by a culture that drew nourishment from the same sources, we do not necessarily have either the same idea of society or the same aspirations.

However, I am convinced that the pluralist nature of our Assembly can serve to enrich our work and not act as a brake on the continuing construction of Europe. Whatever our differences of temperament, I feel that we share the same desire to achieve a Community founded on a common heritage and the shared respect for fundamental human values. In this spirit I invite you to embark in fraternal fashion on the work that awaits us.

# 18
# It Is Necessary to Work Together

*Jacques Delors*

## Speech to Trades Union Congress, Bournemouth, 8 September 1988

*The election in 1979 of a Conservative government, under Margaret Thatcher opened a difficult period in British relations with the European Community. It coincided with the discovery that, despite the re-negotiation of British membership terms under Harold Wilson, the British financial contribution was set to grow disproportionately large. Mrs Thatcher reacted violently to this, thumping the table at the Dublin summit in December 1979 and demanding 'our money back'. It took nearly five years of ill-tempered haggling before a settlement (involving large rebates) was reached at the Fontainebleau summit in 1984. Unfortunately, the Labour Party, together with the trade unions, had reverted to outright hostility, and fought the 1983 election on a platform of withdrawal. A crucial stage in coaxing them back was the speech made by Jacques Delors, who had become President of the Commission in 1985, to the Trades Union Congress. In a subtle speech, ostensibly in support of the 1992 programme for completing the EC's internal market, he emphasized the Community's concern for social issues, and made it clear that the TUC's voice would carry weight in Brussels, even if it was effectively ignored by Mrs Thatcher's government. The delegates responded with enthusiasm, giving him a standing ovation and serenading him with a chorus of 'Frère Jacques'.*

President, dear friends,
It was with great pleasure that I accepted the invitation to address congress today. Europe is again on the move. This is confirmed by your report '1992: Maximizing the benefits – minimizing the costs', and the wide interest in the topic, evident from the large number of motions that have been put forward. I look forward to hearing the debate that follows.

Europe matters to each and every one of us. As your general secretary says things have changed, there will be more change, as your excellent report demonstrates. We are living through a peaceful revolution in which we must all participate. We must all adapt. This is why the challenge of 1992 is now being taken up by Trades Unions across Europe. The commission will respond.

Today I wish to concentrate on four main themes:

First, there is the challenge before us. The potential benefits of completing the internal market by 1992 are very large. But we must, as your report says, maximize these benefits while minimizing the costs, we must also preserve and enhance the uniquely European model of society.

Second, we must again become masters of our destiny. It is only by relying on our own strengths that we will be able to resist adverse external pressures.

Third, close co-operation and solidarity as well as competition are the conditions for our common success.

Fourth, the social dimension is a vital element, your report shows that you are ready to be involved.

## 1. The challenge

Your organization has played a pioneering role in the history of the trade union movement. It has served as a model for other trade unions in neighbouring European countries in their fight for the rights of workers and for the defence of their dignity. This historic achievement helped to forge in Europe a new model for society, a model based on a skilful balance between society and the individual. This model varies from country to country, but throughout Europe we encounter similar mechanisms of social solidarity, of protection of the weakest and of collective bargaining. This model was associated with three decades of expansion following the Second World War. In recent years it had been threatened by adverse economical developments, some of which have an external origin. Europe has grown increasingly vulnerable. We must now rely on our own forces.

The globalization of markets and new technologies affect our perceptions and our way of life. All those concerned with the organization of our society must adapt. This of course includes the Trade Unions of Europe.

The countries of Europe are responding to the challenge in more or less the same way. They have rejected drastic reductions in wages and levels of social protection. They have sought to adapt to the new world situation through an increase in productivity. They have succeeded in part, but at the price of *massive unemployment.*

Unemployment is our major challenge. It is particularly young people and the disadvantaged who are suffering. A number of policies have been tried. There have been successes: but the problem is far from being solved. The policies tried have not been adequate.

## 2. Mastering our destiny

It is essential to strengthen our control of our economic and social development, of our technology, and of our monetary capacity. We must rely on our own resources, and preserve our European identity. We must pool our resources. In keeping with this spirit, there must be full and broad consultation with those involved in the production of wealth. Since we are all closely dependent upon each other, our futures are linked. Jointly, we can enjoy the advantages to be derived from this situation.

It is necessary to give a broader framework to this co-operative action, 1992 *does this*.

The governments and Parliaments of the 12 member states have solemnly committed themselves through the Single European Act to such a framework. European unions and employers have also approved the objective of a truly common market, with their own conditions. This shared objective calls for a concrete and productive social dialogue at the European level. That is the reason why I invited those concerned to relaunch this dialogue in January 1985.

Many of the major decisions necessary for the completion of the internal market have already been taken or are in the pipeline, as explained clearly in your report. The Heads of State and government at the European Council in Hanover in June agreed that implementation of the 1992 programme has become an irreversible process.

Your report rightly points out that there will be far-reaching consequences for industry and the economy. The potential benefits are enormous. Realizing that potential depends on all of us.

There are a number of ways of reacting to 1992.

First, there are the *sceptics*. They doubt that the potential benefits are large. They also fear that increased competition will only put at risk our social achievements. These people are already pointing an accusing finger at the single market and blaming it for all difficulties.

Second, there are the *enthusiasts*. They see the completion of the internal market as the answer to all their problems. They maintain that it, alone and unaided, will result in the convergence of economic policies, the creation of millions of jobs, and spectacular growth.

Third, there are the *architects*. They see the opportunities that it creates and are ready to tackle the difficulties to which it might give rise. I am in this camp: and I hope that you will join it. Your report gives me confidence that you will do so.

Membership of the camp requires constant effort and imagination. Without these, the reality will not correspond to the dream.

### 3. Co-operation – solidarity

The European Community will be characterized by co-operation as well as competition. It will encourage individual initiative as well as solidarity. If these characteristics are not present, the goals will not be achieved.

A large market of 320 million will increase competition. It will benefit the consumer, and allow European industry to compete on a world scale. It will create new job opportunities and contribute to a better standard of living. These benefits will only be fully achieved with increased co-operation, and they must be spread throughout the Community.

It was by no means a foregone conclusion that the governments of the 12 member states would reach the agreement that they concluded in Brussels in February of this year. The measures agreed will increase the solidarity of the Community. Between now and 1992 about £40bn will be devoted by them to following five objectives:

- The development of the backward regions of the Community
- The restructuring of regions in industrial decline
- The fight against long-term unemployment
- The provision of jobs for young people
- Rural development

You will notice that most of these objectives concern all member states. Some have expressed a fear that the North/South problems of a nation like the United Kingdom would be neglected at the Community level. This is not the case, as the list of objectives clearly shows.

With these accompanying policies and with an increased co-operation in areas like technology and the environment, 1992 will not only be a factor contributing to additional growth and employment: but it will also be possible to ensure that the advantages of the single market spread to all regions.

## 4. The social dimension

Our Europe also needs clear rules and respect for the law. While we are trying to pool our efforts, it would be unacceptable for unfair practices to distort the interplay of economic forces. It would be unacceptable for Europe to become a source of social regression, while we are trying to rediscover together the road to prosperity and employment.

The European Commission has suggested the following principles on which to base the definition and implementation of these rules:

First, measures adopted to complete the large market should not diminish the level of social protection already achieved in the member states.

Second, the internal market should be designed to benefit each and every citizen of the Community. It is therefore necessary to improve workers' living and working conditions, and to provide better protection for their health and safety at work.

Third, the measures to be taken will concern the area of collective bargaining and legislation.

Now we have to make concrete progress. For this we need the contribution of the architects. In May last year, when addressing the European Trade Union Congress, I made three proposals, which were designed to clearly show the social dimension of the European construction. You have noted these in your report. They are:

- The establishment of a platform of guaranteed social rights, containing general principles, such as every worker's right to be covered by a collective agreement, and more specific measures concerning, for example, the status of temporary work.
- The creation of a Statute for European Companies, which would include the participation of workers or their representatives. Those concerned could opt, on the basis of their traditions and wishes, between three formulae.
- The extension to all workers of the right to lifelong education. This would be done on the basis of existing provisions, and after a full consultation of unions and management.

These initial proposals should be studied and discussed. Other suggestions from both sides of industry are welcome. In my opinion social dialogue and collective bargaining are essential pillars of our democratic society and social progress.

Dear friends,
Europe must reassert itself. The world is looking at us. It is watching you, the British; it is watching the Germans, the French, the Italians and all the others. It is wondering how these nations, which have fought each other over the centuries, have managed to rise up again when so much was pointing to their decline.

The answer is that Europe is reaffirming itself by managing its diversity. You, dear friends, will remain British. More precisely some, like you President will remain Welsh: others will remain Scottish, Irish or English, and I am not forgetting the others. You Mr Breit [Chairman of the German Trade Union Federation] will remain German. We will all maintain our individual ways of life, and our valued traditions. Thanks to co-operation and solidarity between Europeans, we will succeed in preserving our identity and our culture. Through the richness of our diversity and our talents, we will increase our capacity for decision and action.

I did not come here with a miracle cure, with promises of millions of jobs, and general prosperity. There are no easy solutions. This world is harsh, and rapidly changing. Properly managed, 1992 can help us to adapt, to meet the challenges and reap the benefits. It will re-invigorate our European model of development, 1992 is much more than the creation of an internal market abolishing barriers to the free movement of goods, services and investment. To capture the potential gains, it is necessary to work together.

# 19
## Our Destiny Is in Europe

*Margaret Thatcher*

### Extract from speech to the College of Europe, Bruges, September 1988

*Margaret Thatcher's conduct during the 11 years of her premiership, from 1979 to 1990, and even more during the subsequent decade, has led to her being widely depicted as anti-European or at least as anti-EU. This is a misleading over-simplification. There is little doubt that she valued British membership, for which she voted in favour in what was for Conservative MPs a free vote, in October 1971. As Prime Minister, although she fought her corner hard for what she believed to be the British interest, she was by no means invariably resistant to proposals to extend the competence of the European Community. For example, she signed the Single European Act, in 1986, which greatly enlarged the scope for majority voting within the Council of Ministers. Thereafter, she seems to have concluded that this process had gone far enough, and she became increasingly suspicious that other member states, notably Germany, were conspiring to reduce British influence. The turning point may well have been the famous Bruges speech, in September 1988, which was taken as a defiant neo-Gaullist affirmation of national sovereignty. The speech, however, was not all of one piece. The opening section, reprinted here,[1] is a warm evocation of British links with Europe, which she described as 'the dominant factor in our history'.*

Mr Chairman, you have invited me to speak on the subject of Britain and Europe. Perhaps I should congratulate you on your courage. If you believe some of the things said and written about my views on Europe, it must seem rather like inviting Genghis Khan to speak on the virtues of peaceful co-existence!

I want to start by disposing of some myths about my country, Britain, and its relationship with Europe. And to do that I must say something about the identity of Europe itself.

Europe is not the creation of the Treaty of Rome. Nor is the European idea the property of any group or institution. We British are as much heirs to the legacy of European culture as any other nation. Our links to the rest of Europe, the continent of Europe, have been the *dominant* factor in our history. For 300 years we were part of the Roman empire and our maps still trace the straight lines of the roads the Romans built. Our ancestors – Celts, Saxons and Danes – came from the Continent.

Our nation was – in that favourite Community word – 'restructured' under Norman and Angevin rule in the eleventh and twelfth centuries.

This year we celebrate the three hundredth anniversary of the Glorious Revolution in which the British crown passed to Prince William of Orange and Queen Mary.

Visit the great churches and cathedrals of Britain, read our literature and listen to our language: all bear witness to the cultural riches which we have drawn from Europe – and other Europeans from us.

We in Britain are rightly proud of the way in which, since Magna Carta in 1215, we have pioneered and developed representative institutions to stand as bastions of freedom. And proud too of the way in which for centuries Britain was a home for people from the rest of Europe who sought sanctuary from tyranny.

But we know that without the European legacy of political ideas we could not have achieved as much as we did. From classical and medieval thought we have borrowed that concept of the rule of law which marks out a civilized society from barbarism. And on that idea of Christendom – for long synonymous with Europe – with its recognition of the unique and spiritual nature of the individual, we still base our belief in personal liberty and other human rights.

Too often the history of Europe is described as a series of interminable wars and quarrels. Yet from our perspective today surely what strikes us most is our common experience. For instance, the story of how Europeans explored and colonized and – yes, without apology – civilized much of the world is an extraordinary tale of talent, skill and courage.

We British have in a special way contributed to Europe. Over the centuries we have fought to prevent Europe from failing under the dominance of a single power. We have fought and we have died for her freedom. Only miles from here in Belgium lie the bodies of 120 000 British soldiers who died in the First World War. Had it not been for that willingness to fight and to die, Europe *would* have been united before now – but not in liberty, not in justice. It was British support to resistance movements throughout the last war that helped to keep alive the flame of liberty in so many countries until the day of liberation.

Tomorrow, King Baudouin will attend a service in Brussels to commemorate the many brave Belgians who gave their lives in service with the Royal Air Force – a sacrifice which we shall never forget.

It was from our island fortress that the liberation of Europe itself was mounted. And still today we stand together. Nearly 70 000 British servicemen are stationed on the mainland of Europe.

All these things alone are proof of our commitment to Europe's future.

The European Community is *one* manifestation of that European identity. But it is not the only one. We must never forget that east of the Iron Curtain peoples who once enjoyed a full share of European culture, freedom and identity have been cut off from their roots. We shall always look on Warsaw, Prague and Budapest as great European cities.

Nor should we forget that European values have helped to make the United States of America into the valiant defender of freedom which she has become.

This is no arid chronicle of obscure facts from the dust-filled libraries of history. It is the record of nearly 2000 years of British involvement in Europe, co-operation with Europe and contribution to Europe, a contribution which today is as valid and as strong as ever. Yes, we have looked also to wider horizons – as have others – and thank goodness for that, because Europe never would have prospered and never will prosper as a narrow-minded, inward-looking club.

The European Community belongs to *all* its members. It must reflect the traditions and aspirations of *all* its members.

And let *me* be quite clear. Britain does not dream of some cosy, isolated existence on the fringes of the European Community. Our destiny is in Europe, as part of the Community. That is not to say that our future lies only in Europe. But nor does that of France or Spain, or indeed any other member.

The Community is not an end in itself. Nor is it an institutional device to be constantly modified according to the dictates of some abstract intellectual concept. Nor must it be ossified by endless regulation.

The European Community is the practical means by which Europe can ensure the future prosperity and security of its people in a world in which there are many other powerful nations and groups of nations.

We Europeans cannot afford to waste our energies on internal disputes or arcane institutional debates. They are no substitute for effective action.

Europe has to be ready both to contribute in full measure to its own security and to compete commercially and industrially, in a world in which success goes to the countries which encourage individual initiative and enterprise, rather than to those which attempt to diminish them.

## Note

1. The full speech is included in Martin Holmes (ed.), *The Eurosceptical Reader* (London: Macmillan, 1996).

# 20
## There Will Be One Europe

*Neil Kinnock*

**Extract from speech to the German Social Democratic Party, Berlin, 18 December 1989**

*Neil Kinnock had been a long-time critic of the European Community and had campaigned against British membership up to and including the time of the 1975 referendum. Yet he gradually came to the conclusion that the nature of the Community was changing, largely due to the influence of left-centre governments on its development. He also began to fear the consequences of British isolation if it were to withdraw from membership, as the Labour Party was committed to do under its manifesto in the disastrous 1983 general election. Kinnock became party leader following this election defeat, and soon began to try to nudge the party back into a more positive stance, beginning with the decision to fight the 1984 European election on a common programme with the Socialist parties of the other member states. When he led the party into the 1987 general election, there was no mention of withdrawal in the Labour manifesto, though the party continued to be critical of aspects of EC policies. Kinnock's growing enthusiasm for European unity was resoundingly expressed in the speech which he made in Berlin, shortly after the fall of the Wall, when he greeted the prospect of 'one Europe, with boundaries but no barriers, with borders, but without walls'. In 1995 Kinnock gave up his parliamentary seat to become a member of the European Commission, and in 1999 was promoted to Vice-President, in charge of the Commission's reform programme.*

The great shift in the fate of the world which happened here in Berlin on 9 November and the tumultuous events which have followed since face us all with a new reality. It is a reality of hope that exceeds the bounds of any optimism of the last 45 years.

It is a reality, too, of challenge that is greater in size and nature than anything that has faced us and faced our continent in all of that time. It is the reality that Europe will never be same again.

Before 1939 there were many Europes. Since 1945 there have been two Europes. Now we are at the beginning of the time when it is possible that there will be one Europe, with boundaries, but without barriers, with borders, but without walls.

Twenty-six years ago a great democrat came to this place to look over the concrete scar that split this city and its people and gave his testimony to freedom by saying: 'Ich bin ein Berliner.' Now, such is the passage of time and progress, that it is possible for us to come to this city, to look through those beautiful holes in the wall and to say in our testimony to freedom 'Ich bin, du bist, jene im Osten sind, wir im Westen sind Europaer.'

'Wir sind Europaer.' We are Europeans.

That is the basis upon which we must construct the common future. No one should fail to recognize the great chances that it offers. No one should underestimate the great challenge that it brings. For 45 years since the war fought against fascist barbarity devastated so much of this continent and shattered the lives of so many of its people, all of Europe has lived with division and tension and much of Europe has lived under oppression.

Those conditions were dangerous to all, cruel to many and massively costly to West and to East. But the age had its own certainties, it produced its own habits. It was never comfortable. But it was customary, it was usual. It appeared to have its own sort of dependable stability.

Now that age has gone. We celebrate its passing. We rejoice at the victories for freedom which the peoples of the East are winning in an advance which is not so much a march of progress as a cavalry charge. But since we know that we want, and all people need not only progress but *progress with stability*, we have to work now to achieve that.

We have to ensure that the old, settled state of this continent is, in the wake of the joyous upheavals of this year, replaced by a new form of steadiness that propels change and sponsors progress. We want a stability of community in place of a stability of rivalry. You in the Federal Republic and – most particularly – in this Party, as well as people in the DDR, are already demonstrating your readiness to help in that design.

You do it by the way in which you show your understanding that the question of the future of Germany, whilst being obviously a matter of greatest interest and concern for the German people is also a matter of great interest and concern for your neighbours to the West and to the East too. The specific commitment by your Party, the SPD, to the fixture of present neighbouring borders 'with no ifs and buts' is the most direct and uncompromising expression of that.

Those who carry their placards in East and West and say in those simple words 'Kein Gross Deutschland' are expressing the great ideal and the great potential for a Germany that has unity in freedom and peace with itself and with its neighbours. Those attitudes and the strong body of feeling behind them are part of the formula for the stability with progress that Europe must develop.

No one has the complete formula yet, of course. But what we do know is that it must be built *in* the East and West and *between* the East and West around the cores of:

Freedom for the individual and liberty under just laws.

Co-operation to build the prosperity that is the essential bond of democracy.

Solidarity amongst nations and between nations to ensure the balance of development that is vital to the conquest of poverty in East and West.

Negotiated disarmament to strengthen security and to release the precious resources needed for economic advance.

Freedom, co-operation, solidarity, disarmament – they are amongst the most essential features of any strategy for the European future, any 'architecture' – in US Secretary of State James Baker's words – 'continued peaceful change'.

I use the words with hope. More important, I use them with confidence and a strong sense of purpose. So should we all. First, because to us Socialists freedom, co-operation, solidarity, negotiated disarmament are not just decent concepts, they are basic convictions.

Secondly, because it is just those values, just those ideals, just that determination to make common cause and take common action that are now more relevant than ever in response to the obligations and opportunities of our times.

Without that common cause and common action, the growth of democracy will be stunted. Without that common cause and common action the old enemies of introversion and nationalism will continue to fracture and threaten communities.

Without that common cause and common action, there is no practical means of protecting the national or the continental or the global environment. Without that common cause and common action, poverty and underdevelopment in East and West, North and South will never be effectively combated, let alone defeated. People everywhere know that.

And they know too, that in order to make that common cause they cannot rely on either the absolute of capitalism or the absolute of collectivism. In East and West there is a great convergence of agreement about that. I have seen that convergence expressed in my own country and elsewhere in the European Community. I have watched it in the interviews and demonstrations in the East of Europe.

In the last 12 days in meetings I have had with Lech Walesa of Poland, Miklos Nemeth of Hungary and people from Neues Forum, Demokratischer Aufbruch and Ibrahim Böehme of the SDP, here in Berlin, the convergence of means and objectives has been impressive and encouraging.

People everywhere, West and East, want the beneficial dynamic of the market, the rights of choice in consuming, the impetus of competition in producing. People everywhere, West and East, also want to live in a socially responsible community. A community where care and opportunity, protection from poverty and crime and pollution, access to transport, housing and education, equal treatment and opportunities between women and men are rights of citizenship regardless of individual wealth. And people everywhere, West and East want the regulation of the market and the organization of social justice to be done by Governments that can be elected and dismissed by democracy.

In the West of Europe where the great majority support the values embodied in the Social Charter of the European Community and in the East of Europe where the people forging freedom want economic efficiency and social equity, there is a harmony of objectives even though there is a great disparity of conditions. The call is for *the mixture* – the mixture of private freedom and public responsibility, of individual liberty and collective provision – the combination that is the essence of democratic socialism.

West and East, this is the time that needs that mixture. It is the time in which the only capitalism that should and could succeed is the capitalism that meets the social and environmental needs of the mass of the people. It is the time in which the only socialism that should and could succeed is the socialism that enables, the socialism that makes the state the servant of the people, the socialism for which democracy is both the means and the end of its purpose.

In the Labour Party, in the SPD, in the parties that are in the Socialist International now and the parties that will join the Socialist International as the politics of Eastern Europe clarify and crystallize, that is our kind of socialism.

That is why I speak of freedom, co-operation, solidarity and mutual disarmament with confidence as well as hope. They are much more than ideals. They are necessities of the progress with stability that is vital to the welfare of all mankind.

I do not claim them as the monopoly of democratic Socialism. I do say that they are our basic and long-established principles. I do say that it is for that reason we are the best equipped to take them forward. And I do say that we shall do it – together.

# 21
# The Common European Home

*Mikhail Gorbachev*

## Extract of speech to Assembly of the Council of Europe, Strasbourg, 6 July 1989

*The rise to power of Mikhail Gorbachev in the 1980s, and his policies of* perestroika *(reform) and* Glasnost *(openness) opened up new possibilities of co-operation between the European Community and the Soviet Union. These were further enhanced by the peaceful renunciation of Soviet domination over the countries of central and eastern Europe, symbolized by the fall of the Berlin Wall in November 1989. Already, some months before, Gorbachev had presented to the Council of Europe Assembly his vision of a 'Common European home' and 'a vast economic space between the Atlantic and the Urals where eastern and western parts would be strongly interlocked'. Although Gorbachev's successor, Boris Yeltsin, appeared to share his views and the European Union established good relations with Russia during his presidency, signing a partnership and co-operation agreement in 1994, and providing technical assistance worth more than €1.2 bn by the end of 1998, there was less coming together than had been hoped. Russia joined the Council of Europe in 1996, but there seems very little prospect of membership of the EU in the foreseeable future, if ever. An EU–Russia free trade area might be a more practicable objective in the medium term.*

For centuries Europe has been making an indispensable contribution to world politics, economy, culture and to the development of the entire civilization. Its world historic role is recognized and respected everywhere.

Let us not forget, however, that the metastases of colonial slavery spread around the world from Europe. It was here that fascism came into being. It was here that the most destructive wars started.

At the same time Europe, which can take a legitimate pride in its accomplishments, is far from having settled its debts to mankind. It is something that still has to be done.

And it should be done by seeking to transform international relations in the spirit of humanism, equality and justice and by setting an example of democracy and social achievements in its own countries. The Helsinki process has already commenced this important work of world-wide significance.

Vienna and Stockholm brought it to fundamentally new frontiers. The documents adopted there are today's optimal expression of the political culture and moral traditions of European peoples. Now it is up to all of us, all the participants in the European process, to make the best possible use of the groundwork laid down through our common efforts. Our idea of a common European home serves the same purpose too.

It was born out of our realization of new realities, of our realization of the fact that the linear continuation of the path along which inter-European relations have developed until the last quarter of the twentieth century is no longer consonant with these realities. The idea is linked with our domestic, economic and political *perestroika* which called for new relations above all in that part of the world to which we, the Soviet Union, belong, and with which we have been tied most closely over the centuries.

We also realized that the colossal burden of armaments and the atmosphere of confrontation did not just obstruct Europe's normal development, but at the same time prevented our country – economically, politically and psychologically – from being integrated into the European process and had a deforming impact on our own development.

These were the motives which impelled us to decide to pursue much more vigorously our European policy which, incidentally, has always been important to us in and of itself. In our recent meetings with European leaders questions were raised about the architecture of our 'common home', on how it should be built and even on how it should be 'furnished'.

Our discussions on this subject with President François Mitterrand in Moscow and in Paris were fruitful and fairly significant in scope. Yet even today, I do not claim to carry a finished blueprint of that home in my pocket. I just wish to tell you what I believe to be most important. In actual fact, what we have in mind is a restructuring of the international order existing in Europe that would put the European common values in the forefront and make it possible to replace the traditional balance of forces with a balance of interests ...

If security is the foundation of a common European home, then all-round co-operation is its bearing frame. What is symbolic about the new situation in Europe and throughout the world in recent years is an intensive inter-state dialogue, both bilateral and multilateral. The network of agreements, treaties and other accords has become considerably more extensive. Official consultations on various issues have become a rule.

For the first time contacts have been established between the North Atlantic Treaty Organization and the Warsaw Pact, between the European Community and the Council for Mutual Economic Assistance [CMEA], not to mention many political and public organizations in both parts of Europe.

We are pleased with the decision of the Parliamentary Assembly of the Council of Europe to grant the Soviet Union the status of a special guest state. We are prepared to co-operate. But we think that we can go further than that.

We could accede to some of the international conventions of the Council of Europe that are open to other states – on the environment, culture, education and television broadcasting. We are prepared to co-operate, with the specialized agencies of the Council of Europe.

The Parliamentary Assembly, the Council of Europe and the European Parliament are situated in Strasbourg. Should our ties be expanded in the future and be put on a regular basis, we would open here, with the French Government's consent, of course, a Consulate General.

It goes without saying that interparliamentary ties have major significance for making the European process more dynamic. An important step has already been made: late last year a first meeting of the parliamentary heads of 35 countries was held in Warsaw.

We have duly appreciated the visit to the USSR of the delegation of the Parliamentary Assembly of the Council of Europe headed by its President, Mr Björck. The delegation could, I hope, feel directly the potent and energetic pulse of the Soviet *perestroika*.

We regard as particularly important the recently initiated contacts with the European Parliament. Among other things, we took note of its resolutions on military-political issues which are seen by the Parliament as the core of the western European consensus in the area of security ...

As far as the economic content of the common European home is concerned, we regard as a realistic prospect – though not a close one – the emergence of a vast economic space from the Atlantic to the Urals where eastern and western parts would be strongly interlocked.

In this sense, the Soviet Union's transition to a more open economy is essential; and not only for ourselves, for a higher economic effectiveness and for meeting consumer demands.

Such a transition will increase East–West economic interdependence and, thus, will tell favourably on the entire spectrum of European relations.

# 22
# The Power of Dreaming

*Václav Havel*

## Speech to Council of Europe Assembly, Strasbourg, 10 May 1990

*The collapse of Communism in central and eastern Europe revealed a deep longing among the newly liberated populations to reunite with the European mainstream. This longing was articulated by Václav Havel, the Czech playwright and dissident leader, in a speech which he made as President of Czechoslovakia to the Assembly of the Council of Europe. His concept of a European Confederation did not materialize, but all the former Communist states, except Serbia, became members of the Council of Europe, and ten of them (including the two successor states to Czechoslovakia, which underwent a 'velvet divorce' in 1993) subsequently applied for membership of the European Union. Membership negotiations began in March 1998 for the Czech Republic, Estonia, Hungary, Poland and Slovenia, and in February 2000 for Bulgaria, Latvia, Lithuania, Romania and Slovakia. The first of these candidates will probably be admitted in 2004.*

The 12 stars in the emblem of the Council of Europe symbolize – among other things – the rhythmical passage of time, with its 12 hours in the day and 12 months in the year. The emblem of the institution in which I now have the honour of speaking strengthens my conviction that I am speaking to people who are acutely aware of the sudden acceleration of time that we are witnessing in Europe today, people who understand someone like myself who not only wants time to go faster but actually has a duty to project this acceleration into political action.

If you will bear with me, I shall once again try some thinking aloud on this subject in a place that is perhaps the environment best suited to such reflections. Let me start with my personal experience.

Throughout my life, whenever my thoughts have turned to social affairs, politics, moral questions and life in general, there has always been some reasonable person ready to point out sooner or later, very reasonably and in the name of reason, that I should be reasonable too, cast aside my eccentric ideas, and acknowledge that nothing can change for the better because the world is divided once and for all into two worlds. Both halves are content with this division and neither wants to change anything. It is pointless to behave according to one's conscience because no one can change anything and those people who do not want a war should just keep quiet.

I often had to listen to this 'voice of reason' following Brezhnev's invasion of Czechoslovakia, after which all the so-called 'reasonable' people felt much revived because it had given them a new argument for their indifference to public affairs. They could say: 'There you are, that's the way it goes, they've written us off, nobody cares, there's nothing we can do about it, it's no use trying, so just learn your lesson and say nothing! Or do you want to go to jail?'

Naturally, I was by no means the only one to disregard this wise advice and to continue doing what I considered to be right. There were many of us in my country. We were not afraid of looking like fools, but went on thinking about how to make the world a better place and we did not hide our thoughts. Our efforts eventually merged into a single co-ordinated flow which we called Charter 77.

All of us together in the charter, and each one of us individually, thought about freedom and injustice, about human rights, about democracy and political pluralism, about market economics and much else besides. Because we thought, we also dreamed. We dreamt, whether in or out of prison, of a Europe without barbed wire, high walls, artificially divided nations and gigantic stockpiles of weapons, of a Europe free of 'blocs', of a European policy based on respect for man and human rights, of politics unsubordinated to transient and particular interests. Yes, the Europe of our dreams was a friendly community of independent nations and democratic states. When I had the chance to snatch a quarter of an hour's conversation with my friend Jiri Dienstbier (now Deputy Prime Minister and Minister for Foreign Affairs) as we changed machines at the end of a shift in Hermanice Prison, we sometimes dreamt of these things aloud.

Later, when he was working as a stoker, Jiri Dienstbier wrote a book called *Dreaming of Europe*. 'What sense is there in a stoker writing down Utopian notions about the future when he can't exert the tiniest influence and can only bring further harassment upon himself?' wondered the friends of reason shaking their wise heads.

And then a strange thing happened. Time suddenly accelerated and what previously took a year suddenly happened in an hour. Everything started to change at surprising speed, the impossible suddenly became possible and the dream became reality. The stoker's dream became the daily routine of the Minister for Foreign Affairs. And the advocates of reason are now split into three groups. The first is quietly waiting for setbacks to occur which will serve as yet another argument in support of' the nihilistic ideology. The second is looking for ways to push the dreamers out of government positions and replace them again by 'reasonable' pragmatists. And the members of the third group are loudly proclaiming that what they have always known would happen has come to pass at last.

I am not telling you of this experience to ridicule my allegedly reasonable fellow citizens, but for a very different reason: to show that one is never wrong to think about alternatives, however improbable, impossible or quite simply fantastic they may seem at the time. We don't dream, of course, just because the results of our dreams might come in handy one day; we dream, as it were, on principle. Apparently, however, there can be moments in history when the fact of having dreamt 'on principle' may suddenly prove useful.

In my opinion, the main disaster of our modern world has been its bipolarity, the fact that the tension between the main powers and their allies was indirectly transferred somehow or other to the whole world. This situation persists to this day. The whole world seems constantly torn apart by this tension and stifled by the existing superpowers. The victims of this unfortunate state of affairs are above all the hundred or so states inaccurately called 'the Third World', 'the developing world', or 'the world of the non-aligned'. Their understandable anxiety over the possibility that the emergence of a united 'Helsinki' security zone could widen the gap between North and South is unjustified. The very opposite is true. It would be an important step from bipolarity to multipolarity!

In addition to the powerful North American continent and the rapidly changing and liberating community of nations of today's Soviet Union we have the emergence of a large European connecting link. These three entities, living in peace and mutual co-operation, would indirectly open up a new chance of a full life to other countries or communities of countries.

The whole international community would start changing from an area of mutual competition and of direct or indirect expansion of two superpowers into an area of peaceful co-operation among equal partners. The North would cease to threaten the South through the export of its interests and its supremacy but would beam towards the South the idea of equal co-operation for all. Against the broad background of this large

'Northern' or 'Helsinki' security zone, and simultaneously with its emergence, obstacles which until recently seemed insurmountable would fall away and Europe could quite swiftly achieve political integration as a democratic community of democratic states.

This process would no doubt go through several stages and involve a number of different mechanisms simultaneously. It may be that initially, say within five years, a community will be established on European soil that we might call the Organization of European States, by analogy with the Organization of American States. Then, at the beginning of the third millennium, we could with God's help start to build the European confederation proposed by President Mitterrand.

With the consolidation, stabilisation and growing competence of the future confederation, the whole 'Helsinki' security system would gradually become redundant, and in the end Europe would be capable of ensuring its own security.

At which point the last American soldier could leave Europe because Europe would have no further cause to fear Soviet military might and that powerful country's unpredictable policy.

In my view, every move leading to this goal should be encouraged. The more varied the endeavours made in different quarters the better, because the chances of one of them succeeding will be all the greater. Czechoslovakia therefore supports all manner of initiatives such as the small regional working groups including 'Initiative 4' (Danubian-Adriatic Community), and is studying such projects as Prime Minister Mazowiecki's scheme to set up a permanent political body of ministers for foreign affairs of all the European states.

You will certainly understand why I speak so extensively of these ideas, and why I do so in this Assembly, before the representatives of Europe's oldest and largest political organization, which has such firm, sound foundations and has already done so much useful work. Yes, the spiritual and moral values on which the Council of Europe is based and which are the best of all possible foundations for a future integrated Europe.

I can see no reason why your Parliamentary Assembly and your executive bodies should not be the crystallizing core of the future European confederation. Czechoslovakia considers all the criteria for the admission of new states to the Council of Europe as excellent, recognizes them unreservedly and rejoices that the Council of Europe is responding attentively to the emerging democracies in the former Soviet satellites who are now building their relations with the Soviet Union on the principles of equality and full respect for the sovereignty of individual states.

I am firmly convinced that the day will come when all European states will fulfil your criteria and become full members. The Council of Europe was, after all, founded as a Europe-wide institution, and only the sad course of history turned it for so long into an exclusively western European organization.

I come back to what I said at the beginning about dreams. Everything seems to indicate that we must not be afraid to dream of the seemingly impossible if we want the seemingly impossible to become a reality. Without dreaming of a better Europe we shall never build a better Europe.

To me, the 12 stars in your emblem do not express the proud conviction that the Council of Europe will build heaven on this earth. There will never be heaven on earth. I see these 12 stars as a reminder that the world could become a better place if, from time to time, we had the courage to look up at the stars.

# 23
# Ancient Fallacies

*Geoffrey Howe*

## Extract from House of Commons speech, 20 November 1991

The conflict of loyalty – of loyalty to my right hon. Friend the Prime Minister, and, after all, in two decades together that instinct of loyalty is still very real, and of loyalty to what I perceive to be the true instincts of the nation – has become all too great. I no longer believe it possible to resolve that conflict from within this Government. That is why I have resigned. In doing so, I have done what I believe to be right for my party and my country. The time has come for others to consider their own response to the tragic conflict of loyalties with which I have myself wrestled for perhaps too long.

*These were the concluding words of the devastating resignation speech made by Sir Geoffrey Howe on 13 November 1990, which provoked the leadership contest which led to Margaret Thatcher's replacement by John Major some two weeks later. Howe had been a central figure throughout the 11 years of Thatcher's premiership, serving as Chancellor of the Exchequer, Foreign Secretary and latterly as Deputy Prime Minister and Leader of the House of Commons. Increasingly irritated by her growing hostility to the European Community, and her intemperate way of expressing it, his patience finally snapped after she had given a highly tendentious report to the House of Commons on the recent Rome summit discussions on progress towards introducing a single currency, concluding with the emphatic words: 'No, no, no.' As a backbencher, Howe became one of the strongest opponents of the growing Eurosceptical forces within his party, and – one year later – made another highly effective speech in the Commons, extracted here, in which he dismissed their 'negative' approach to sovereignty and refuted a number of 'ancient fallacies'.*

**Sir Geoffrey Howe (Surrey East):** ... Underlying the debate, a number of ancient fallacies have begun to re-emerge in this country and elsewhere. One that keeps recurring is that the Community to which we still belong remains an economic community, devoted only to economic objectives. That was never its purpose. It was one of the great post-war institutions whose central purpose was political – to put an end to the frightful nationalistic quarrels which had for decades, indeed centuries, seen the people of Europe tearing each other to pieces and spreading havoc far and wide.

The Community has gone a long way towards achieving that central purpose; towards taming nationalism without suppressing patriotism; towards sharing sovereignty without destroying nations; and towards putting the magic of markets to work for society in a stable democratic setting. In that way it has used economic means to promote the central political objective of 'ever closer union among the people of Europe'. That was at the heart of the process at the outset, and it mains so.

The next fallacy that causes some confusion in the discussion is the persistence of what I regard as a narrow outdated approach to the notion of sovereignty. Such an approach was repudiated by Harold Macmillan, the then Prime Minister, when we applied to join the Community, as it had been by Winston Churchill before that. That idea is that sovereignty is something to be guarded, preserved and held in splendid isolation, the idea that we must always think of sovereignty as something that we are required to hand over, required to lose, to surrender or to sacrifice – conceding, in the words of my right hon. Friend the Member for Finchley [Margaret Thatcher], powers demanded by the Community.

That strikes me as an unduly negative approach. Sovereignty is not an undivided thing. If it were, the only ruler who was absolutely sovereign and monarch of all he surveyed was Robinson Crusoe. But he was sovereign of everything and master of nothing.

There is a great confusion involved in regarding sovereignty as in some way akin to virginity – 'Now you have it, now you don't.' It is not a zero sum game, or some kind of single-entry book-keeping exercise, related to 'graph-paper economics'. Sovereignty is an asset to be used, deployed, exploited, committed and joined in partnership with that of others.

I make no apology for reminding the House of the quotation from Sir Winston Churchill upon which I drew last year [in his resignation speech]:

It is said with truth that this involves some sacrifice or merger of national sovereignty. But it is also possible and not less agreeable to regard it as the gradual assumption by all the nations concerned of that larger sovereignty which can alone protect their diverse and distinctive customs and characteristics and their national traditions.

That is a more positive and valuable view of sovereignty.

The historic deepening process of the Community was foreseen from the outset, which is why those who recommended it to the country 20 or 30 years ago took care to see that it was not misunderstood. Harold Macmillan, at the time of the 1962 party conference at Llandudno, when he applied to join the Community, described it as 'perhaps the most fateful and forward-looking policy decision in our peacetime history'.

And so it remained.

'Ever closer union' is an objective which has been reaffirmed and defined time after time in successive meetings of the European Council. I remember that at the first European Council which my right hon. Friend the Member for Finchley and I attended together, in Stuttgart, it was reaffirmed as a clear objective. The Single European Act in 1985 reaffirmed the need to make concrete progress towards European unity in accordance with the Stuttgart declaration.

There has always been a temptation to regard the successive recommitments to the central political purpose of the Community as being confined to the small print, to be accepted only through gritted teeth and only on our terms. But it was never thus. It was always part of the process whose importance was made clear at the outset. My right hon. Friend the Member for Old Bexley and Sidcup [Mr Heath] echoed Harold Macmillan's theme when he spoke to the House on 28 October 1971:

> I cannot over-emphasise ... the importance ... the scale and quality of the decision ... whether we are going to decide that Western Europe should now move along the path to real unity ... our decision tonight will vitally affect ... the sort of world in which we British people and many generations to come will live their lives. [*Official Report*, 28 October 1971, Vol. 823, c. 2202–3]

It was more than an event; it was the start of a process. It is a fallacy to regard that process as some kind of negative slippery slope along which each reluctant step should be seen as more sinful than the last. That negative, apprehensive, fearful, even sometimes hostile tone with which some Eurosceptics approach and discuss the question is wholly contrary to the best interests of Britain. Those who most confidently claim to speak for British interests sometimes seem to have the least confidence that those interests are likely to prevail. All too often they see the European enterprise as one huge thicket of hostility and conspiracy. They far too seldom see it as a field in which British talents and interests can prevail and multiply. We need to see the process as a series of opportunities to be exploited and carried forward in good faith.

My hon. Friend the Member for Cambridge [Sir R. Rhodes James], in his biography of Robert Boothby, quotes something that Churchill said to Boothby: 'We are not making a machine, we are growing a living plant.' That is the reality. It is our task, now as ever, to nurture the growth of that plant in the right way.

I am glad that my right hon. Friend the Prime Minister [John Major] dealt so firmly with one of the most gravely misleading illusions of the Eurosceptics – that Britain can exercise a veto that will stop the process in its tracks. I was dismayed that my right hon. Friend the Secretary of State for Trade and Industry [Peter Lilley] told the Confederation of British Industry a couple of weeks ago: 'This train cannot leave the station unless we are on board.'

That is not the position. A veto exercised at Maastricht will not bring the intergovernmental conferences to an end. They remain in place and will continue until member states reach common accord. So the issues could and would return – in Lisbon next June, and in Edinburgh the following December. If that were the course of events, I must tell my hon. Friends that a pointless attempt to veto Maastricht would make it much more likely that those IGCs would resume under the guidance of the Labour Party, heaven forbid. An even more serious delusion is to believe that our veto could bring the whole process to a halt. That overestimates the leverage of this country, and underestimates the weight and momentum of the others in support of the agenda. It is a further error to believe – the Prime Minister made this clear – that, if the veto were deployed, others could thereby be prevented from going ahead on their own. As my right hon. Friend said, there is nothing in Community law to prevent a smaller group of countries from pressing ahead with a separate treaty, outside the existing Community structure, to pursue policies that go further and faster.

That does not mean that we are without support for our arguments in the negotiations. So long as we take part in good faith, with respect for the common objectives, we may take part with the utmost vigour. If our arguments are good, we shall find supporters and allies. However, if we seek partners for a suicide pact in those negotiations, we will look in vain.

**Mr Ivan Lawrence (Burton):** Is it not right that such actions can be taken by our European partners only outside the treaty? It is totally illegal for them to take such action within the treaty.

**Sir Geoffrey Howe:** That is precisely my point. I am glad that my hon. and learned Friend has grasped it so clearly. There is nothing to stop a smaller group of nations, such as 11 out of the Twelve, going ahead with objectives that would leave us to one side and deprive us of the ability to contribute.

# 24
# Britain at the Heart of Europe

*John Major*

## Extract from speech at Bonn, 11 March 1991

*When John Major succeeded Margaret Thatcher as Prime Minister in December 1990 the way seemed open for a fresh start in Britain's badly strained relations with its European partners. Major lost little time in moving to repair the damage, establishing a good rapport with German Chancellor Helmut Kohl, and making a striking speech in Bonn, in March 1991, where he claimed that his aim was for Britain to be 'where it belongs – at the very heart of Europe'. Despite his undoubted good intentions it was, unfortunately, downhill nearly all the way after this promising start. In December 1991 he agreed to the Maastricht Treaty, preparing the way for economic and monetary union with a single currency. In hard bargaining, however, he secured an opt-out for Britain, both from the single currency and the 'social chapter', to which all the other member states were committed. He went on, unexpectedly to win the 1992 general election, but his small parliamentary majority (subsequently eroded by by-election losses and defections both to Labour and the Liberal Democrats) left him largely at the mercy of the initially small, but fast growing minority of Eurosceptic Tory MPs. Despite their opposition, he managed with great difficulty to secure ratification of the Maastricht Treaty, but thereafter his government took an increasingly nationalistic and anti-EU line. This culminated in his vetoing the appointment of Belgian Prime Minister Jean-Luc Dehaene as President of the European Commission, despite his being supported by all the other 11 member states. Worse was to follow, with his abortive attempt, in the summer of 1996, to block decision-making in the EU Council of Ministers in retaliation for the banning of British beef exports following the BSE affair. A possibly terminal crisis in British–EU relations at the Amsterdam summit in June 1997 was only averted by the defeat of Major's government in the May 1997 general election.*

My aims for Britain in the Community can be simply stated. I want us to be where we belong – at the very heart of Europe, working with our partners in building the future. That is a challenge we take up with enthusiasm.

Today the Community is contemplating the course of its future development. That is natural and right. The Community is a living institution: it must continually adapt and change to meet new circumstances.

We are bringing our own ideas to the Intergovernmental Conferences on economic and monetary union and on political union. We are willing to discuss both our own ideas and the ideas of our partners openly and positively.

Britain will relish the debate and the argument. That is the essence of doing business in today's Community. And we want to arrive at solutions which will enable us to move forward more united, not less. That is why we think it better that change in the Community should be of an evolutionary rather than a revolutionary kind.

It would be a tragedy if Europe tried to move so that in the cause of unity it provoked disunity.

Konrad Adenauer, that great supporter of a united Europe, knew that diversity and difference were essential. In his memoirs he wrote:

> It was clear to me that a united Europe could only arise if a community of the European peoples could be reconstructed, a community in which each people made its own irreplaceable contribution to the European economy and culture, to Western thought, imagination and creativity.

There are many things we can and must do in common with our European partners. At the same time, Europe is made up of nation states: their vitality and diversity are sources of strength. The important thing is to strike the right balance between closer co-operation and a proper respect for national institutions and traditions.

We want the Community to move forward harmoniously. To do that, we need to build from economic strength and confidence. The debate on economic and monetary union will have a real impact on our future prosperity. The stakes are high. So let me set out a British agenda.

First, price stability must be the prime objective of monetary policy. Whether or not it is sensible to use the same money, surely we can all agree on the need for sound money. As Finance Minister, I took sterling into the Exchange Rate Mechanism because I knew membership would help drive inflation down. Germany's own record is of course exemplary;

we fully understand the German determination not to move to new arrangements which are less effective.

Second, economic and monetary union must be based on free and open markets. Stage One still has a long way to go before we can proclaim that Europe is truly open for finance. As the President of the European Commission made clear last month, the Community must devote the same energy to its programme for the single financial area as to proposals for subsequent stages of the EMU process.

Third, the development of monetary co-operation must depend on much greater progress towards economic convergence between member states. The gaps at present are simply too wide. To rush forward and ignore them would be to risk economic failure.

We must ensure that the economic ground is fertile before we contemplate planting the seed of a completely new monetary discipline. We should establish clear and objective performance criteria for moving between the stages of the EMU process.

Britain has proposed that the Community should use the period after Stage One to learn by action, through the development of a new common currency, the hard ecu. We are pleased that it is now generally accepted that the strengthening of the ecu will be a central feature of Stage Two. At the same time, monetary policy should remain firmly in national hands in Stage Two.

Finally, though others in the Community may take a different view, we in Britain think it best to reserve judgement on a single currency until later. We cannot accept its imposition. But we are confident that the Intergovernmental Conference will be able to work out arrangements which protect the right of a future British Parliament to make a decision later.

The key to a common policy is the convergence of interests. All member states have a common interest in building up the Community's standing in the world. We must punch our weight politically as well as economically. That is why Britain has set out ideas for a common foreign and security policy. But this notion has its limits. Are Germany's relations with the Soviet Union really going to be governed by Europe? What about France's relations with Algeria? Or Britain's responsibilities for Hong Kong?

One only has to ask the question to know the answer. A common foreign and security policy requires consensus. Another necessary condition is recognition of the vital need to keep Atlantic ties strong. As we look at the wider world, the pivotal role of the United States is clear

– and in the last few dangerous months it has become clearer still. The Community must get its relationship with North America right.

Germany and Britain have a crucial role here. We understand the importance of the United States to security in Europe. For the last 40 years, the American troops on our soil have been the visible guarantee of our continued peace and prosperity.

The US must remain in Europe. We must therefore build up the European defence identity in a way which sustains a long-term American presence. Both Germany and Britain believe that the WEU [Western Economic Union] is the right organization for this. It can act as a bridge between NATO and the Twelve.

Last week I visited Moscow for talks with Mr Gorbachev. The Soviet Union is in crisis. Economic failure is adding to the forces pulling the Union apart. There is a danger of a return to isolation. We should do all we can to prevent that. We should redouble our support for all those working for a more enlightened Soviet Union.

We are not seeking to prescribe the future shape of the Soviet Union, still less to undermine its stability. But we do have a special concern for the Baltic states. In Moscow, I met representatives of the Baltic states and discussed their position with President Gorbachev. I found both ready to negotiate. We should play our part in promoting a peaceful solution that meets the aspirations of the Baltic people.

Steady relations with a reforming Soviet Union are the best background to tackling the problems of Eastern Europe. The ultimate destiny of Eastern Europeans is membership of the Community. I hope Germany, which has particularly strong ties to the East, will join Britain in advocating this course.

There are 80 million people in Eastern Europe who have recently gained their freedom. The 16 million who live in the Eastern part of Germany already enjoy EC membership. Sixty-four million Europeans have still to make the same leap. If they made the leap too soon, it would not only be expensive for us, but perhaps damaging to them. We would be doing them no service if we held out false hopes of membership in the next three or four years; but we should make it clear that the option of full membership exists in due course. It is open to them, as soon as they can sustain the political and economic obligations that it entails. And in the meantime we must help them prepare for that day.

Your experience in bringing a Socialist command economy to the new life of the free market will be invaluable. It will be an example to other East Europeans struggling to achieve the same difficult transformation – and to the Soviet Union itself.

Forty-five years ago a great predecessor of mine looked forward to our post-war future with a prophetic challenge. He saw our task as 'to recreate the European family, or as much of it as we can, and provide it with a structure under which it can dwell in peace, in safety and in freedom'.[1]

That challenge was taken up magnificently by men such as Konrad Adenauer. But it still rests on the table before my political generation.

We did not have to take up arms in a European war. We grew up in the armed peace that followed. Now we have the chance to recreate more of the European family. To build on those post-war structures. To construct a safe and prosperous home for European generations to come. It is a chance that we must not miss.

## Note

1. Zurich, 19 September 1946.

# 25
# A New Start

*Romano Prodi*

## Extract from speech to the European Parliament, 14 September 1999

*The European Commission suffered a heavy setback in March 1999, when it was forced to resign in the face of a threatened vote of censure by the European Parliament. This followed a critical report by an independent committee into allegations of fraud, mismanagement and cronyism allegedly involving several commissioners, notably Edith Cresson, the former French Prime Minister, who was responsible for research and education. Although the committee turned up little in the way of active corruption, it strongly criticized Mrs Cresson for jobbery and lax management, and contained the damning phrase 'it is becoming difficult to find anybody who has even the slightest sense of responsibility'. Commission President Jacques Santer and his 19 colleagues immediately resigned, and two weeks later at their summit in Berlin, the EU heads of government nominated the highly respected former Prime Minister of Italy, Romano Prodi, to head a new Commission. Prodi and his colleagues were 'vetted' by the European Parliament, which in September 1999 voted to appoint them to serve out the remaining four months of Santer's term and then another five years until January 2005. In his final speech to the Parliament, seeking approval, Prodi set out the main challenges facing the new Commission, and promised a 'new start'.*

Madame President, Honourable Members of Parliament,
The time for the vote has come. I have explained to you why I believe this is the right team to lead the European Commission over the next five years. You have scrutinized the team, both through their written responses to your questionnaires and through the hearings you have held with each Commissioner-designate. I should like to pay tribute today to the dignified and business-like way in which those hearings were conducted. I hope your vote tomorrow will mark a new beginning in relations between our two institutions ...

Today, I would like to give you a broad overview of three fundamental challenges facing us:

- Enlarging the EU and how this affects our relations with neighbouring countries.
- Reforming the EU institutions and planning the next intergovernmental conference.
- Securing economic growth, creating jobs and achieving sustainable development.

We have inherited an adventurous, visionary project, and as we plan the future, it is important to recall what we have already achieved. We have created a customs union and a single market based on the free movement of goods, services, capital and people. We have built an economic and monetary union with a single currency. We have laid the foundations of a political union with shared institutions and a directly elected European Parliament.

What we now need to build is a union of hearts and minds, underpinned by a strong shared sentiment of a common destiny – a sense of common European citizenship.

We come from different countries. We speak different languages. We have different historical and cultural traditions. And we must preserve them. But we are seeking a shared identity – a new European soul.

It was the vision of the founding fathers 50 years ago to create a European Community based on peace, stability and prosperity. And that European ideal is as relevant to our citizens now as it was then. As I stand before you today, peace, stability and prosperity are still our common goal. That is why enlarging the EU is such a tremendous challenge. Our attitude to enlargement is the mirror we must hold up to ourselves. Can we rest content with having achieved peace, stability and prosperity only for ourselves, the 15 member states? I think not.

The question therefore is: do we have the courage, the vision and the ambition to offer a genuine prospect of peace, stability and prosperity to an enlarged Union and, beyond, to the wider Europe? Terrible conflicts have divided our continent this century. We in the EU have put them behind us, and we must help our neighbours to walk the same path.

I do not pretend that the task is easy. It requires a comprehensive strategy setting out how, over the next 25 years, we are going to enlarge the European Union from 15 to 20 to 25 to 30 member states. This strategy must take account of three things. First, the fact that, inevitably, enlargement will happen in stages: some countries will join before others.

Second, the specific needs of those countries who face a longer wait for membership. Third, the way in which this process of enlargement affects our other neighbours, for whom membership itself is not an issue but with whom we want close and constructive relations.

With regard to the first point, I am very clear – we need a political vision, not a technocratic one. We need to set a genuine enlargement strategy looking beyond accession to our life together in the enlarged family of European nations. This means, first of all, that we need to give serious consideration in Helsinki to setting a firm date for the accession of those countries which are best prepared, even if this means granting lengthy transition periods to deal with their social and economic problems. And there is the fundamental question of how enlargement will affect our common policies. The more we enlarge, the harder it will be to say what really needs to be dealt with at European level. I do not pretend to have the answers on this, but we must have the courage to address the question seriously and honestly.

The second point is that we have to think creatively about meeting the needs of countries for whom membership is a more distant prospect. I am thinking of closer co-operation with those countries, perhaps granting them 'virtual membership' in certain areas as a prelude to full membership. They could, for example, be offered the fullest possible participation in economic and monetary union, new forms of security co-operation adapted to their needs, and new forms of consultative and observer relationships with the European institutions.

The situation in the Balkans deserves special mention, because although the prospect of EU membership for those countries is not imminent, we must nonetheless use it to spur them towards peaceful co-existence and greater inter-regional partnership. Let me be clear. The peoples of the Balkans have to resolve their conflict themselves before they can enter the European Union. They should not think they can import it into the EU so we can resolve it for them. However, they certainly need our assistance, and I want to underline the European Commission's special responsibility for the reconstruction effort. Our citizens expect the EU to take a moral lead, particularly in a region which is on our very doorstep. I do not want to disappoint them.

The third element of the strategy must be a clear and comprehensive approach towards our near neighbours whose contribution to the peace and stability of the wider Europe is vital. Such a strategy will succeed only if it is inclusive. All of us – the European Union, the applicant countries, and our neighbours in the wider Europe – must work together towards our common destiny: a wider European area offering peace, stability and prosperity to all. A 'new European order'. This should include 'Strategic Partnerships' with Russia and Ukraine, adapted to the geopolitical dimensions of these countries. And it should include a 'Partnership of Cultures' – the term I am tempted to suggest for a new and more ambitious commitment towards the Mediterranean, where we Europeans are dedicated to promoting a new, exemplary harmony between peoples of the three religions of Jerusalem. A resounding 'No' to the clash of civilizations.

Finally, I must say a word about the importance of our strategic relationship with the United States. We need to build a reinforced transatlantic partnership capable of showing real joint leadership. Our first opportunity to do this will be the launch of an ambitious and comprehensive Millennium Round in Seattle offering a balance of benefits to all WTO members: let us seize this opportunity!

Let me now turn to the second immediate challenge facing us: the next intergovernmental conference (IGC).

We always knew that enlargement would raise the question of how the institutions function. But the recent crisis in the Commission and the poor turnout in the 1999 European elections have shown that a genuinely ambitious reform of the European institutions is now imperative. And the Treaty of Amsterdam – positive on some issues – has fallen far short of what was required on directly institutional matters.

In my view, to proceed by stages, with a series of intergovernmental conferences, is particularly unappealing. It would plunge Europe into a state of perpetual constitutional reform. This would be incomprehensible to our citizens and our neighbours. And it would be a huge waste of energy much needed elsewhere.

So we cannot afford to settle for a minimal reform that fails to equip us for powerful, efficient, decision-making. As you know, I have asked Messrs Dehaene, Von Weizsäcker and Lord Simon, to prepare a report which the Commission will draw upon in forming its own position on the issues which the IGC must tackle. This report will be made available to you, and I look forward to a constructive debate in the run-up to Helsinki.

We have to express our views clearly and loudly, because the coming months will be crucial in determining whether we enter a new era strong and well equipped or weak and inward-looking.

But Europe isn't about institutions: it's about people. Prosperity in Europe depends on European people having jobs, and we need to get Europe back to work! Jobs depend on a healthy economy, so the third

122 The Pro-European Reader

key challenge facing us is how to achieve environmentally and economically sustainable growth that creates new jobs.

After a difficult period, the European economy is now recovering. Growth is back, even if not yet uniformly spread. The sometimes painful process of convergence towards economic and monetary union – combined with the responsible attitude of the two sides of industry towards wage increases – has created the macroeconomic conditions for healthy growth. The introduction of the euro has consolidated this achievement. The member states' stability programmes will deepen it.

This is good news. But it also places upon us a huge responsibility. The economic upturn provides us with a golden opportunity to make structural adjustments at lower costs. Modernizing Europe's economy today means more European jobs tomorrow. We cannot afford to miss this opportunity, as we have too often done in the past.

We must therefore use the more favourable years ahead to ensure that growth remains strong for as long as possible, that it generates the jobs we need, and that we combine it with a renewed and meaningful commitment to sustainable development. We must also tackle the long-term problems resulting from demographic trends and their impact on the fabric of our societies. Ultimately, this means increasing both productivity and the number of people actively participating in the labour force. If we can do this, we have a real opportunity to build an equitable and sustainable society for present and future generations.

The single market has given a new vitality to our economies and is contributing to the present recovery. But we must continue restructuring the single market and promoting liberalization to bring even more competition in the goods and, especially, the services sector. This will help us to maximize the job-creating potential of growth and, in the longer term, will support a higher growth in our productive capacity.

This is not the place to list the structural reforms needed: they have already been outlined in many Commission reports. I would, however, like to mention one specific challenge facing us. Information technology is transforming the way in which we live and work and the way in which firms operate. It enables individuals and firms to do things unthinkable only a few years ago.

The current stunning performance of the American economy owes much to the gusto with which the United States has embraced information technology. I am concerned that European countries seem reluctant to fully exploit the potential of this technology. Modern economies are increasingly knowledge-based, and this is an area where we have a competitive advantage at world level. Encouraging the use and development of information technologies will therefore be a priority for the new Commission. I propose to launch an initiative in this area for the Helsinki summit.

Finally, we must take advantage of economic recovery and stronger growth to adapt our welfare systems to current demographic trends. We can no longer ignore the problems or postpone the decisions: the pensioners of 2050 are already among us!

A highly developed welfare system is one of the distinctive features of our European societies, and we must preserve it. However, we owe it to our children to adapt it so that it will offer them credible promises as close as possible to those that it held out to our generation. The Commission recently proposed an ambitious strategy for further EU co-operation in this area, and this is something to which I will be attaching particular importance.

In all these difficult tasks, the European Union has a crucial role to play. First, because it is more effective to address long-term issues through concerted European strategies – such as the European employment process – than at purely national level. Second, because action at European level often makes it easier to avoid the more immediate pressures of the national electoral cycle.

We have the tools to do the job. For example, following the Luxembourg summit, solid progress has been made in building a genuine European employment strategy in which the combination of guidelines, peer review and recommendations is providing a powerful European stimulus to change.

We have to continue driving this process forward, deepening co-operation at European level so as to focus people's minds on the major structural reforms needed to revitalize our economies.

Madame President, Honourable Members of Parliament,
You are democratically elected representatives of the European citizens. You represent the different European political families in all their diversity. I hope that in your vote tomorrow you will give the new Commission your strong support. For my part, I stand by the political commitments I gave to the Conference of Presidents last week, which now have to be integrated into a new framework agreement that will govern our future work.

Let us therefore turn the page. Let us foster a new spirit of co-operation between our institutions. A new balance, based on mutual respect. A new partnership, working for the people of Europe. A new Commission. A new European Parliament. A new start.

# 26
# For Britain's Sake I Am a European

*Michael Heseltine*

## Speech at the launch of Britain in Europe, 14 October 1999

*It was a Conservative government which took Britain into the European Community in 1973, and successive Conservative leaders – including Margaret Thatcher during most of her time as Prime Minister – sought to foster the further development of European integration. Yet by the end of the twentieth century, fired by a largely visceral hostility to the prospect of a single European currency, the bulk of the party, with the encouragement of its then leader, William Hague, had swung towards a Eurosceptic, if not Europhobic position. A significant minority, however, led by such senior figures as former Deputy Premier Michael Heseltine and former Chancellor of the Exchequer Kenneth Clarke, stood firm in their pro-European beliefs. They strongly supported the all-party campaign, Britain in Europe, which was launched in October 1999 with the primary object of rallying support for a 'yes' vote in the projected referendum on British adoption of the euro. In his speech to the launch meeting, Heseltine drew on the shades of Winston Churchill to justify his conviction, as a Tory, that Britain's destiny continued to lie in Europe.*

It is impossible to overstate the overpowering impact on young Conservatives of my generation of the masterful vision and political generosity of Sir Winston Churchill's great post-war speeches.

On 19 September 1946, speaking in Zurich, he foresaw the future of our Continent as a European family. He sought to kindle a new hope amongst the shattered nations in the aftermath of the horrors of the Second World War.

On the 14 May 1947, in the Royal Albert Hall in London, he went further:

> We are ourselves content, in the first instance, to present the idea of United Europe, in which our country will play a decisive part, as a moral, cultural and spiritual conception to which all can all rally without being

disturbed by divergences about structure. It is for the responsible. statesmen, who have the conduct of affairs in their hands and the power of executive action, to shape and fashion the structure. It is for us to lay the foundation, to create the atmosphere and give the driving impulsion.

This was no mean search for the lowest common denominator of economic self-interest. In the same speech, he spoke of the contribution of Europe that history reveals:

Here is the fairest, most temperate, most fertile area of the globe. The influence and power of Christendom have for centuries shaped and dominated the course of history. The sons and daughters of Europe have gone forth and carried their message to every part of the world. Religion, law, learning, art, science, industry throughout the world all bear, in so many lands, under every sky and in every clime, the stamp of European origin, or the trace of European influence.

Many will debate what he meant and question where he would have led us. The controversy about Britain's place in Europe was no less present and in every way more understandable then than it is today.

We had stood alone. We had defended these islands and provided the springboard from which America and the Commonwealth were to join us in the liberation of the Continent. We were the head of the greatest empire the world had ever seen or will see again. We enjoyed the special relationship of the Atlantic Alliance. But slowly, remorselessly, a new awareness gained ground in the body politic.

From the early 1960s every Conservative Prime Minister has had to wrestle with the defence and enhancement of our national self-interest. Each of these people has been very different by instinct and background. From the great aristocratic families to men and women of humble origin, they brought their own very different experiences and judgement to bear. Macmillan himself, Alec Home, Ted Heath, Margaret Thatcher and John Major. Only their convinced and instinctive commitment to the Conservative party gave them a common theme.

And yet in over 40 years in which they served their country in the highest office in the land, each weighed our national self-interest and took us further, deeper and more irrevocably towards that vision that Churchill himself had so confidently predicted.

Britain's three major political parties share this platform today. I can only speak as a Conservative. I stand on this platform with Ken Clarke this morning because all our lives we have shared the same belief in a combination of practical national self-interest with political vision that has guided our party for more than half a century. By the shared sovereignty of the NATO alliance we have enjoyed prosperity and well-being on a scale without precedent. As the world shrinks and the regional market place of Europe assumes ever greater significance in our industrial and commercial lives, I cannot understand those who think we can fight our corner or protect our legitimate interests in the everyday conferences of Europe that determine our fortunes, if Britain is detached or absent from the process.

Whether we like it or not, what happens in Europe *is* inseparable from what happens to our own trade, employment, investment and industry. They are talking about *our* jobs, *our* prosperity, *our* way of life. I say with no disrespect to our neighbours, if we aren't there, they'll fix the rules their way. I want to fix the rules our way. You can't wield a handbag from an empty chair.[1]

So, for Britain's sake I am a European.

We will need, in the not too distant future, to determine how we exercise the discretion, that John Major negotiated so brilliantly at Maastricht, as to whether or not to enter the single currency.

As to the decision itself, I have one test. Is it in our own national interest? As to timing, I will judge by the facts of the matter. There can be no predetermined moment. There could be a time to act. It could well be necessary, then, so to act.

I have no doubt that, in or out, the converging market of Europe is now inseparable from our future as a trading nation and a financial centre. The coming of the single currency will unleash a wave of competitive pressure, which will sweep through this huge common market. Our companies will be forced to trade in euros. That is why they *must* prepare – and they must do so now. Overseas investors will weigh the exchange rate risks of investing here, if they perceive we will remain outside. Our interest rates will remain higher outside than inside.

I welcome the establishment of Britain in Europe. It represents the widest spectrum of opinion. It brings together the men and women who have very different philosophies, a quite different political perspective and who do not share the same vision on society. We will continue to disagree.

But on one thing we are *all* agreed. The dawning century will see Britain moving closer to Europe. That is an opportunity, *not* a threat.

## Note

1. A dig at Lady Thatcher.

# 27
# Britain Can't Be Anywhere Else

*Charles Kennedy*

## Speech to launch meeting of Britain in Europe, 14 October 1999

*The Liberal Party, and its successor, the Liberal Democratic Party, has been the most consistent supporter of British membership of the European Community ever since the founding of the Coal and Steel Community in 1951. Successive Liberal leaders, from Jo Grimond onwards, have all stressed their strong European credentials, and – unlike their main rivals – their party has never harboured a significant minority of anti-Europeans. So it was entirely fitting and logical that Charles Kennedy, who became leader of the Liberal Democratic Party in 1999, in succession to Paddy Ashdown, should share the platform with Blair and Heseltine at the launch of the pro-European pressure group, Britain in Europe, in October 1999.*

Britain in Europe. The name says it all. Britain can't be anywhere else. Britain is in Europe. Part of its rich culture and heritage. Part of its history.

You know, it always amazes me, when the Eurosceptics talk about 800 years of Britain's independent history. Of course, they can never quite agree whether it is 800 – sometimes it's 1000, sometimes 600. But they do say it's a long time. They talk of Britain standing alone, standing strong. And they are right to do so. We have a proud history. We have often shown the Continent the way.

But it's a partial view of the past. It only tells part of the story. There's an equally strong record of British involvement in Europe. Go back even to the Middle Ages. When the east coast had far closer links with the Low Countries by sea, than it did with the rest of Britain.

Those trading contacts began another 800-year long story. Of Britain in Europe. Of cultural dialogue. Of shared values. Of common struggles. It's a story of music, and art, and literature. Of blood spilt by Britain and France on Flanders fields to save the Continent from tyranny. A story of a 50-year mission, through the European Union, to ensure that Europe is never again ravaged by poverty, unemployment and war.

I am proud to stand here, as the Leader of the Liberal Democrats. So I am proud to commit the Liberal Democrats to Britain in Europe. To give the campaign our 100 per cent support. It is a vital campaign for Liberal Democrats. It embodies two long held Liberal Democrat principles. First, because it is putting forward a positive view of Britain's role in Europe. We have done that for decades. Second, the campaign is a model of the new politics of co-operation which Liberal Democrats have long espoused. We have here today a genuine coalition of political leaders.

The leaders are joined by thousands of people across the country. Who have registered their support for this campaign. I am glad to see some of you here today. The campaign brings together people from across Britain and from across society. Business people and trade unionists. Leaders from the voluntary sector, local government and academia.

We have a shared mission. To explain why Britain is in Europe. To explain that it is good for British business. Good for British jobs. Good for British people. So it is patriotic to be pro-European.

To paraphrase someone, I forget who:[1] We will get the pro-European message across before breakfast. We will get the pro-European message across before lunch. And we will get the pro-European message across before dinner.

There is another challenge. And that is to put the Eurosceptics under the spotlight. We all know how destructive withdrawal from Europe would be for Britain. That is why we must ensure that the British people reject the views of anti-Europeans. There's a clear question to put to them. When you talk about renegotiating treaties, will you admit that you are advocating either British withdrawal from Europe, or at least disengagement by 90 per cent? That's the reality of their case. And it needs to be shown up for what it is.

The unprecedented nature of what we are doing together today becomes clear when you realize that this moment is not an end, but a beginning. It is the beginning of a long-term campaign to change the way that Britain thinks about Europe. A campaign which will shape the attitudes and future of Britain as we enter the new millennium.

The Britain in Europe campaign can change the face of British politics. And it can change our relations with Europe. The Liberal Democrats will work to ensure we seize this chance with both hands.

## Note

1. An ironic reference to a well-known speech made, in a different context, by Michael Heseltine.

# 28
# The New Challenge for Europe

*Tony Blair*

## Extract from acceptance speech for the Charlemagne Prize, Aachen, 29 September 1999

*'Once in every generation, the case for Britain in Europe must be made' said Tony Blair at the beginning of his speech to the launch of Britain in Europe in October 1999. He had, perhaps, put the case rather more fully two weeks earlier in his speech at Aachen, accepting the Charlemagne Prize. This prize had been awarded to Blair in recognition of the much more positive attitude to Europe showed by his government from the day of its election in May 1997. This enabled the Treaty of Amsterdam to be signed six weeks later, and ended Britain's virtual isolation within the EU. The governments of the other member states also welcomed the Blair government's decision to recommend British participation in the euro, subject to certain economic conditions being met, but there was some disappointment that a firm date was not set for a referendum to be held. Blair and his colleagues evidently felt that more time was needed to convert the British public which – according to opinion polls – remained largely sceptical on the issue.*

My argument today is this: Britain must overcome its ambivalence about Europe. Then our creativity and our practical common sense can be accepted as the contribution of a partner, not an outsider. This is in Britain's interests. It is in Europe's interests too.

For Europe the central challenge is no longer simply securing internal peace inside the European Union. It is the challenge posed by the outside world, about how we make Europe strong and influential, how we make full use of the potential Europe has to be a global power for good. To achieve this, we must accept our economy needs reform to compete; our European defence capability is nowhere near sufficient; we do not yet wield the influence in global issues that we should. We are less than the sum of our parts.

This requires us to work more closely on the big issues, and to use subsidiarity to get out of many of the small issues. Integrate where necessary. Decentralize where possible. The European Council, the leaders of Europe, then must return to its original role, setting clear strategic direction and vision and working in partnership with the Commission to achieve it.

The first time I voted was in the referendum for Britain joining the Common Market. I voted yes. As a student in France, one of the best parts of my education, I felt liberated by the sense that here, in our common market, I could work and earn a living in another country. I want to be very frank about my feelings about Britain and Europe. I am a patriot. I love my country. The British, at their best, have two great characteristics: creativity and common sense. As history shows, we have never lacked boldness, or courage. But our sense of adventure has always been tempered by practical realism. We are pragmatic visionaries, rather than utopians.

We have sometimes found it hard to come to terms with the Europe the last 50 years has created. Maybe history would have been different had we been there at the very beginning, if we had felt we were creating it rather than joining it. But we weren't. However, my generation has a new opportunity. We have, I hope, much to contribute to the European Union. But I know we can only give it on the basis of partnership and by playing our part fully. Half-hearted partners are rarely leading partners.

The practical part of the British character accepts we should be in Europe but worries about Europe's direction. Is the European economy efficient enough? Does the Brussels bureaucracy function well? Many of these questions are reasonable, echoed in countries whose European commitment is never remotely questioned. My point to my own country is this: if we wish Europe to be guided by the common sense part of our character, we must also use our creative vision to see that only by participating can we shape and influence the Europe in which we live.

To be pro-British you do not have to be anti-European. We treasure our national identity, as you do. But in creating the European Union we have the chance not to suppress our national interest, but to advance it in a new way for a new world by working together.

Since our election, I believe relations between Britain and the rest of the European Union have been transformed. At the IGC in Amsterdam in June 1997, in Cardiff in 1998, in Berlin this March we have acted constructively. In our joint statement at St Malo with our French colleagues, we helped initiate a long-overdue debate about the future of European defence. In February this year we published a national changeover plan for Britain to join the single currency. We have declared our support in principle for UK membership, though stressing the necessary conditions that have to be met for us to join. The intention is real. The conditions are real.

I have a bold aim: that over the next few years Britain resolves once and for all its ambivalence towards Europe. I want to end the uncertainty, the lack of confidence, the Europhobia. I want Britain to be at home with Europe because Britain is once again a leading player in Europe. And I want Europe to make itself open to reform and change too. For if I am pro-European, I am also pro-reform in Europe.

We should lay to one side the theological debates about European super-states. No one I know wants some overblown United States of Europe. People who believe France, Germany, Spain, Italy, for example, do not have a clear sense of nationhood, have little understanding of them. We are proud nations and we work together.

The European ideal is best seen in terms of values rather than institutions; of a European society in which our key values of freedom, solidarity, democracy and enterprise are shared and reinforced together; in which our diversity becomes a source of strength; our cultural heritage enriches us, and where by representing those values to the outside world, we fulfil our global responsibility.

Our first phase was peace within the EU; our second phase is meeting the new global challenge The next era must be about how we build Europe's strength, power and responsibility *vis-à-vis* the outside world. The challenges are now external: in the economy; in defence; enlargement.

Now, rather than beginning with theory about structures and then asking what the structures can do, we must begin with what we want to be done and create structures to do it. This will require fundamental reassessment of our basic objectives and the means of achieving them.

So what do I mean by reform?

We are living through an economic revolution: global finance; technological change; the Internet and e-commerce; workplace revolution, mass production ended, new consumer tastes, infinite variety and change. The European social model is about values, not rigid and fixed policy prescriptions. The values – a society combining enterprise and social justice – remain. But today the focus has to be on competing with the outside world, in a new knowledge-based economy. This means investment in education and skills; support for small businesses; active not passive welfare states; reforming tax and benefit systems to encourage work. It means less regulation, more labour market flexibility, fewer costs on labour. It may mean fewer pieces of social legislation. But it may mean also far more co-operation in areas of technology, communication and enterprise.

In the new fields of enterprise and in small businesses, we aren't competing favourably with the US. That's a fact and we must face it. The way to deal with long-term unemployment and social exclusion is not old-style demand management. It requires targeted measures closely linked to welfare reform. EMU, so far from diminishing the need for reform, makes reform essential. Economic and structural reform is the key to success for the single currency. I believe we are now moving in this direction. But it needs to be further and faster.

Then in areas like the WTO and the international financial architecture, Europe should make its voice count. We should be a powerful force for free trade, an outward-looking EU and a leader in the search for sensible reform in global finance. We should be providing leadership in the easing of Third World debt and in providing effective help to Russia.

When we began the European defence debate at Poertschach in Austria and then followed it with the St Malo Declaration, there was rightly a sense of optimism. It was a breakthrough. But it is only a start. There is much talk of structures. But we should begin with capabilities.

To put it bluntly, if Europe is to have a key defence role, it needs modern forces, strategic lift, and the necessary equipment to conduct a campaign. No nation will ever yield up its sovereign right to determine the use of its own armed forces. We do however need to see how we can co-operate better, complement each other's capability, have the full range of defence options open to us. This also means greater integration in the defence industry and procurement. If we were in any doubts about this before, Kosovo should have removed them.

Events in Kosovo also bring home to us the urgency of enlargement. The thing the frontline states want from us above all else is the prospect of membership of the European Union. I do not underestimate the difficulties involved in extending enlargement to these countries, or in the necessary transition for their economies. But I do believe we have a moral duty to offer them the hope of membership of the EU and move as fast as we can to make that prospect a reality. In return for that offer, they must, with our help, build their economies and democratic structures and, above all, learn to live and work together in peace.

This does not mean slowing down the process of accession for the existing central European and Mediterranean applicants. On the contrary we should intensify our negotiations. Enlargement offers us the chance of a market of 500 million consumers and the inestimable advantage of political stability for the Continent. We must take it and make the changes necessary to secure it.

Then there is the challenge of crime and drugs. A half century ago the major challenge of serious crime was to prevent gangs establishing networks of corruption and vice in our major cities. Today we have to tackle the threat from international drug barons who establish parastatal despotisms in countries with weak or non-existent governments, run supply lines across the globe in order to peddle their wares of self-destruction on our streets and recycle these profits of evil through banks that are beyond the reach of national financial regulators.

Is it not self-evident that a European Union acting decisively together in partnership with other countries has far more power to counteract this menace than any member state acting on its own initiative? The issue that should primarily concern us is how we pool our efforts for the common good.

The same is true of the environment. Global warming is a threat to the prosperity, ecology and security of all mankind. At Kyoto it was Europe that took the lead – with my Deputy, John Prescott, playing a vital role. Now it is Europe's task to see that the Kyoto commitments are implemented with all that means for our approach to conservation, energy use and transport policy. Europe acting together can achieve far more than nation states acting on their own.

In all these areas I am suggesting Europe gets greater cohesion, strength and influence and uses it. In some areas, it will need greater integration. But it is for a purpose. To serve our own interests, by building up the European Union in order for us to engage with the outside world. Europe should do the big things better; and it should get out of as many of the small things as possible.

Our citizens will support the EU. But the one thing they will unite on, in opposition, is where the EU appears to interfere in the minutiae of everyday life for purposes that appear obscure. Europe could legislate less in some areas and achieve more.

As I say, integrate where necessary, decentralize where possible. Subsidiarity is a vital part of creating the new Europe. It is making Europe work, keeping it in touch with the people of Europe.

So my case is that we need in this next era of Europe to focus on building external strength. Does this mean we avoid internal reform? No, of course not. We are at a moment of transformation in Europe. To meet the global challenge, we need reform of our own workings too.

I do not believe Europe is likely to grow into a replica of the United States of America. But no more do I think Europe will simply be a mere free trade area. It will be a new and different sort of entity. Power will be diffuse – with decisions taken at the European level when they need to be, and taken at the local or national level when they can be.

In reforming our European structure, we should not imitate the constitutional theory of a sovereign state, but rather build the structures we need to achieve our objectives, recognizing the unique nature of the Union.

We need a strong Commission able to hold off vested interests. It must, on enlargement, be streamlined, with a Commission chosen on ability. Romano Prodi has indicated he will carry through reform. After recent events, our citizens expect it. Now is the time to make it fundamental.

We need a new partnership between Commission and Council. Of course the Commission must have the right to propose. But there should be a real change in the role of the European Council. At the moment it acts as a court of appeal, arbitrating disagreements from lower councils. We discuss omnibus concluding declarations of no legal and little political force. The European Council should return to its original conception of looking at the major strategic questions, on which it can issue clear guidelines to carry out agreed political tasks. It should set the strategy and review the Commission's progress in meeting the agreed priorities.

The European Parliament then examines detailed policies, scrutinizes the Commission's effectiveness in delivering the plan the European Council has set out and holds the Commission to account. In this way we can have effective government and democratic legitimacy, both through the Council, in which all elected governments are represented. and through the Parliament.

And we have a great opportunity on appointing Mr or Mrs CFSP.[1] The person needs to have the weight and authority to make Europe count, make its voice heard. A serious person for a serious job.

So my vision of Europe is this. A Europe looking out to the world, not in on itself. A Europe scaling the heights of ambition, not seeking the lowest common denominator. A Europe that does what it needs to do well; and what it doesn't need to do, it doesn't do at all. A Europe that matters – by focusing on the things that matter. A Europe, that wins the battles that matter.

We compete and win in markets abroad. We win in the fight against drugs and crime. We win in the fight to save our planet from environmental deterioration. We win in the battle for peace and security.

Jobs and competitiveness. Crime. Environment. Enlargement. Defence and foreign policy. That is an agenda that matters for a Europe that counts. Get these things right. And we win. We build a Europe of winners.

I am honoured to receive your prize. In return, let me say this: once Britain commits itself as a friend and ally, it is a friend for life. Of all the challenges we face, none is more important than how we develop our relations with the rest of Europe, and how Europe rises to the new challenges I have described. Get this right, and the new Britain can take its rightful place in the new Europe, and the new Europe can fulfil its potential as that global force for good.

## Note

1. In the autumn of 1999, the former Spanish Foreign Minister, Javier Solana, was appointed as the EU's High Representative for its Common Foreign and Security Policy.

# Part III

# The Future Shape of Europe: The Political Case in the Twenty-First Century

# 29
# Network Europe[1]

*Mark Leonard*

It is not difficult to understand why people saw European federalism as the answer to the Continent's political and economic problems 50 years ago. Fiercely independent and aggressive states were the only political model we understood – and nobody wanted to live through another war between them. The priorities for the founders of the European Union were very clear: the need to pacify and reconstruct a continent of over-powerful states which had been devastated by a cycle of wars. That is why European co-operation began with the heavy industries which had provided the raw material for weapons of destruction, and which, after the war, lay at the heart of the continent's economic future. Federalism was deliberately not based on popular democratic aspirations, it was more about saving European citizens from themselves.

It is more difficult to see why European federalism should be seen as an answer to problems of democratic legitimacy today. With Euroscepticism on the rise across the European Union, a crisis of confidence in its institutions, and a revival of regional and local identities, people seem more worried about the intrusive nature of European integration than the lack of a political infrastructure to support it. That is not to say that we should roll back European integration and opt for a European free trade area. The political arguments for European integration are very powerful, but in order to be convincing, European leaders must persuade a sceptical public that we can combine the military and environmental protection, the large markets, and the global power which only European integration can deliver, with the flexibility, strong national identities and democracy that we enjoy at a national level.

This means building on the political identity which is rooted at the level of the nation state rather than trying to supplant it. There is a delicate balance to be maintained between delivering efficient European action – and respecting peoples' opinions and priorities.

That is why we cannot create a system of politics where the majority view can ride roughshod over the preference of the minority. Majoritarian systems depend on having a clear community of interest that sees itself as such – if there are not strong ties that bind, and people feel consistently ignored the legitimacy of a political system will haemorrhage. British people need look no further than their own country to see this process in action – many Scots began to question the viability of a United Kingdom in the face of a perpetual Conservative government that did little to respect the priorities of those north of the border. That is why there is not, and can never be, a central figure or body like a President of Europe or Prime Minister drawn from a European Parliament who is solely responsible for setting the agenda and driving it forward. Similarly, a constitution with a classic division of powers between a single executive, legislature and judiciary would emasculate the national political systems that we cherish.

Despite the fact that it often tries to look like one, the EU is not an embryonic nation state in its own right. Its institutions do not have the extensive powers of coercion, the hierarchical bureaucracy or large welfare budget that states have. Even if you include interpreters and translators, the Commission employs only 22 000 officials – less than a third of the number employed by Birmingham City Council.

The reason that the EU has been accepted, and succeeded in getting this far, is precisely because it has maintained many centres of power rather than a single one. It has developed creative ways for member states, European institutions and other actors to share power horizontally, rather than vertically according to the rigidly predefined blueprint of a constitution. Member states are all interdependent, and though they have different weight on different issues, none, however powerful, can ignore the others. This is a pioneering form of governance.

That is why we need a new model to understand the EU: the network. Though most people don't realize it, or talk in these terms, this is already the model which is closest to the EU we have and it is very different from the two alternative models. Networks do not figure prominently in political theory, but we all benefit from them in our everyday lives – in friendships, clubs, churches, trade unions, political parties or the Internet. Instead of being planned by a central authority, they come about from the interactions of decentralized actors. The rules and order that govern them are not overarching but depend on reciprocal relationships, shared values and a common identity.

The key to a network system is that it is about much more than instrumental co-operation. Networks need common values, a common style of decision-making and a shared set of objectives to maximize their benefits. The fact that the EU's system is inclusive has allowed it to get beyond the 'zero-sum' competitive bargaining of many international organizations when each individual issue is considered in isolation, and success for one state is seen to be achieved at the expense of its opponents.

But our 'Network Europe' has not come about as a result of a conscious plan – it is a fluke. It is the product of an uneasy truce between the traditional visions of Europe as a free trade area and federal state, in which everybody sees Network Europe as a transitional phase – to be replaced by one of the other visions of Europe when conditions allow.

This ambiguity about the EU has enabled us to progress to where we are now. But, with reform at the top of the European agenda, it is now time to pause to understand the nature of the extraordinary system we have created and to see 'Network Europe' as a desirable goal that we can unite around, and one which can help the EU reach its full potential – rather than an unfortunate staging post on the road to a federal state or a free trade area. We can then start to reform it rationally.

We need Network Europe to deliver many goods that might seem to be in conflict with each other – co-operation between states which compete and innovate; decentralization and integration; internal diversity and a single voice on the world stage. To get this right we need to start with an understanding of networks and what makes them work rather than with the traditional theory of state-building. There should be three central areas for the reform agenda: reinventing democracy; creating a framework for competition and co-operation between states; and galvanizing the EU around a shared identity. If we look at each of these areas, we can see where the EU is falling short, before looking at possible ways forward.

## Reinventing democracy

The European Union must be seen as a force for democracy and not a threat to it if it is going to succeed. In the past it was enough to entrench democracy within the region. Today people expect it to embody democratic practice as well. But too often the debate about democracy is confused. In the future we must concentrate less on aping national institutions and more on delivering the two dimensions of legitimacy on a European stage: democratic outcomes (giving citizens the policies they want), and democratic inputs (giving citizens a sense that politicians are accountable). This involves major reform, of the entire culture of the European Union as well as the institutions – and depends on turning Europe into a political space where there is competition between policies rather than institutions.

Table 29.1: Different models of Europe's future

| | Federal State | Free Trade Area | Network Europe |
|---|---|---|---|
| **Constitution** | Single centre of power; single Executive (president of EU Commission to run European government); bicameral legislature (European Parliament to take on equivalent role of national parliament; European Council to take on role of senate); Federal judiciary | No centre of power to police single market; intergovernmental meetings with decisions taken by unanimity; very limited political integration | European Council sets strategic agenda; increased role for European party groups; clear frameworks for competition and co-operation; strong commission to drive through Council's agenda; European Parliament restricted to scrutiny role; benchmarking and policy competition to drive accountability agenda; direct democracy |
| **Economic Policy** | Central direction of economic and monetary policy including industrial, environmental and regional policy; dual taxation including European direct taxes; tax harmonization; national implementation | National economic and monetary policy; national currencies; national fiscal policy | Co-ordination of national economic policies; peer-review benchmarking; single currency with European monetary policy; national taxation with contribution to European budget |
| **Foreign Policy and Defence** | European army and single foreign policy | No capacity to work together; national defence base | Constructive abstention; co-operation between national armies; defence consolidation |
| **Justice and Home Affairs** | Federal police and intelligence bureau; single judicial system; single border controls; single sentencing policy | National | Interoperable policing; non-binding charter of fundamental rights; co-ordinated immigration with burden-sharing |
| **Identity and Citizenship** | European identity replaces national identity; melting pot; European citizenship; European football team | National identity; cultural quotas; national citizenship; national football leagues | European identity builds on national identity; hybridization; dual citizenship; European football league |

## Focus on outcomes

Political systems exist to match public policy to citizens' priorities by making trade-offs between competing interests, bundling them into strategic programmes which voters can choose between. Within Europe many of the things that we want depend on common action: a safe environment on shared measures against pollution, peace on spreading democratic values and intervening together to avert humanitarian disasters, prosperity on the dynamism of the largest single market in the world, and security on police co-operation and other measures against international crime and drugs. Too often the EU does not deliver on its potential. The gulf between what people expect from the EU (solutions to cross-border problems) and what they get (half of the budget spent on the CAP) is much more damaging than the formal democratic deficit. To restore legitimacy in the institutions we need to find ways of proving that the EU will only act in areas where it can add value. Of course, getting the right policies is not enough. People need to feel that they are part of the process that makes them – and that they can hold the institutions that implement them to account.

## Accountability through competition

The reason that we need to reinvent politics is that we are trying to create the first political system that is not tied to a single state, one that allows us to have political debates across frontiers. This will mean thinking about politics very differently. Instead of seeing EU politics as a bolt-on extra that can be confined to the European Parliament, we need to ensure that the political debate runs through all the EU institutions and member states.

## The power of the European average

It is a heretical thought, but it is possible a European Statistics Office could do more for political accountability in Europe than a directly elected European Parliament. Access to comparative European figures on prices, taxes, economic performance and public services has vastly increased accountability for national governments. The reason the recent fuel crisis sparked such animosity was not just the level of prices consumers faced in the UK but the fact that British consumers could see that they were paying above the European average. The fact that people see their national policies within a broader context is creating a genuine competition for policies across Europe. So far the competition between governments has often been seen as regressive on the centre-left: people have talked of the dangers a Dutch auction on corporation tax and social protection, or interest groups picking issues off, one at a time, like fuel tax.

But the European average could be tremendously empowering. The single market for companies meant that uncompetitive industries had nowhere to hide. A European policy space could mean that sub-standard polices have nowhere to hide. The task of the centre-left is to transform European governance into a progressive quest for the best policies: the finest hospitals, the most creative schools, the most efficient measures against crime. To do this we will need to find better ways of sharing good practice. The European Commission should have a role in this, but we should also reconfigure national embassies and diplomatic services to systematically gather information on what works and feed it into domestic departments. We will also need to publicize data in a progressive way: measuring the European average so that people can assess policies across the board and understand the trade-offs that need to be made rather than picking issues off one at a time. Politicians will be at the heart of this process.

### Reinventing representation to deliver policy competition

There is a genuine need to maintain national identity and national priorities in the EU, but our attempts to protect them must not be allowed to squeeze out the vital debates on social and economic priorities and values that cut across national boundaries. There is no clear way for citizens to vote for, or debate, the kind of Europe they want and what values and socioeconomic priorities it should promote. We have seen that we cannot have a European government, so the biggest challenge is reforming the European Council so that it can give political direction to the whole EU system. It is the EU institution with the most power and legitimacy because it contains Europe's best-known and most powerful political leaders. It is time for these leaders to remember that they are party leaders as well as heads of government, and to treat the European Council as a political forum, not only somewhere that they defend their national interests. By acting as a more political body, the European Council can develop tools for strategic decision-making and leadership, and provide the political and policy framework for the Commission's legislative, financial and administrative proposals. We will need some institutional changes such as replacing the six-monthly rotating Presidency with one that can deliver leadership for a longer period of time. One idea might be for governments to elect a three-country team Presidency (one for each pillar) for a two-year period. We will also need to create a back-up for the Council in the form of a new Council of Europe Ministers with deputy PM status who would meet monthly in Brussels and co-ordinate the work of the different Councils of Ministers to ensure that a co-strategic agenda is being followed through.

But even more important will be cultural change. Building on the now established practice of party caucusing before summits, party leaders and heads of government need to use and develop the transnational party infrastructures to feed their agenda into the Council of Ministers, national parliaments and European Parliament. This will overcome some of the institutional rivalry and promote greater coherence. The Commission will again be able to fulfil its central role of encouraging member states to stick to the commitments which they sign up to in front of the cameras, rather than posing as a European government in waiting. And the Parliament will act as a democratic check within the system – scrutinizing legislation and the running of the commission, rather than lobbying for more legislative power.

### Direct democracy

Of course, improving representative democracy will not be enough. It will make the EU system more strategic, and allow citizens to see a link between the way they vote in national elections, and the policies being pursued at a European level. But people will also want a more direct way of participating and voting for what we want Europe to do. Because the EU will never have a single government or president that citizens can vote out, we should consider supplementing representative politics with forms of direct democracy. In the long term, we could explore Simon Hix's idea of holding Europe-wide referendums giving citizens the chance to overturn an existing piece of EU legislation, or to put a new legislative issue on the agenda in policy areas of EU competence. We should also investigate the idea of a European People's panel which policy-makers in the EU's institutions or in national governments could draw upon to test public attitudes to what the EU's priorities should be, and how service delivery could be improved from the point of view of the user.

## Creating a framework for competition and co-operation between states

Network Europe should be about having our cake – and eating it too. We need to be able to co-operate on a continental scale to deliver solutions to the problems which need cross-border solutions, speak with a single voice on global issues where we share interests, and create a large and dynamic single market and currency. But at the same time we need to preserve the competition between countries and companies that has acted as a spur to innovation over the centuries.

At the moment, EU member states often co-operate in areas where they should compete, and compete in areas where they should be speaking with a single voice.

Our historical inheritance is a European Union that often seems to be most integrated where it is least relevant. The core projects in the history of European integration – the Coal and Steel Community, Euratom or the CAP – are now either redundant, or in desperate need of reform. But the fragmented nature of the Council of Ministers and the inertia of sectoral councils has made it difficult to move co-operation out of these increasingly defunct traditional areas of integration.

At the same time, the EU has not yet developed the capacity to deal with international crime, drugs, or the environment – let alone a crisis such as Kosovo. In fact, the EU is particularly weak at providing its member states with the external security they need – because instead of co-operating and coming up with common solutions – it often works against itself on the world stage. While able to protect our trading interests very effectively by speaking with one voice, its foreign and defence identity has been undermined by 15 separate foreign policies.

Internally, EU institutions have competed over which should have more power, instead of working together towards a shared agenda. Widespread institutional change is needed to make the institutions more responsive, flexible and capable of working in a joined-up way. We also need to challenge the mindset which assumes that harmonization and minimum standards will provide a solution, and develop the institutional capacity to structure competition between countries: only the structure of a network can ensure this. But for it to function effectively we need to have connections that work.

The EU's traditional techniques for co-operation were innovative in their time. It now needs to develop new models suitable for today's cross-border problems.

Above all, we need to build the EU's capacity for policy competition to create a single market for government and ideas. The EU's role will increasingly not be to drive the policy agenda, or devise 'one-size-fits-all' solutions, but to collect information, monitor progress, bench-mark countries' achievements and highlight their shortcomings. Each EU member should see its partners as common learning resources across the full range of policy – so that the European Union becomes a laboratory for policy innovation.[2]

The new emphasis must be placed on 'joined-up government', not sectoral representation. We need vastly to reduce the number of sectoral councils to just four, allowing strategic decision-making and the focusing of political attention on key issues. The European Council should create European Ministerial Taskforces, made up of a range of ministers from different departmental backgrounds to tackle other issues. This will help to break up the departmental fiefdoms which have come to dominate in EU decision-making. The Commission also needs streamlining and should be reformed to match a reformed European Council with four divisions dealing with Finance and Economics; Foreign and Security Policy; Justice and Home Affairs, and Structural Reform which would be chaired by Commission Vice-Presidents. There also needs to be a focus on outcome-led reform, not intergovernmental conferences, achieved through themed 'reform summits' which tackle one key challenge at a time. We have seen that the EU is most likely to progress by focusing on specific agreed challenges, such as defence, rather than trying and failing to solve everything at once.

## European identity and direction

Network Europe needs to develop shared values and a common set of objectives if it is to effectively promote co-operation and competition. Perhaps as a result of its functionalist roots, the European project has not succeeded in developing a sense of identity which inspires its citizens. Instead of building on the Europe that we live in our everyday lives – in holiday snapshots, on supermarket shelves, in history lessons, on school exchanges, in novels, films, music and restaurants – politicians have tended to employ abstract and elitist ideas from European history. In so doing they have at best limited Europe's appeal to elites, and at worst increased Euroscepticism and fear of the EU with its nation-building symbols.

An EU that seeks to compete with our national identities will fail. Instead, the EU should be working with the genuine European identities which already exist – and show how Europe is adding something to the identities we cherish. To do this, it needs an attractive overarching narrative which gives the identity a content and shows why it delivers something that we want. The European identity which we are striving for will have to be very different from the national identities which it will supplement. It will not be powerful enough to raise taxes or conscription. It must be based on a set of common values and objectives rather than ethnicity or religion. A European identity, which values all of the diversity which Europe contains – based on democracy, diversity, solidarity, quality of life, multilateralism and compromise – can provide a beacon of what Europe stands for which attracts those queuing up to join; can help to provide the social capital to lubricate particular transactions; and bring Europe to life for its citizens.

To do this, we have to understand what it is that makes Europe different. Above all, we value our rich diversity but would reject a US-style melting-pot; we want prosperity, but understand quality of life in less materialistic terms; we value social solidarity as well as social change; we believe in sharing power as well as projecting it. These can underpin a specifically European identity which could be embodied in a new preamble to the Treaty of Rome. Just as the Labour Party modernized by abolishing Clause IV, the EU could rewrite the Treaty so it doesn't imply a limitless march towards 'Ever Closer Union'. What it should say is that we have agreed to work together towards a set of common objectives, using the most democratically accountable and effective means to do so. That could mean setting up supranational institutions where necessary but it could mean reserving powers to nation states in other cases.[3]

If we understand the nature of Network Europe and reform it in the right way, we have a unique opportunity to build a broad coalition for Europe. But to do this we must first bury the ghosts of federalism and free trade areas so that we can start to define a European dream which is appropriate for our age.

The pro-European case must once again convince Europe's peoples that European integration is something that they need to improve their lives rather than something imposed upon them for political reasons. The test of European legitimacy will not be the precise structure of the EU's institutions – they should just be a means to an end. The real test will be the EU's ability to deliver the things that its citizens expect of it. In 2020, people will want to see an EU that is powerful enough to defend its security, to tackle organized crime, to promote jobs and a clean environment. But they will also expect to retain a strong sense of national identity and to have control over the key decisions which affect their lives.

*Mark Leonard is Director of the Foreign Policy Centre*

## Notes

1.  This is an edited extract from the essay which draws on my longer report *Network Europe* (Foreign Policy Centre in association with Clifford Chance, 1999).

2. Ben Hall, 'A new model of integration' (London: Centre for European Reform Briefing, Centre for European Reform, 1999).
3. See *New Visons for Europe: The Millennium Pledge* (Foreign Policy Centre, 1999; full text available at http://www.fpc.org.uk) for one attempt at a commitment which Europe's governments could make to their peoples.

# 30
# Europe and Security

*Robert Cooper*

The year 1989 marked a break in European history. It was more significant even than the events of 1789, 1815 or 1919. These dates stand for revolutions, the break-up of empires and the re-ordering of spheres of influence. But until 1989, change took place within the established framework of the balance of power and the sovereign independent state. The year 1989 was different. In addition to the dramatic changes of that year – the revolutions and the re-ordering of alliances – it marked an underlying change in the European state system itself.

To put it crudely, what happened in 1989 was not just the end of the Cold War, but also the end of the balance-of-power system in Europe. This change is less obvious and less dramatic than the lifting of the Iron Curtain or the fall of the Berlin Wall, but it is no less important. And, in fact, the change in the system is closely associated with both of these events and perhaps was even a precondition for them.

What is now emerging into the daylight is not a re-arrangement of the old system but a new system. Behind this lies a new form of statehood, or at least states which are behaving in a radically different way from the past. Alliances which survive in peace as well as in war, interference in each other's domestic affairs and the acceptance of jurisdiction of international courts mean that states today are less absolute in their sovereignty and independence than before.

The purpose of this essay is to explain the changes that have taken place and to offer a framework for understanding the post-Cold War world. The central focus will be on Europe, for a number of reasons. It is Europe that has dominated, first actively and then passively, the international stage for about 500 years. Secondly, it is in Europe that systemic change has taken place: the nation state balance-of-power system came into being first in Europe; and now the post-balance system (which I call the postmodern) has also begun in Europe. Thirdly, this essay is written primarily for Europeans; they face the twin challenge of making the new model of security work on their own continent while living with a world that continues to operate on the old rules.

## The new world order

What came to an end in 1989 was not just the Cold War, nor even in a formal sense the Second World War – since the 2+4 Treaty (ending the post-war arrangements for Berlin and Germany) represents a final settlement of that war, too. What came to an end in Europe (but perhaps only in Europe) were the political systems of three centuries: the balance-of-power and the imperial urge. The Cold War brought together the system of balance and empire and made the world a single whole, unified by a single struggle for supremacy and locked in a single balance of terror. But both balance and empire have now ceased to be the ruling concepts in Europe; and the world consequently no longer forms a single political system.

We live now in a divided world, but divided quite differently from the days of the East–West confrontation. First there is a pre-modern world, the pre-state, post-imperial chaos. Examples of this are Somalia, Afghanistan, Liberia. The state in these countries no longer fulfils Weber's criterion of having the legitimate monopoly on the use of force. In such places we have, for the first time since the nineteenth century, a *terra nullius*. It may remain so or it may not. The existence of such a zone of chaos is nothing new; but previously such areas, precisely because of their chaos, were isolated from the rest of the world. Not so today when a country without much law and order can still have an international airport. While such countries no longer stimulate greed, they may excite pity: television pictures can bring their suffering into our homes. And, where the state is too weak to be dangerous, non-state actors may become too strong. If they become too dangerous for the established states to tolerate, it is possible to imagine a defensive imperialism. If non-state actors, notably drug, crime, or terrorist syndicates take to using non-state (that is, pre-modern) bases for attacks on the more orderly parts of the world, then the organized states may eventually have to respond. Occasionally they do so already.[1]

The second part of the world is the modern. Here the classical state system remains intact. States retain the monopoly of force and may be prepared to use it against each other. If there is order in this part of the system it is because of a balance-of-power or because of the presence of hegemonic states which see an interest in maintaining the *status quo*. The modern world is for the most part orderly, but it remains full of risks. An important characteristic of the modern order (which I call 'modern' not because it is new – it is in fact very old-fashioned – but because it is linked to that great engine of modernization, the nation state) is the recognition of state sovereignty and the consequent separation of domestic and foreign affairs, with a prohibition on external interference in the former. This is still a world in which the ultimate guarantor of security is force, a world in which, in theory at least, borders can be changed by force. It is not that, in the modern order, might is right so much as that right is not particularly relevant; might and *raison d'état* are the things that matter. In international relations, this is the world of the calculus of interests and forces described by Machiavelli and Clausewitz.

The concepts, values and vocabulary of the modern world still dominate our thinking in international relations. Palmerston's classic statement that Britain had no permanent friends or enemies but that only its interests were eternal is still quoted as though it were a lasting truth of universal application. Theories of international relations are still broadly based on these assumptions. This is clearly true for 'realist' theories, of the calculus of interests and the balance-of-power; it is also true for 'idealist' theories – based on the hope that the anarchy of nations can be replaced by the hegemony of a world government or a collective-security system. The United Nations, as originally conceived, belongs to this universe. It is an attempt to establish law and order within the modern state system. The UN Charter emphasizes state sovereignty on the one hand and aims to maintain order by force. The veto power is a device to ensure that the UN system does not take on more than it can handle by attacking the interests of the great powers. The UN was thus conceived to stabilize the order of states and not to create a fundamentally new order.

The third part of the international system may be called the postmodern element.[2] Here the state system of the modern world is also collapsing; but unlike the pre-modern it is collapsing into greater order rather than into disorder. Modern Europe was born with the Peace of Westphalia. Postmodern Europe begins with two treaties. The first of these, the Treaty of Rome, was created out of the failures of the modern system: the balance-of-power which ceased to work and the nation state which took nationalism to destructive extremes. The Treaty of Rome is a conscious and successful attempt to go beyond the nation state.

The second foundation of the postmodern era is the Treaty on Conventional Forces in Europe (the CFE Treaty): this was born of the failures, wastes and absurdities of the Cold War. In aspiration at least the Organization for Security and Co-operation in Europe (OSCE) also belongs to this world. So, in different ways, do the Chemical Weapons Convention

(CWC), the Ottawa Convention banning anti-personnel mines and the treaty establishing an International Criminal Court.

The postmodern system does not rely on balance; nor does it emphasize sovereignty or the separation of domestic and foreign affairs. The European Union is a highly developed system for mutual interference in each other's domestic affairs, right down to beer and sausages. The CFE Treaty also breaks new ground in intrusion in areas normally within state sovereignty. Parties to the treaty have to notify the location of their heavy weapons (which are in any case limited by the treaty) and allow challenge inspections. Under this treaty, more than 50 000 items of heavy military equipment – tanks, artillery, helicopters and so on – have been destroyed by mutual agreement, surely an unprecedented event. The legitimate monopoly on force, which is the essence of statehood, is thus subject to international – but self-imposed – constraints.

It is important to realize what an extraordinary revolution this is. The normal logical behaviour of armed forces is to conceal their strength and hide their forces and equipment from potential enemies. Treaties to regulate such matters are an absurdity in strategic logic. In the first place, you do not reach agreements with enemies, since, if they are enemies they cannot be trusted. In the second place, you do not let the enemy come snooping round your bases counting weapons. What is it that has brought about this weird behaviour? The answer must be that behind the paradox of the CFE Treaty lies the equal and opposite paradox of the nuclear age: that in order to defend yourself you had to be prepared to destroy yourself. The shared interest of European countries in avoiding a nuclear catastrophe has proved enough to overcome the normal strategic logic of distrust and concealment. The mutual vulnerability that provided stability in the nuclear age has now been extended to the conventional end of the spectrum where it becomes mutual transparency. (The Cold War nuclear stalemate already contained some elements of the postmodern. It relied on transparency; for deterrence to work it has to be visible.)

The path towards this treaty was laid through one of the few real innovations in diplomacy – confidence-building measures. Through the fog of mistrust and deception, the Cold War states began to understand late in the day that the others might not, in fact, be planning to attack them. Measures to prevent war through miscalculation grew out of this, for example, observation of manoeuvres. The progression has proceeded logically to observation of weapons systems and to limitations on them. The solution to the prisoners' dilemma lies in ending mutual secrecy.

In one respect, the CFE Treaty collapsed at an early stage under its own contradictions. As originally designed, the treaty embodied the idea of balance between two opposing blocs. The underlying assumption was one of enmity: balance was required to make it unlikely that either side would take the risk of making an attack. Transparency was required to make sure that there was really a balance. But by the time you have achieved balance and transparency it is difficult to retain enmity. The result is that transparency remains but enmity and balance (and one of the blocs) have effectively gone. This was not, of course, the work of the CFE Treaty alone but of the political revolution that made that treaty possible. It does suggest, however, that there is a basic incompatibility between the two systems; the modern based on balance and the postmodern based on openness do not co-exist well together.

Intrusive verification – which is at the heart of the CFE system – is a key element in a postmodern order where state sovereignty is no longer seen as an absolute. But far-reaching as they may be, the CFE Treaty and the CWC are only partial approaches towards a postmodern order.

Although their acceptance of intrusive verification breaks with the absolutist tradition of state sovereignty, the field in which sovereignty has been sacrificed is limited to foreign affairs and security. Thus what is permitted is interference in the domestic aspect of foreign affairs.

The aspirations of the OSCE go rather further. OSCE principles cover standards of domestic behaviour – democratic procedures, treatment of minorities, freedom of the press – which are distant from the traditional concerns of foreign and security policy. Whether the OSCE will develop – as it aspires to – into a system for international monitoring of domestic behaviour remains to be seen. If it does, this will be a break with the tradition of the European state system which will take all the OSCE countries (or all those who play by the rules) decisively into a postmodern world.

The characteristics of this world are:

- the breaking down of the distinction between domestic and foreign affairs
- mutual interference in (traditional) domestic affairs and mutual surveillance
- the rejection of force for resolving disputes and the consequent codification of rules of behaviour. These rules are self-enforced. No one compels states to obey CFE limits. They keep to them because of their individual interest in maintaining the collective system. In the same way the judgements of the European Court of Justice are

implemented voluntarily, even when they are disliked, because all EC states have an interest in maintaining the rule of law
- the growing irrelevance of borders: this has come about both through the changing role of the state but also through missiles, motor cars and satellites. Changes of borders are both less necessary and less important
- security is based on transparency, mutual openness, interdependence and mutual vulnerability.

The most prominent postmodern institutions are mentioned above but this list is by no means exclusive. The Strasbourg Court of Human Rights belongs in this category: it interferes directly in domestic jurisdiction. No less striking, within the Council of Europe framework is the Convention on Torture, which permits challenge inspection of prisons without warning and without visas. In the economic sphere, the IMF and the OECD operate systems of economic surveillance. The Non-Proliferation Treaty (NPT), taken together with the International Atomic Energy Agency (IAEA) safeguards and special inspection regimes, aspires to be a part of the postmodern system, although the lack of openness on the part of the nuclear powers themselves means that it does not fully qualify.

The International Criminal Court is a striking example of the postmodern breakdown of the distinction between domestic and foreign affairs. If the world is going to be governed by law rather than force then those who break the law will be treated as criminals. Thus, in the postmodern world, *raison d'état* and the amorality of Machiavelli have been replaced by a moral consciousness that applies to international relations as well as to domestic affairs: hence also the renewed interest in the question of whether or not wars should be considered just.

The new security system of the postmodern world deals with the problems identified earlier that made the balance of power unworkable. By aiming to avoid war it takes account of the horrors of war that modern technology represents; indeed, it depends to a degree on the technology and on the horrors. It is also more compatible with democratic societies: the open society domestically is reflected in a more open international order. And finally, since security no longer depends on balance, it is able to incorporate large and potentially powerful states. The peaceful reunification of Germany is in itself a proof that the system has changed.

A difficulty for the postmodern state – though one that goes beyond the scope of this paper – is that democracy and democratic institutions are firmly wedded to the territorial state. The package of national identity, national territory, a national army, a national economy and national democratic institutions has been immensely successful. Economy, law-making and defence may be increasingly embedded in international frameworks, and the borders of territory may be less important, but identity and democratic institutions remain primarily national. These are the reasons why traditional states will remain the fundamental unit of international relations for the foreseeable future, even though they may have ceased to behave in traditional ways.

## The postmodern world

What is the origin of this change? The fundamental point is that 'the world's grown honest'.[3] A large number of the most powerful states no longer want to fight or to conquer. This gives rise both to the pre-modern and to the postmodern world. France no longer thinks of invading Germany or Italy although it has nuclear weapons, and these should theoretically put it in a position of overwhelming superiority. Nor does it think of invading Algeria to restore order there. Imperialism is dead, at least among the Western powers. Acquiring territory is no longer of interest. Acquiring subject populations would for most states be a nightmare.

This is not altogether a novelty. Imperialism has been dying slowly for a long time. Britain was inventing dominion status in the nineteenth century and – admittedly under intense pressure – was letting Ireland go early in the twentieth. Sweden acquiesced in Norwegian independence in 1905. What is, however, completely new is that Europe should consist of states which are no longer governed by the territorial imperative.

If this view is correct, it follows that we should not think of the European Union or even NATO as the reason we have had half a century of peace in Western Europe; at least not in the crude way that this is sometimes argued – that states which merge their industries or armies cannot fight each other. This proposition seems to be neither a necessary nor a sufficient condition for peace. After all the EFTA countries did not fight each other even though most were members of neither NATO nor the EU. And on the other side, Yugoslavia has shown that a single market and a single currency and integrated armed forces can be broken up if those concerned want to fight.

NATO and the EU have, nevertheless, played an important role in reinforcing and sustaining the basic fact that Western European countries no longer want to fight each other. NATO has promoted a greater degree of military openness than has ever existed before. Force planning is done in the open even if it is not quite so much a joint procedure as it is supposed to be. Joint exercises and an integrated command structure reinforce this openness. Thus within Western Europe, there has been a kind of internal CFE Treaty for many years – except that most of the times, states were urging each other to increase rather than to cut defence spending.

No doubt the solidarity created by having a common enemy also played a part initially; so did the presence of US forces, which enabled Germany to keep forces at lower levels than its strategic position would have warranted; and so did the US nuclear guarantee – which enabled Germany to remain non-nuclear. But for Germany to have pursued these policies in isolation would not have been enough: France or the UK might still have suspected a secret German troop build-up or a nuclear weapons programme. What mattered above all was the openness NATO created. NATO was and is, in short, a massive intra-western confidence-building measure.

This is why the reunification of Germany within NATO was so important. In a curious way, it is part of how NATO won the Cold War: not by beating Russia but by changing the strategic position of Germany. NATO provided a framework within which Germany – the epicentre of the Cold War – could be reunited. The balance-of-power system broke down in Europe because of Germany and, for a while, it seemed that the solution to the problem was to divide Germany. And – in the same logic – the Cold War was needed to maintain the division. Balance in Europe seemed to require a divided Germany and a divided Germany required a divided Europe. For Germany to be reunited, a different security system was required: in effect a post-balance, postmodern system, of which NATO was one key element.

The EU was another. Its security role is similar to that of NATO though this is harder to see since it is further from the sharp end of military hardware. It is not the Coal and Steel Authority (which did not integrate the industry so much as the market – German coal mines remained German and French steel mills remained French) that has kept the countries of Europe from fighting each other, but the fact that they did not want to do so. Nevertheless, the existence of the Coal and Steel Authority and the Common Market and the Common Foreign and Security Policy and the Common Agricultural Policy and so forth, has served important reinforcing functions. They have introduced a new degree of openness hitherto unknown in Europe. And they have given rise to thousands of meetings of ministers and officials, so that all those concerned with decisions over peace and war know each other well.

They may or may not agree; they may or may not like each other, but they do belong to the same organization and work together and make deals together over a wonderful range of subjects. By the standards of the past this represents an enormous degree of what might be called administrative integration. (This is neither complete political integration – which would require *inter alia* European political parties – nor economic integration, which takes place at the level of the firm, the investor and the workforce.) Again, compared with the past, it represents a quality of political relations and a stability in political relationships never known before. To create an international society, international socialization is required and one of the important functions of the Brussels institutions is to provide this.

A second important function is to provide a framework for settling disputes between member states. Since force is no longer available some mixture of law, bargaining and arbitration is required: the EU provides this in most cases (not all since, for example, territorial disputes remain outside its ambit). The same framework of bargaining and law also regulates a good deal of transnational co-operation. As one (disappointed) observer noted, the EU is an organization not for pursuing a European interest, but for pursuing national interests more effectively. In the postmodern context 'more effectively' means without being obliged to resort to military means.

The EU is the most developed example of a postmodern system. It represents security through transparency, and transparency through interdependence. The EU is more a transnational than a supranational system. Although there are still some who dream of a European state (which would be supranational), they are a minority today – if one takes account of ordinary people, a very small minority. The dream is one left over from a previous age. It rests on the assumption that nation states are fundamentally dangerous and that the only way to tame the anarchy of nations is to impose hegemony on them. It is curious that, having created a structure that is ideally adapted to the postmodern state, there are still enthusiasts who want to replace it with something more old-fashioned. If the nation state is a problem then the superstate is certainly not a solution.

Nevertheless, it is unlikely that the EU, as it is at the start of the twenty-first century, has reached its final resting place. Perhaps the most important question is whether integration can remain a largely apolitical process. It is striking that monetary integration has been achieved precisely by removing monetary policy from the hands of politicians and handing it over to the technocrats. This may be no bad thing but, in the deeply democratic culture of Europe, the development of the EU as a continuation of diplomacy by other means rather than the continuation of politics by other means may in the end exact a price. International institutions need the loyalty of citizens just as state institutions do.

## State interests

To say that the EU (or for that matter the Council of Europe or the OSCE) is a forum in which states pursue their interests should not be misunderstood. 'Interests' means something different for the modern state and for its postmodern successor. The 'interests' that Palmerston referred to as eternal were essentially security interests. They included such notions as the Russians should be kept out of the Mediterranean; no single power should be allowed to dominate the continent of Europe; the British Navy should be bigger than the next two largest navies combined and so forth. Even defined in these terms, interests are by no means eternal, though they can have a shelf-life measured in decades at least. These interests are defined by the security problems in a world of fundamentally predatory states. It is the essential business of a state to protect its citizens from invasion: hence the absolute, if not eternal, nature of these interests; hence the adjective 'vital'. Such interests still exist for the West today: it is probably a vital Western interest that no single country should come to dominate world oil supplies, perhaps also that nuclear weapons should not get into the hands of unstable, aggressive or irresponsible hands. Or if Japan, for example, should come under serious military threat there would be a general Western interest, probably a vital interest, in defending it.

These are problems about encounters between the postmodern and modern world. Within the postmodern world, there are no security threats in the traditional sense; that is to say its members do not consider invading each other. The 'interests' that are debated with the European Union are essentially matters of policy preference and burden sharing. There is no fundamental reason why in the last GATT negotiations France should have been ready to sacrifice the interests of its software companies in favour of its farmers; France's 'interests' are defined by the political process. Such interests may change with governments. These are vested interests rather than national interests. In the UK, the Thatcher government brought with it a stronger commitment to open markets than its predecessor had shown. The 'interest' in free markets was born in 1979 – it was certainly not eternal. The vital national interests that are defended under the Luxembourg compromise are almost certainly neither vital nor national and they are not even 'interests' in the Palmerstonian sense – none of which is to say that they are unimportant. If the second half of Palmerston's proposition, that interests are eternal, no longer applies in the postmodern world, the first half, that no country has permanent friends is equally alien. Although friendship is hardly a concept that applies between states, institutions like the EU and NATO constitute something analogous to a bond of marriage. In a world where nothing is absolute, permanent or irreversible, these relationships are at least more lasting than any state's interests. Perhaps they will even turn out to be genuinely permanent.

At all events we should beware of transferring the vocabulary of the modern world into the postmodern. Germany may (occasionally) exercise a dominant influence in the EU, or the US may dominate NATO policy making, but this kind of dominance, achieved by persuasion or bought in some other way, is quite different from domination by military invasion. (These two countries are not, of course, mentioned by accident – but the significant fact in each case is probably not their size but the fact that they are dominant financial contributors to these two institutions.)

## Who belongs to the postmodern world?

It is certain that there is a new European order based on openness and mutual interference. The EU countries are clearly members. Whatever happens to the European Union, the state in Western Europe will never be the same again.

Although these postmodern characteristics apply among the states of the EU they do not necessarily apply between them and other states: if Argentina chooses to operate according to the rules of Clausewitz rather than those of Kant, Britain may have to respond on the same level. Similarly, in the days of the Cold War, all the European states had to operate on the old logic *vis-à-vis* the Warsaw Pact although among themselves the postmodern logic increasingly applied.

Outside Europe, who might be described as postmodern? Canada certainly; the US up to a point perhaps. The US is the more doubtful case since it is not clear that the US government or Congress accepts either the necessity and desirability of interdependence, or its corollaries of openness, mutual surveillance and mutual interference to the same extent as most European governments now do. The United States's unwillingness to accept the jurisdiction of the International Criminal Court and its relative reluctance about challenge inspections in the CWC are examples of US caution about postmodern concepts. The knowledge that the defence of the civilized world rests ultimately on its shoulders is perhaps justification enough for the US caution. Besides, as the most powerful country in the world, the US has no reason to fear any other country and so less reason to accept the idea of security based on mutual vulnerability, except of course in the nuclear field. Here the US is unavoidably vulnerable. Hence one very emphatic piece of postmodern diplomacy in an otherwise rather uncompromising insistence on sovereignty: START[4] and all the other nuclear treaties with Russia – not least the anti-ABM[5] Treaty which is designed to preserve mutual vulnerability. (The occasional bouts of longing for a Strategic Defence Initiative astrodome show, however, that the US is not necessarily reconciled to postmodernism even in the nuclear field.)

Russia poses an important problem for us. Is it going to be a pre-modern, modern or postmodern state? It embodies all three possibilities. A collapse into pre-modernism is perhaps the least likely: the urbanized and industrialized landscape of Russia has a low tolerance for disorder. The risk is more of the state becoming too powerful than of it disappearing altogether. But there are also postmodern elements in Russia trying to get out. And Russian acceptance of the CFE Treaty and of OSCE observers in Chechnya during the first Chechen war, but not during the second, suggests that it is not wholly lost to the doctrine of openness. How Russia behaves in respect of its postmodern treaty commitments will be a critical factor for the future: so will the behaviour of the rest of Europe as it decides how to build its security relationship with Russia.

Of non-European countries, Japan is by inclination a postmodern state. It is not now interested in acquiring territory, nor in using force. It would probably be willing to accept intrusive verification. It is an enthusiastic multilateralist. Were it on the other side of the world, it would be a natural member of organizations such as the OSCE or the EU. Unfortunately for Japan it is a postmodern country surrounded by states firmly locked into an earlier age: postmodernism in one country is possible only up to a point. If China develops in an unpromising fashion (either modern or pre-modern), Japan could be forced to revert to defensive modernism.

And elsewhere? What in Europe has become a reality is in many other parts of the world an aspiration. ASEAN,[6] NAFTA,[7] MERCOSUR,[8] even the OAU[9] suggest at least the desire for a postmodern environment. This wish is unlikely to be realized quickly. Most developing countries are too unsure of their own identity to allow much interference in domestic affairs. Nevertheless, imitation is easier than invention and perhaps rapid post-modernization could follow the rapid industrialization that is already under way in many parts of the world. Europe's military power may have declined but the power of example remains. Perhaps that is the postmodern equivalent of imperialism.

## The hegemony of the postmodern?

The postmodern group is a powerful and growing collection of states. If we add to that the partially postmodern US and the would-be postmodern Japan it is more or less a dominant group, in economic terms at least. It exerts a strong influence on the way the world is organized. Even those who insist on sovereignty find themselves enmeshed in a range of co-operative institutions and agreements governing trade, transport, communications and so on. Sometimes – as the price of access to financial markets rises – they may find themselves having to accept interference in their economic affairs from the IMF. Those who want trade agreements with the EU find that there is a human rights clause attached.

The strongest of the modern states resist this. China has accepted relatively few binding international commitments; India is notoriously resistant to arrangements that might infringe her sovereignty but most go along with, and all profit from, the multilateral organization of the world.

The multilateral system that has grown up in the post-war world could be seen as the hegemony of the postmodern. In fact it hardly runs so deep. The multilateral systems concerned are vital to prosperity but, unlike the key treaties in Europe, they are not essential to security. For most non-European states the co-operative world system, though highly beneficial to them in many ways, is resented because it interferes with their full exercise of sovereignty. In a security crisis where state sovereignty was under real threat the multilateral links would place little constraint on violent action; at worse they would simply be blown away.

Thus the image of domestic order and international anarchy is false on one level. The world is in fact a highly structured and orderly system (though without a central authority). On the other hand, anarchy remains the underlying reality in the security field for most parts of the world just as it did in Europe before the First World War despite the high levels of economic interdependence.

In contrast, the co-operative structures in Europe reinforce sovereignty by reinforcing security. Indeed European states now effectively define sovereignty in a different way from hitherto: the state monopoly on law-making no longer exists as far as EU members are concerned; and even for others it is limited by as many treaties such as those in the Council of Europe framework. The state monopoly on force is also constrained by alliances, the CFE and other arms controls treaties. In some cases, the monopoly on force has been modified by EU agreements about policing (police are the domestic arm of the monopoly of legitimate force). What in these circumstances does sovereignty amount to for the postmodern state? The answer is probably a mixture of elements: the ability to make and enforce laws is a part of the picture but there is also a second part, which is the right to sit at the table when international co-operative agreements are worked out.

*This chapter is an extract from Robert Cooper,* The Postmodern State and the World Order *(2nd edition, Foreign Policy Centre and Demos, 2000)*

## Notes

1. For an excellent general description of the pre-modern state see *Troilus and Cressida*, Act I, Scene iii, 115–124.
2. I am not alone in choosing this terminology, see, for example, Christopher Coker 'Postmodernity and the End of the Cold War', *Review of International Studies*, July 1992, or S. Toulmin, *Casomopolis: The Hidden Agenda of Modernity* (Chicago: University of Chicago Press, 1990).
3. *Hamlet*, Act 2, scene ii, 235.
4. Strategic Arms Reduction Treaty.
5. Anti-ballistic missiles.
6. Association of South East Asian Nations.
7. North American Free Trade Area.
8. Mercado Commun del Sud (South America).
9. Organization of African Unity.

# 31
# A Third Way for the European Union?

*Anthony Giddens*

Joschka Fischer's speech attracted so much attention not because he said anything particularly new, but because of the context in which he delivered it. Here was a German foreign minister proclaiming the need for greater federalism in Europe, speaking in a historic setting in the new capital of a reunified Germany. Fischer insisted that he was talking in a personal capacity, not an official one. Yet this fact gave what he had to say even greater weight, because he was 'speaking frankly'.

Fischer set out his stall in a cogent and effective way. With the coming of the euro, the economic integration of Europe is more or less complete. What remains is to complement it with greater political integration. How else, in the longer run, can the European Union tackle its problems? Enlargement might eventually double the current EU membership. The EU is marked by its notorious democratic deficit, which seems to be producing declining levels of public support in member countries for its aims and policies. Monnet, Schuman and the other early founders of the EU dreamed of a society that would overcome the divisions that had led to two world wars. As Fischer points out, they foresaw that such developments should encompass Eastern as well as Western Europe. The time has come to move towards making that vision a reality.

Fischer made clear that progress towards a federal Europe should depend in the future, as it has in the past, upon Franco-German collaboration. France and Germany have been the vanguard through each of the main phases of development of the Union. The next stage, enlargement and political integration, will in his words also 'depend decisively on France and Germany'. After all, it was largely the enmity of these two countries that sparked the great wars.

I write as someone strongly committed to the EU. Yet I don't believe that we should be thinking along the lines Fischer advocates. We need a different model of the future of Europe today from the federalist one, for reasons I shall try to spell out in what follows. Neither of the two main models of the EU – federalism or a minimalist free-market – offer appropriate means of thinking about either what the EU is or what it should become.

I think British intellectuals and policy-makers could make some contribution to working out what such a future for Europe might involve. At first sight this looks an unlikely proposition. The British famously have been the 'reluctant Europeans'. The UK has not as yet adopted the Euro and the majority of the population is at best indifferent towards Europe.

Yet Britain has been the source of some of the most lively thinking in politics in recent years, at least so far as the centre-left is concerned. Effective analysis of the big changes affecting our lives, such as globalization and the advent of the new economy, began earlier in the UK than in most other countries. So did the attempt to create a framework of policy response to these transformations, in the shape of third way politics. The term 'third way' has by no means been universally adopted. But the basic ideas and policies which that term subsumes have been taken up by left of centre parties almost everywhere.

Ideas about the likely development of the EU, of course, do not break down cleanly along a left–right dimension. Thus, federalist views have been supported by Continental politicians and parties from both left and right. However a 'third way view' of Europe should stem from the same considerations that underlie the wider political debate – the need to respond to far-reaching processes of social and economic change.

Fischer said he looked for an alternative term to 'federalism', but in the end used it because he could not find one. The main reason he seemed to give for seeking a different concept is that talk of a 'federal Europe' doesn't go down too well in some countries – most notably, Britain. However, there are much more important reasons why 'federalism' is an inappropriate term:

1. It implies that further political integration in EU should move Europe in the direction of forming a state, with the institutions appropriate to such a political order. But one doesn't have to be a Eurosceptic to see that the EU is not a state at all, and will never become one. It is (or should now be seen as) a new form of supranational authority, characterized by a voluntary sharing of aspects of sovereignty.

2. Talk of federalism always encourages comparison with the US. In a widely syndicated debate with Jean-Pierre Chevenèment, which followed on from his Berlin speech, Fischer cites the US as his basis for thinking about the future of Europe. Larry Siedentop's influential

recent book, *Democracy in Europe*, does much the same. But there are no close parallels. James Madison and his fellow constitution-builders were creating a sovereign state, whereas the EU is seeking to help transform sovereignty in a newly interdependent world.

3. The EU, as Fischer accepts, is founded upon 'a rejection of the European balance of power principle' that used to prevail. In the age of globalization, cosmopolitan co-operation has to be the prime force in the world order. However, talk of federalism can easily imply readmitting power politics by the back door – creating a balance of power on a larger scale. The point of the EU should not be to counter the dominance of the US, but to help tie the United States into a wider cosmopolitan order.

We need a vision of the future of the EU that stresses Europe's wider role in a world that is being transformed by globalization; places an emphasis upon pluralism and the decentralisation of power; responds to the demands of the new economy; and sits comfortably with the need to find a renewed role for the nation in the global age. I do not think a federalist model fits any of these requirements particularly well.

Fischer says 'we are at the start of the age of globalisation', and this is something I agree with. But he doesn't follow through this thought properly. The new global era is not just an extension of the past. It is in many respects a break with it – nowhere more obviously so than in the case of the dissolution of Soviet communism and the ending of the Cold War period. The EU was strongly shaped by the Cold War – it was constructed in a Western Europe that was a buffer zone between the US and USSR. The fact that the EU can or has to 'expand towards the east', is not just a contingency of history, as Fischer makes it appear. The events of 1989 both reflected globalization and contributed to its further advance. Hence the issue of enlargement has to be seen in the context of these transformations, which mean that the EU today faces a very different world from that in which it was originally shaped.

What matters about the European Union today is not primarily that it is European, but that it forms a bridgehead towards global governance. If we think of the EU as spanning a territory worth calling 'Europe', or as representing some distinctive 'European past', we face intractable difficulties. There is no 'natural' border of Europe to the East. It is a positive step to propose that Turkey, as a 'non-European', Islamic nation, should be a serious medium-term contender for membership. In the longer-term the involvement of Russia should also be considered.

Fischer says that we have 'put into place the last building block' of economic integration of the EU, and now we should do the same politically. But this is not a valid way of looking at things. The troubles of the euro indicate, among other things, that there has been too little structural reform in the core European economies. The way to defend the 'European social model' is not through encouraging developments which will protect existing welfare institutions, capital and labour markets. We need a reformed European social model today, of the sort signalled in the Lisbon declaration – one geared again to the demands of globalization. Countries like the UK, Denmark, Holland and Spain are showing the way forward here, rather than France and Germany.

France and Germany were the dominant countries driving the EU project during its Cold War days. Against the background in which the EU was established this was understandable, as was the need to 'contain' Germany. However, in the contemporary world these factors have lost most of their relevance. The chances of war between nations in Europe are virtually non-existent, and the same can be said for nations in many other parts of the world too.

The threat of 'old wars' is diminishing massively. It is the 'new wars' that are going to dominate the future.[1] They will often be extremely difficult to prevent or manage, as Europe has found to its cost in Bosnia-Herzegovina and Kosovo. The new wars, however, concern fragmenting nations, not nations whose power is too strong. 'Containing Germany' is no longer an issue. The Franco-German relationship, important although it is because of the size of the two countries, no longer needs to have a privileged position.

To the question 'what is the EU?', if it is neither merely a marketplace nor a stage on the way to federalism, I would say the following. The EU (today) is, above all, an experiment in transnational governance, of great consequence to the rest of the world, not just to Europe itself, and capable of being emulated elsewhere. Given the diversity of nations and cultures involved, the EU is inherently diverse, and its institutions must reflect that.

This position suggests a fairly clear architecture for the future development of the Union. The European Council should have a core directive role, something that is happening anyway. A strong Commission and Parliament are needed to provide stabilizing influences. Enlargement will only happen in a progressive way, which gives time to adapt decision-making processes in the Council and in other bodies. The identity of the Union, as Jürgen Habermas argues – and Fischer also agrees – should be developed around civic values, not around attempts to find a common heritage. It makes sense, as Fischer suggests, to think of a second chamber for the European Parliament, but this has no necessary connection to federalism. Such a chamber could allow national parliaments greater involvement in EU policy formulation. However, for reasons already given, the European Parliament will contribute more to horizontal than to vertical democracy.

In its relations with its member nations, the Union is (should be) concerned neither merely to defend the nation, nor to supersede it in a federal system. Rather the EU should contribute to the *restructuring* of nations, as they become less concerned with territory and more with peaceful collaboration. It is not a coincidence that – again not just in Europe but almost everywhere – nations are busy rethinking their identities and reinterpreting their past. The reason is that the factors which shaped nations in earlier periods, including the bipolar world, have become altered or transformed with the intensifying of globalization. Most found their identities in opposition to others. 'Nations without enemies' must necessarily be different from those of the past, they cannot define themselves through hostility to 'the other'.

With intensifying globalization, nations have to face problems, and embrace opportunities, that demand collaborative action. The EU can help supply the goods without which a self-governing society is difficult or impossible to sustain in the global era. Moving towards a federal model would exacerbate the problems of political legitimacy which most nations now face – manifest in voter apathy, volatility of political support and the declining influence of parliaments. The democratic deficit of the EU cannot be addressed by further draining the democratic capacities of member countries through channelling more power to the EU level. We should tackle the issue by recognizing that (a) the means of reducing the democratic failings of the EU and its constituent nations are directly parallel and (b) mechanisms of democracy appropriate at the national level can be no more than partially relevant at a supranational one.

The democratization of the EU in some key respects needs to be the same as the democratization that nations themselves have to deploy. Within nations, as in the EU, we need a 'second wave' of democratization, or what I call the 'democratizing of democracy'. Existing political structures, including orthodox national parliamentary systems, even the most democratic of them, are not democratic enough in a globalizing information age. Poor transparency of public institutions, the undue influence of corporate power, 'media politics', backstage deals, old-boy networks, straightforward corruption, lack of representation of women and ethnic minorities – these are found even in the most democratic of countries. Most are very evident in EU institutions too. While some progress has been made in confronting them, there is a great deal of scope for further improvement.

Governance in a global age must of course continue to feature parliamentary mechanisms and electoral democracy. This applies on the level of the EU as well as nationally, even if there are reasons why the European Parliament is never likely directly to reflect the concerns of electorates. But 'vertical democracy' needs to be complemented, and in principle enhanced, by 'horizontal democracy', taking the form of discourse democracy and pluralism. The proponents of 'new governance theory' have pointed out that we are experiencing a transition towards governance by network, and away from governance by hierarchy. Horizontal democracy depends upon the making of decisions through negotiation between different bodies and agencies. Rather than receiving a direct democratic mandate, and after that having the power to enact decisions, decisions must be reached through open processes of negotiation. The separation of powers helps prevent oligarchy, while the demand to negotiate stops any one agent or set of agents from achieving a dominant position. As Christopher Lord puts it 'EU institutions should be read as a supranational version of deliberatist ideals and interpreted with a view to compensating some of the shortcomings of the constitutional nation-state'.

Devolution is a crucial part of an active response to globalization. As one of its influences, globalization exerts a 'push-down' effect, creating strong pressures for local autonomy. How far EU institutions can effectively be connected with local and regional government will be fundamental in defending, or enhancing, the popular legitimacy of the EU. Yet this issue is barely touched upon in Fischer's speech. And more generally it must be said that the concepts of subsidiarity and a 'Europe of the Regions' remain poorly implemented. A transfer of authority downwards, including the handing back of some powers to nations or localities, should surely be basic to the future evolution of the EU. Right at the end of his dialogue with Chevènement, Fischer says that he 'can well envisage that certain competencies would be given back to member states'. But this appears as an afterthought, not as generic to how he sees the development of the Union.

It is now generally accepted in the EU that there has to be flexibility in how far nations adopt some forms of policies rather than others. However, we should say firmly that there should be no avant-garde. The very idea of having an avant-garde, 'moving ahead' of the rest, only makes sense if there is a unilinear path that the EU is going to follow, towards federalism. Europe will certainly look more diverse in the future than it does now, but this should best be understood as 'bounded pluralism' rather than a few 'in front' while others 'lag behind'.

The prime basis of the legitimacy of the EU has to be achieved in the nation, since nations will continue to be the main source of both identity and citizenship. How far the Union commands popular support will depend primarily upon whether citizenries are convinced that it benefits national communities, in terms of democracy, security and economic development. But this cannot be the traditional nation, built around geopolitical imperatives. We need to construct 'cosmopolitan nations', which find their identity in mutual collaboration.

The American political scientist, Joseph Nye, has remarked that the EU is more about the 'pooling and sharing' of sovereignty than its transfer to a higher level. I think this is correct, and such a conception, not a federalist one, should be the guiding thread of our thinking about the Union's future.

## Note

1. See Mary Kaldor, *New and Old Wars* (Oxford: Polity Press, 1999).

# 32
## Can Britain Lead in Europe?

*Charles Grant*

Britain should join France and Germany in forming a triple alliance to lead the European Union, suggested Gerhard Schroder, the German Social Democrats' candidate for Chancellor, in April 1998. Joschka Fischer, the leader of the German Green Party, reacted swiftly. 'If Schroder tried to widen the Franco-German relationship into a triangle with Britain it would be a disaster for Europe', said Mr Fischer. 'Britain just doesn't know what it wants.' He said that Britain's ambivalent position on the single currency and its eager backing of the United States in the recent crisis over Iraq reflected attitudes that had very little to do with the deepest reflexes of France, Germany or their Continental Partners.

Mr Fischer said in public what several Continental leaders say in private. They feel much good will towards Tony Blair's government. But they think it faintly ridiculous for Mr Blair and his ministers to talk of Britain playing a leading role in Europe. They believe that Britain's peripheral geographical position, its Atlanticist and Westminster-centred historical traditions, the Eurosceptical bent of much of its public opinion, the absence of any British vision of the kind of Union it wants and, above all, its decision not to join the first group of countries in the euro all prevent it from being a leading member.

All those arguments have force. But the contention of this booklet is that while Britain cannot in the near future be one of the more influential EU members it can in the longer run count as much as any country. Such an outcome will certainly be difficult to achieve. Few Britons appreciate how low Britain's stock with its European partners had sunk in the 1990s. The governments of Margaret Thatcher and John Major, often anti-European in rhetoric and sometimes in their actions, bequeathed a massive legacy of mistrust. Indeed, if there is one thing that holds together the Franco-German alliance it is that the French and the Germans know that when the chips are down they can normally trust each other to do what is right for the cause of Europe, in a way that they cannot trust the British.

None of this means that restoring British influence is an impossible task. Much of the Continent is moving slowly towards an Anglo-Saxon model of capitalism, with a greater emphasis on, for example, equity as opposed to debt finance, shareholder value and flexible labour markets. The relative economic success of Britain, compared with the high unemployment that still plagues much of the Continent, strengthens Mr Blair's hand. So, undoubtedly, does his government's popularity at home, his influence in Washington DC and the kudos that he has won from the Northern Ireland settlement. With President Chirac looking weak and tired, and Chancellor Kohl departed, the EU is suffering from a leadership vacuum.

Europe's future has never looked so uncertain. Many of the forces which in the past ensured stability – such as the Cold War, America's military presence and a solid Franco-German alliance – have either disappeared or weakened. And there is a multiplication of forces promoting change and uncertainty: the advent of the euro; the enlargement of the EU into Eastern Europe; economic crises in Russia, Asia and elsewhere; and political instability in the Balkans, the eastern Mediterranean and north Africa. But some of these challenges also present opportunities. The EU's structures and future direction are far from set in stone and could be moulded by a country or group of countries that was capable of exerting leadership.

Britain's ability to set the EU's agenda will evidently be limited, so long as it remains outside monetary union. But to minimize that loss of influence, until such time as it embraces the euro, Britain needs to work out a bridging strategy that plays to its strengths. A crucial part of that bridging strategy must be to give a clear indication that, even though Britain will not be in EMU on 1 January 1999, it is preparing to join early in the next parliament.

The bridging strategy will require several other pillars: championing EU enlargement, while recognizing that its institutional implications cannot be ignored; stressing the need for economic reform in Europe, while avoiding smugness over Britain's relative economic success; being prepared to take part in more co-operation on justice and home affairs; helping to build more effective mechanisms for co-ordinating foreign policy; and giving the EU a defence identity, without undermining the Atlantic alliance.

The government cannot shape the EU in ways that suit British interests unless it develops a clearer view of the kind of Europe it wants. This booklet argues that one British objective should be to avoid a 'two-speed' Europe. The EU's members should not be divided into sheep and goats, those in the euro and those outside, for an enlarged Union of up to 25 countries will require more fluid and flexible structures. Britain should also search for new ways of making the institutions less distant from and intimidating to ordinary people. The Commission, in particular, needs to be made democratically accountable.

## Europe's shifting balance of power

The Franco-German alliance, the dominant force in EU politics for the past 35 years, is probably in a shakier state than at any time since de Gaulle and Adenauer formalized it by signing the Treaty of the Elysee which defined that alliance. Whether this axis continues to lead the EU, though with much less strength and clarity of purpose than in the past, or whether it is replaced by a more open system of alliances, with Britain playing an important role, depends on how the British play their cards.

The first thing the British have to do is learn to make friends on the Continent. They have managed brief liaisons on particular subjects, such as budget reform, but have not been good at longer-term relationships. The politics of the EU is a subtle and complex game in which country A may do country B a favour, in return for it supporting A's most cherished policies. But Britain, more than most member states, has a tendency to treat each issue in isolation, thereby missing the chance to make trade-offs and win friends. It has often been reluctant to listen to its partners and unwilling to engage with them in the joint analysis of problems.

Britain's policy on Europe has generally followed Palmerston's comment to the House of Commons in 1848 that 'we have no eternal allies and we have no perpetual enemies. Our interests are eternal and perpetual, and those interests it is our duty to follow.' Britain's only significant strategic alliance is with the United States, particularly on military matters and intelligence.

Is there scope for Britain to form long-term alliances in Europe? For the time Britain probably cannot make a long-term commitment to a country, through thick and thin. In the longer run such alliances might be possible, when Britain has clarified its own vision of the kind of Europe it wants. What Mr Blair can do right away – without trying to supplant either the French or the Germans in each others' affections – is make a big effort to improve bilateral relations with France, Germany and the other EU states. Encouragingly, there are signs that he is trying to do this.

Of the larger EU countries, Germany appears to offer the best prospects. Britain and Germany disagree on whether much more European integration is a good idea. But as the two largest net contributors to the EU budget, they believe in imposing financial discipline on the Union. Both are instinctive free traders. Britain and Germany think it important to maintain America's commitment to European defence and worry that French prickliness may undermine it. They are the strongest supporters of enlarging the EU into Eastern Europe.

Ties with France may prove harder to nurture. France's economy becomes a little more liberal every year, but its politicians are still more inherently protectionist than most others in the EU. Its views on Common Agricultural Policy reform will often be diametrically opposed to those of Britain. Nevertheless Mr Blair and Mr Jospin were starting to get on well. Mr Blair understands that the French prime minister is having to modernize his country under much greater constraints – such as Communist ministers and vociferous trade unions – than he did. The French and British governments want the EU to remain in essence a union of states. And both want to give the Union more legitimacy by boosting the role of national or nationally based institutions (such as the European Council, the Council of Ministers and national parliaments).

They are the only EU members that often have a global perspective and a sense of responsibility for international peace and stability. Both have both talented diplomatic corps and the ability to project military power. Their close collaboration in Bosnia has shown that the two countries can work well together. They should be in the forefront of trying to make the EU's foreign policy machinery more effective, and in developing the European defence identity.

Mr Blair should suggest to the German and French governments that Britain shadow some provisions of the Elysee treaty with each of them. There would be no need for formalities or fanfares. Mr Blair could simply ask his senior ministers to meet their opposite numbers in France and Germany say twice a year, and to stay in touch on the telephone. Similarly, senior officials could meet their equivalents on a regular basis. An effort should be made to find policy areas that are ripe for common analyses. With France, for example, Britain could try to work on a joint approach to Russia's problems, and with Germany it could develop a common line on reforming EU competition policy.

The creation of such 'virtual' Elysee treaties would lead to a lot of extra meetings. That might appear to be an uninspiring way of augmenting British influence. But over a period of time all the meetings should – as the Franco-German relationship has shown – help to create a climate of trust, understanding and consultation that could only be beneficial.

On one matter or another, Britain should be able to forge alliances with virtually all the EU countries. So long as British ministers are willing to make an effort to understand the thinking of other governments, they will find them willing allies. For example, Britain might agree to back the Nordic countries in their campaign for greater openness, in return for their acquiescing to British proposals for reforming the EU's foreign policy machinery.

The construction of alliances would require Britain, on occasion, to give up some of its negotiating positions. The tabloids would be livid. But it should not be beyond the wit of Labour's spin doctors to explain to the tabloids that the point of such tactics is, in the long run, to increase British influence. Ministers must understand that they need to please two audiences. Of course they have to worry about domestic constituencies, including tabloid editors, in order to be re-elected. But in order to promote British interests in the EU they also have to think about how other governments will react to what they do and say.

If making friends is one thing Mr Blair has to do in order to make Britain a country that counts, the second is to take a more positive stance on the euro. His attitude to EMU, more than anything, will determine the degree to which Paris, Bonn and other capitals take Britain seriously. Britain has to appear to be on the road – however slow and circuitous that particular route may be – to monetary union. If Britain's partners thought it had no intention of joining, the best bridging strategy imaginable could not prevent Britain's relegation to the outer rim of a two-speed Europe. The gap would be too wide to be bridgeable. Neither a comprehensive effort to win allies, nor a plethora of proposals for plugging the democratic deficit, nor a clear vision of the kind of Europe it wants would suffice to restore Britain's position. Britain's influence over a whole range of areas – such as reform of the budget, farm policy and regional policy – would diminish, however sensible the policies it proposed. Britain can be a leading member of the European Union, so long as Tony Blair makes it clear that his government intends to join the euro.

## A new British identity

In the long run, a stronger British role in Europe will depend not only on the government changing the way it deals with the EU, but also on the British people learning to view the Union in a different way. They tend to see the EU as the kind of zero sum game that John Major had in mind when he proclaimed 'game, set and match to Britain' on returning from the Maastricht summit. So long as the British people think that their gain is someone else's loss, and vice versa, their governments will be constrained in pursuing more positive European policies.

In most other EU countries people regard the Union as a positive sum game in which what is good for one country is usually good for all of them. An underlying reason for this contrast is that, as Anthony Barnett has argued, Britons tend to see national identity in a different way from other Europeans. In much of the Continent, national identity contains a strong European element. The French use the EU to give them a sense of grandeur on the world stage that they can no longer obtain on their own. The Germans love the EU for containing the nationalism that bedevilled their past. The Italians admire the EU for imposing efficient financial management on their government. The Spaniards still view the EU as a symbol of modernity and freedom from a Francoist past. The Irish nation could not become truly independent until the EU gave it the political recognition and the resources which allowed it to flourish. And so on.

But fewer Britons feel that the EU is anything to do with British identity. This is for reasons of geography and, above all, history: in this century Britain's history has had relatively few utterly shameful episodes. Not many Britons believe that their country needs the EU in order to be whole or respectable.

Thus a crucial but extremely difficult task for Tony Blair's government is to nudge the way the British perceive themselves in a European direction. Ministers have a responsibility to explain that what is good for other EU countries will often be good for Britain, and vice versa. But even the cleverest of spin doctors will find this an uphill struggle so long as many Britons think the EU is a distant, undemocratic and ineffective organization.

Hence the importance of reforming the EU so that it becomes more open and accountable. If the British can start to imagine that the EU belongs to them, they will find it easier to realize that, over a host of areas – such as the fight against crime, the strength of the economy, social protection, environmental quality, equal opportunities and influence in the world – Britain can only gain from working with its partners and those unloved but necessary EU institutions.

*This chapter is an extract from* Can Britain Lead in Europe?, *a pamphlet published in September 1998 by the Centre for European Reform*

# 33
## Should Europe Become a State?
## A Neo-Medieval Solution

*Jan Zielonka*

Joschka Fischer's European vision is overwhelmingly state-centric. And he believes that this federal vision can be achieved through institutional engineering. In my view such a vision is at odds with the postmodern and post-Soviet realities of today. Institutions cannot be a substitute for politics, economics and culture. Statist solutions hamper rather than enhance the process of European integration. And when we look at current trends in Europe we see a neo-medieval empire rather than a neo-Westphalian state in the making. In other words, Joschka Fischer's vision of a European federative state is neither workable nor desirable despite all noble intentions.

I will try to illustrate my argument by looking at two crucial dimensions of European integration: the European Security and Defence Identity, and Justice and Home Affairs. Providing internal and external security is crucial in any state-building effort. A Union without a workable external dimension and with soft and ever moving borders is unlikely to rise to Joschka Fischer's statist expectations. Fischer's vision, I will argue, is also at odds with the forthcoming eastern enlargement of the European Union. A larger and more diversified European Union will find it more difficult than ever to acquire state-like features. Statists would either have to moderate their ambitions or else postpone or water down the enlargement process. Unfortunately, the latter is the more likely outcome of Joschka Fischer's vision, despite all disclaimers and qualifications.

## What would a European state imply?

The problem with the state-centric argument is not that it wants some sort of European superstate. Today, no single mainstream politician would dare to support such a vision, because it would certainly scare the electorate. True, a vision of a European superstate is sometimes presented as a necessary balance to the all too powerful superstate across the

177

Atlantic. However, even in this case the argument is more about making Europe less dependent on America than about balancing it by creating a kind of United States of Europe. After all, the European Community at its inception was to be an antidote to the excessive competition among nation states in Europe and beyond.

Thus what is the essence of the statist argument, and why should one try to counter it? In my view, there are three basic features of the statist argument, and they all create more problems than they solve. First, and most obviously, the state-centred argument always emphasizes the state and its institutional structures rather than a nation, politics or markets. In other words, institutional engineering rather than cultural or economic factors is always given priority. For instance, the democratic deficit is to be tackled by reorganizing the European parliamentary system rather than by creating a truly European demos. Peace and security is to be assured by setting up intergovernmental institutions rather than through the balance-of-power politics or by mitigating cultural prejudices and historical fears. Trade is more about central regulations (positive and negative alike) than about spontaneous exchanges of economic actors. Of course, it is easier to engineer or manipulate state institutions than culture, politics or economic markets. One can probably envisage the creation of a European state, but not a European nation. However, institutional engineering would be unable to enhance European integration on its own if there were only little progress in terms of cultural identity, political solidarity and economic interdependence. One does not need to endorse cultural or economic determinism to see that all institutions have their social, economic and cultural prerequisites which are usually ignored or underplayed by statists.

Second, the state-centric argument suggests giving the Union more and more responsibility for market, money, security and solidarity across all member states. Ultimately the Union should have a single central government in charge of a given territory with clear-cut borders, a common European army and police, a single European citizenship, a common market, and a common social policy. The government may well have a federative rather than unitary nature, but it will basically resemble a modern version of the sovereign, territorial state that emerged in Europe following the 1648 Treaty of Westphalia. When the Union's efforts to acquire all these functions and powers are staggered, the friends of a European state talk about a dangerous stalemate in the process of European integration as if no other more flexible solutions could suit the purpose of integration. In other words, statists believe that European integration is making progress only when the Union is gradually acquiring all the major prerogatives of a Westphalian type of state.

Third, the state-centric argument would like the Union to provide an overlap between its functional and geographical borders. If one looks at the historical process of state formation following the Treaty of Westphalia, success has largely been determined by the degree to which states were able to assure overlap between administrative borders, military frontiers, cultural traits and market fringes. And so the friends of a European state oppose a Union acting in concentric circles and along variable geometric patterns resulting from various opt-outs negotiated by individual member states in the areas of foreign, monetary or social policy. They believe that the European integration should be about increased convergence across various functional fields and within a given territory. Since such convergence is unlikely in a broader European setting, the idea of a 'core group' has been launched in many forms and shapes by the statists.

All these three major features of state-centric argument can easily be found in Joschka Fischer's speech to the Humboldt University in Berlin, even though Fischer implicitly denies any ambition to create a European superstate.

A vision of a neo-Westphalian European state is better comprehended if contrasted with a vision of a neo-medieval empire that preceded the creation of the Westphalian system of territorial, sovereign states. This is because these two visions or models offer totally opposite solutions for organizing public life in a broader European space. The Westphalian model is about concentration of power, hierarchy, sovereignty, clear-cut identity and about fixed and relatively hard borders. The neo-medieval model is about overlapping authorities, divided sovereignty, diversified institutional arrangements, multiple identities and soft border zones that undergo regular adjustments. The latter model is often labelled a postmodern one, but the term 'postmodern' has been used and abused by many authors and I therefore prefer the neo-medieval metaphor put forward by Ole Weaver. Table 33.1 illustrates differences between these two contrasting models of the future EU system.

## Why it is difficult to build a European state

It is impossible to have a Westphalian type of state without a centrally governed army and relatively hard external borders. A superficial first look at the current trends suggest that the friends of a European state are close to achieving these objectives. As a result of the single market and the Schengen Agreements internal borders are gradually being abolished

**Table 33.1: Two contrasting models of the future EU system**

| Neo-Westphalian State | Neo-Medieval Empire |
|---|---|
| Hard and fixed external border lines | Soft border zones in flux |
| Relatively high socioeconomic homogeneity | Socioeconomic discrepancies persist without consistent patterns |
| A pan-European cultural identity prevails | Multiple cultural identities co-exist |
| Overlap between legal, administrative, economic and military regimes | Disassociation between authoritative allocations, functional competencies and territorial constituencies |
| A clear hierarchical structure with one centre of authority | Interpenetration of various types of political units and loyalties |
| Distinction between EU members and non-members is sharp and it is most crucial | Distinction between the European centre and periphery is most crucial, but blurred |
| Redistribution centrally regulated within a closed EU system | Redistribution based on different types of solidarity between various transnational networks |
| One single type of citizenship | Diversified types of citizenship with different sets of rights and duties |
| A single European army and police force | Multiplicity of various overlapping military and police institutions |
| Absolute sovereignty regained | Divided sovereignty along different functional and territorial lines |

while the external borders of the EU are being tightened up. External borders are also increasingly being run by the Union rather than by individual member states. For instance, the Treaty of Amsterdam moved immigration, asylum and visa policy from (intergovernmental) pillar III to (communitarian) pillar I. The Schengen Manual for the External Frontiers envisages common rules for border controls. Co-operation between national police units responsible for border controls and supranational intelligence agencies are also being developed. The Union is also in the process of acquiring a surrogate of its own army: by the year 2003 some 50 000–60 000 soldiers will be put at the EU's disposal to perform the full range of Petersberg peace-keeping and peace-enforcing tasks. In addition, a special EU military committee has been set up, and the Union has promised to enhance its command-and-control capabilities, logistics and other combat support sources including naval and air elements.

However, a closer look at the current trends suggests that a neo-medieval rather than a Westphalian pattern is in the making. In other words, the Union is far from possessing any effective military forces or relatively hard external borders. In the defence field this is not so much because the official language of EU documents implicitly denies any ambition to create a European army and insists that national units will not be transformed into the European ones. The problem is that Europe's defence identity is being built upon Europe's foreign policy failures which have repeatedly manifested themselves in the Balkans. One cannot help but ask whether a common EU defence policy is possible without a workable common foreign policy? After all, it is important to know how, when and for what purposes the Union is going to use its soldiers. If the Union's common foreign policy is often in a state of paralysis, especially when faced with a crisis, how can a common defence policy ever work?

The military capabilities currently envisaged are also quite modest even for the purpose of performing the Petersberg tasks. But if the Union wants to be a state it would have to go much further and provide credible defence of its vital interests (and territory) against any foreign attack. Are the EU's citizens ready to undertake the defence task on their own? Are they prepared to shoulder the financial costs of such defence? Does the European Union enjoy enough legitimacy for sending soldiers into combat? Without giving positive answers to these questions, one can hardly talk about a genuine defence capability of the Union as envisaged by the Westphalian state model. This is not to suggest along with Eurosceptics that people are willing to die for their own country, but not for Europe. Most probably, they want to die for neither. However, defence policies are not merely a matter of available hardware and command structures; they are also, if not primarily a matter of collective political will in a situation of crisis. Unfortunately, such a collective will, let alone the necessary endurance and determination, has so far been in short supply within the European Union when faced by a serious crisis.

Prospects for acquiring relatively fixed and hard external borders as envisaged by the Westphalian state model are not bright either. This is not so much due to the persistent opposition to communitarization of the border regime that exists either in some countries (Great Britain most notably) or in some cross-border political circles (the 'party of territoriality' to use Charles Maier's term). This is because increased global economic pressures and cascading interdependence make it difficult for any political unit to install a hard border regime able to perform tasks envisaged by a Westphalian type of state. The difficulty of maintaining any hard border regime is most visible when we look at the issue of cross-border economic transactions. It is now generally acknowledged that the policy of open borders for goods, services and capital is more profitable for the Union than a protectionist policy of constraining such exchanges and transactions. Borders as a line of territorial defence have also been rendered largely obsolete by modern weapons and satellite intelligence technology. Arguments for a hard border regime are more forcefully pronounced in the context of migration, but the Union is losing its battle with migrants pouring in from all parts of the world, partly because of desperation and partly because of the persistent demand for certain kinds of (semi-legal) labour within the Union as such. The concept of a hard border is not even very useful for combating cross-border crime. Most experts agree that improving police and security co-operation between countries is a more efficient alternative to investing in large numbers of border guards or in expensive surveillance technology. The term 'remote policing' exemplifies the most efficient way of combating organized transnational criminal activities, and this policing is not done at border checkpoints but in a broader border zone or even within the entire territory of crime exporting and crime importing countries.

All this suggests that a hard border regime as envisaged by the Westphalian state model is at odds with economic rationale, it is damaging for Europe's broader strategic interests, and it is only partially effective as a means of curbing migration or combating cross-border crime. This is why the Union is more likely to end up with soft border zones in flux (neo-medieval solution) than with hard and fixed external border lines as envisaged by the single market and Schengen (neo-Westphalian solution).

Nor would it be easy for the Union to provide an overlap between its geographic and functional borders. In the defence field the multiplicity of various overlapping military and international security institutions is likely to persist. Most notably, NATO is likely to remain the major pillar responsible for Europe's security regardless of the EU's progress in creating its own army. This is not only because the American military capabilities will remain superior to the European ones or because neither France nor Britain is willing to extend its nuclear umbrella to other European countries. This is largely because EU involvement in any conflict is likely to lack political credibility (both within and outside the EU) as long as the Americans are unwilling to get involved in this conflict in one way or another. It is also very likely that EU member states will occasionally choose to act via other than European and geographically much broader international institutions responsible for maintaining peace and security. The United Nations and the OSCE (Organization for Security and Co-operation in Europe) are the most obvious candidates here. Nor is it possible to exclude security involvement outside the EU framework via different sort of 'coalitions of the willing' or 'contact groups' including some EU and some non-EU states. For many years to come frameworks of security co-operation in Europe will resemble flexible and overlapping circles along the neo-medieval model rather the single command and combat structure of a neo-Westphalian state.

Providing an overlap between geographic and functional borders is not only a matter of deciding to co-operate within a single European framework. More often than not it is a matter of the degree of homogeneity existing within certain geographical borders. In other words, a neo-Westphalian European state could only work in a relatively convergent environment. Free trade zones can admittedly operate in a vastly diversified setting. However, this does not equally apply to more ambitious projects of political, economic and social integration. Common laws and administrative regulations cannot cope well with a highly diversified environment, and various complicating opt-outs and multi-speed arrangements are therefore required. A degree of common values and habits is also needed for a system to function efficiently and legitimately. The existence of largely incompatible members multiplies the EU's internal boundaries, however informal, and creates incentives for some smaller groups of countries to 'go it alone'.

So far, the European map of convergence and divergence remains very complex despite all efforts to bridge it. For instance, there are large countries and small countries in the European Union, interventionists and anti–interventionists (or neutrals). There are the original six and the latecomers; the federalists and the intergovernmentalists; the Atlantic and the Mediterranean; those with socialist governments and those with conservative ones. There are unitary nation states and others are states with powerful regions. In many respects, Great Britain resembles America more than Germany or France. Average support for democracy in Finland is much lower than in any other EU member state (and lower than in some post-communist states), while in Spain the average rejection of violence as a political instrument is strikingly below the EU average. Austria's GDP per capita is more than double that of Portugal. Some reasons for this divergence are historical, while others are cultural. The European integration was able to reduce some divergence, but its 'polling power' was always limited. For instance, how can one drastically reduce economic discrepancies within the Union with a common budget for assistance and redistribution not exceeding 1.2 per cent of the total budget of all member states? The various opt-outs negotiated by individual member states in the areas of foreign, monetary and social policy have not helped either. The Union lacks a strong and coherent sense of cultural identity, let alone of a European demos or patria. The Union is trying hard to increase its institutional, economic, social and cultural homogeneity, but there are reasons to believe that globalization (or if you wish, Americanization) is having a greater homogenizing impact. The persisting divergence has prompted calls for the creation of a hard core within the European Union within which there can be much more internal convergence. Joschka Fischer has advocated the creation of a 'centre of gravity', while Jacques Chirac has talked about a 'groupe pionnier'. However, there are good reasons to believe that such a hard core would only complicate rather than simplify the European map of convergence/divergence. The links between EU member states belonging to the hard core and those outside it would not disappear, after all, but they would probably fall prey to fierce political bargaining.

## No state, no regrets

Friends of a European state argue that a failure of their vision would undermine the efficiency of European institutions, and may even lead to a total paralysis of the Union. But this is a very selective way of looking at the issue of efficiency. For instance, one can argue that forcing convergence and squeezing diversity within the Union is at odds with the prerequisites of efficiency. Today only highly diversified and pluralistic societies acting in a complex web of institutional arrangements are able to succeed in conditions of modern competition. Effective governance requires institutional diversity – 'for a multitude of relatively independent European arrangements with distinct statuses, functions, resources and operating under different decision rules'.

And we should not forget that diversity is Europe's great historical and cultural treasure. Moreover, diversity by another name – pluralism – is the basic prerequisite of democracy. Diversity is a liability only when we look at it from the perspective of a Westphalian type of state. The neo-medieval perspective views diversity as an asset.

The state-centred argument is also at odds with the original purpose of European integration. As Joseph Weiler rightly argued:

> It would be more than ironic if a polity set up as a means to counter the excesses of statism ended up coming round full circle and transforming itself into a (super)state.

One may hope that the acquisition of some state-like characteristics by the Union would solve certain problems, but it would also create other ones. As argued earlier, the hard border regime as envisaged by Schengen is only partially effective in taming migration and combating cross-border crime. At the same time, Schengen has become a symbol of exclusion and discrimination within countries bordering on the Union. In the Union itself Schengen has justified mixing crime and migration in a variety of forms and measures. Populist politicians trying to curb flows of even genuine asylum seekers have exploited it.

Similarly, acquiring military status may help the Union to cope with local violence, but it might also raise suspicion and induce balancing efforts. Because the current Union's power is not military and hegemonic in nature, it does not drive other states out (through the balancing mechanism). Its civilian power attracts; it does not repel. But when the Union becomes a military power, both internal and external actors will watch its policies as never before. To have a 'gun at hand' not only widens opportunities for action. It also puts on one's shoulders much greater responsibility for one's actions, and it is far from certain whether the Union is ready for this.

Finally, and probably most crucially, efforts to build a European state will hamper integration of Eastern Europe with Western Europe. Joschka Fischer recognizes the prime importance of two parts of Europe coming together, yet his proposals are basically in conflict with the idea of the Continent's reunification.

Fischer and other friends of a European state fear that enlargement will greatly enhance diversity within the Union and result in an ever greater disjunction between the EU's geographic and functional boundaries. They also fear that an enlarged Union will increasingly act in crosscutting circles and along a variable geometry more closely resembling a neo-medieval empire than a neo-Westphalian federal state. This is why they suggest the creation of a hard core in the Union within which a Westphalian state model will be easier to achieve. However, this would deprive Eastern European countries of the greatest benefit of the enlargement project, that is, joining the more advanced countries of Western Europe on equal terms. This would also condemn them to the peripheral status. After all the concepts of 'core' and 'periphery' are like two sides of a coin that cannot be separated.

In order to secure his statist vision Joschka Fischer is prepared to inflate the entire meaning of enlargement. This would be neither good for Europe nor for the European integration project. Enlargement and not creation of a European state is, in my view, the key to the European Union's prosperity and peace. The enlarged European Union will indeed resemble a neo-medieval empire, but there is no reason to be afraid of it. A neo-medieval solution can offer an alternative to absolute sovereignty, facilitate overlapping authorities and help to recognize multiple identities. Postmodern empires should not be confused with the pre-modern ones because they exercise political power in a totally different manner and are embedded in a dense global network of communication and exchanges.

# Part IV

# Beyond Politics:
# The Everyday Case for Europe

# 34
# The Quest for a European Identity

*Philip Dodd*

It is easy to date the emergence of the adjective European: Pope Pius II first used it during the Renaissance. It is much harder to describe who or what a European now is, and what a European identity might be. Yet at present these are pressing questions, particularly as we emerge from the shadows of the revolutions of 1989. Indeed, the current interest in the question of what it means to be European may be a testimony to the collapse of old identities (as well as of the Berlin Wall) and to anxiety over the forging of new ones.

At moments such as this, the ghosts of past identities haunt the present and claim our allegiance. This essay attempts to sketch a usable European identity, but also describes some of the inherited thinking within Europe about the Continent. And it will give particular emphasis to a negative tendency that emphasizes an introspective, at times defensive identity, based on the assumption that the rest of the world is a threat to Europe's traditional values and way of life. This is manifested less in trade (where the EU is more liberal than it used to be) than in culture, where anxieties about the Decline of the West, the Americanization of Europe, the emergence of multiculturalism and the place of Islam, among others, have produced, at times, a fortress mentality. That this introversion is more evident in culture than in economics makes it more rather than less powerful, since culture is less about the formal aspects of our lives than our everyday experience of which we are only half-conscious. It is a sign of the times that in the summer of 1996 both John Birt, the BBC's director-general, and Jean-Marie le Pen focused on American cultural imperialism as a threat to European national cultures.

Of course, one polemical way of thinking about European identity would be to claim that the only identity Europeans share is one derived from a common indebtedness to the United States. It is axiomatic that post-1945 Western Europe has been economically, militarily and culturally indebted to America, but even the countries of the Soviet bloc, prior to 1989, had to define themselves against the United States, and since that date have been embraced by it. Although an over-simplification, this point about the United States reminds us that European identity has never been forged on some self-contained island, neither in the present nor the past. If, in the words of the former Soviet president Mikhail Gorbachev, Europe is our common home, it is a home more like an airport or a seaport than a shelter.

After all, the briefest glance at history would show that from the time of Columbus, Europe's sense of itself has been shaped by its engagement with – and sometimes subjection of – large parts of the rest of the world. It is simply impossible, or ought to be, to think of the history and identity of France outside of its relationship to north Africa. Or Spain outside of its relationship to Latin America. Or Britain outside of its relationship to India. And what about other countries, such as Turkey or Russia, which have as often belonged to the history of Asia as to that of Europe? This engagement is not simply something which happened in the past. The imprint of abroad is visible in Europe's quotidian life, whether in Ruud Gullit, the Dutch former manager of Chelsea FC, born of Indonesian parents; or in Ridley Scott, who went from Hartlepool art college to Hollywood, reinvented popular American cinema with films such as *Alien* and *Thelma and Louise* and then saw them exported to Britain; or in Jacques Derrida, the king of post-structuralism, who was born in Algeria and now rules over Parisian intellectual life.

The tragedy is that no one would recognize this mobile, 'promiscuous' Europe in the cloud of arguments that has enveloped Brussels and the European Union. The rest of the world can seem to go hang while one side of the argument claims that Europe (that is the Union) has become a synonym for an over-centralized and wasteful supra-state, denying national sovereignty to its members, while the other argues that Brussels can deliver answers to economic and social questions that can no longer be tackled by the nation state.

Even in the debates that have followed the collapse of the Soviet bloc, the Europeans have been so concerned to wed together a fraught and divided continent that 'Europe-in-the-world' has scarcely been visible. It only seems to surface as a negative term, when immigration becomes a political issue. Or when there are appalling acts such as the ethnic cleansing of Muslims in the former Yugoslavia; the historical equation of Christendom and Europe – which took a settled form in 1492 when the expulsion of Moors from Granada 'purified' the continent – can still take a deadly form.[1] These days European identity is generally imagined to be a matter of political structures – and ones that are wholly European, owing little to historical links with elsewhere. Thus a recent pamphlet from a British think-tank, 'Social Democracy at the Heart of Europe' considers Europe to be a matter of internal political structures, required to deliver full employment, a welfare state and material prosperity.[2] Not that these issues are not critical. Indeed, they are necessary to any vision (although whether 'Europe' can deliver them is another matter). But to use the philosopher's distinction, they are not sufficient.

The starved character of this vision of Europe (and any vision which is only political is inevitably starved) makes it possible to see why Raymond Aron's comment in 1952 – made soon after the birth of the European Coal and Steel Community – still has some force: 'The European idea is empty ... It was created by intellectuals, and that fact accounts at once for its genuine appeal to the mind and its feeble echo in the heart.' Raymond Aron's cynicism may in the end be wrongheaded. But his comment does remind us that a European identity, if it is to be inhabited by people who feel it as their own, must be able to provide them with stories which help them to make sense of more than the political part of their lives. After all, for some people 'Europe' may be gathered up – to take some random examples – in memories of holidays or certain sports; in music or literature; or in buildings or landscape. And of course people are never only European: whatever the European stories we are told, they must not make us choose between belonging to Europe and our other identities, whether national or more local. Loyalty in Europe has to be multiple rather than singular. Any European identity must be inclusive rather than exclusive and conjure up ideas of civil society at least as much as politics.

So how did the dominant vision of European identity become so introspective and political? As far back as the seventeenth century, thinkers were seeing Europe as a political idea and assuming that it had nothing to learn from the rest of the world. As Voltaire put it, Europeans shared 'the same principle of public law and politics unknown to other lands'. More recently, the trauma of the loss of empire among the colonial powers (as well as their continuing failure to relate to former colonies other than in paternal terms) has led them into an imaginative retreat from the world. As the Europeans have withdrawn, they have had to teach themselves to be European much as they had taught others, elsewhere, before them. It is noteworthy that 'European history' was not taught in European universities until the 1960s, after decolonization. But among the many influences on the current sense of European identity, the most potent is the shadow of war, which has lain across the continent in the twentieth century. Think how many of the resonant names of Europe are bound up with war: from the Somme to Dresden; from Stalingrad to Sarajevo; from Guernica to Auschwitz.

One might say, crudely, that some of the most important European institutions were invented in the aftermath of the Second World War: NATO, the European Union (in its earlier manifestations) and the Warsaw Pact. These bodies represented political projects – whether the taming of Germany; the invention of a supranational entity to control the nationalisms that had fuelled wars; the attempt to invent a Third Force between the superpowers of the United States and the USSR; or the desire to build powerful economic and military blocs.

Thus European identity, post-1945, fragmented along political lines, and Europe became less of a term of reference, at least in the West, than Western Civilization or the Atlantic alliance. During this period the earlier historical intermingling of East and West – Joseph Conrad and Appollinaire, Bartok and Janacek, all East Europeans, were key figures in modernist European culture – was forgotten. Memories of such cultural promiscuity could hardly be encouraged in the new divided Europe.

Crude ideological battles arrested thinking about European identity and ensured that such imagining as there was looked inwards rather than outwards. Even benign manifestations of the Cold War divisions, such as the European Union, are now having trouble making sense of the post-Berlin Wall Europe – one with proliferating states, rampant nationalisms and economic, cultural and political imperatives that are wildly different from those of 1945. For example, once upon a time the United States was the powerful economic presence haunting Europe; now the source of anxiety is just as likely to be the booming economies of the Pacific Rim.

An identity born in the immediate post-war years is no longer desirable or useful as we enter the third millennium. The post-war project of European integration has come to an end, and left us two choices: either we struggle to shore up that project; or we try to *re-imagine* it within a Europe less introspective, and more intent on acknowledging its past and present intimacies with the rest of the world – but without its earlier sense of superiority. Given the immense revolutions of 1989 that Europe has experienced, we ought to be doing something more worthwhile than spilling our energy into either defending or attacking modestly amended versions of post-war institutions.

In the current unsettled Europe – in which new regions and countries have appeared, many of them claiming a European identity – it may seem wanton to advocate that our ideas of Europe need to be unsettled rather than settled. But that is precisely the case. For we need to think about European identity in ways that embrace both the complex, perplexed history of Europe, and the ambitions and interests of all those who live here now.

What we need to do now is to imagine Europe anew – and imagine is the right word since, as Benedict Anderson has pointed out, it is simply impossible to know personally more than a few of those with whom you share a national or continental identity. And, this imagining is certainly far from easy, given the range of images about Europe already circulating. *Auf Wiedersehn Pet*, *Rapido*, *Allo Allo*, *Holiday '96* and documentary series such as *Cutting Edge* are just a few of the ways that 'Europe' is imagined in just one space: British terrestrial television.

## The mongrel continent

One way of beginning to imagine a new Europe is to remember that *50* million people, a population not much smaller than Britain's, emigrated from Europe to the United States in the *50* years before the First World War. Thus Europeans have family memories of migration and of ties with the countries concerned. This reminds us that there is nothing settled about Europe and that it has aways been umbilically tied to other continents. In turn, this allows us to offer an alternative vision to Fortress Europe, the place of exclusion that needs to defend itself against a hostile world. This is a vision of Europe as a place of comings and goings, of change and even of excitement. For instance in the late 1940s Luis Buñuel, a great Spanish filmmaker, was making startling movies in Mexico at the same time as the great black saxophonist Lester Young was playing jazz and escaping American racism in Paris.

There is simply no basis for the belief that there were once autonomous national European cultures, and that they have recently been contaminated by alien influences. The idea that there is some common esperanto European culture is equally groundless. Europe, both past and present, is a mongrel place of mixed cultures. Some of the mixing has always happened within Europe. The court of the English king, Charles I, was painted by the Flemish Van Dyck; the great Russian writers of the late nineteenth century spoke French as one of their native tongues; post-war East European poets have been extraordinarily influential on their Western counterparts (for instance Miroslav Holub on Ted Hughes); and French surrealism reanimated Czechoslovakian culture after the Second World War. And this is not to mention the changing political geography of Europe, which has seen regions and even countries come and go – minding us, if nothing else does, that Europe is no monument to stability.

The mongrelness of European culture also stems from Europe's intercourse with abroad. Le Corbusier's buildings stand in France and India; Hollywood is unimaginable without the influx of European refugees from Hitler; the European novel, often cited as one of the continent's great achievements, grew, in part, from the interaction of Europeans with other cultures (think of Flaubert or Joseph Conrad); and the south of both Spain and Italy have been shaped architecturally by their relationship with north Africa.

This insistence on the composite character of Europe and European identity is important, for it opposes the yearning for purification that presently stalks Europe, all the way from British Tory xenophobes to Serbian ethnic cleansers. Each in their own way (and evidently the two should not be equated) sees mixing as adulteration rather than enrichment. But such a mongrel identity does not only have that negative virtue. It also incites us to see Europe's mixing with the rest of the world, and the internal mixing, as its peculiar strength. And not as some deadly disease, for which the only cure would be a period of isolation.

Equally important, the acknowledgment of Europe as a space where cultures have intermingled allows us to welcome change as an opportunity, rather than view it as threat. Once Europe revelled in its acceptance of change and was the spearhead of novelty; now it has grown old and distrusts it. Yet an openness to change will become more valuable, not less, as global entertainment and information technology increasingly undermine national and continental boundaries.

Europe has responded to these developments either defensively, as in France, where the government enforces French language-only or European-only quotas on the media; or by promoting schemes at EU-level (such as EURIMAGES) which have by and large not been successful. Certainly, the status of European culture is a real *Kevin Robins* concern: American films hold three-quarters of the European market. But Europe cannot imagine a useful response to such a situation if it thinks in terms of its pure culture being sullied by Hollywood, or demands an EU-wide film and television industry that has to produce purely European programmes, inspired by European imaginations. Given the history of Europe, dreams of virginity can never be anything other than fantasy.

For, as I have argued, our Europe has been marked by its encounters with its own constituent parts, which have themselves varied through history, and also by encounters with the rest of the world. And these meetings will intensify and multiply in number. This is not the moment to start building walls again, either within Europe or between Europe and elsewhere. We need to think in terms of the birth of a Europe whose parents are many, of mixed origins, and who wish their child to flourish in the world, rather than stay at home with the doors locked.

## Notes

1. John Lukacs, *Decline and Rise of Europe* (1965).
2. Donald Sassoon, *Social Democracy at the Heart of Europe* (IPPR, 1996).

# 35
# Europe and Cities

*Peter Hall*

Europe's history is the history of its cities. From the very start until the present day, the significant part of Europe's history, the worthwhile and important part, was forged in its cities. Despite suggestions to the contrary, its future lies in them also.

A correction: of course, the countryside had to be there too, to grow the grain and press the wine, to provide relief from the noise and heat and sometimes the plagues of the city, to give a sense of arcadian calm for those who could afford to get away, whether to country houses or weekend picnic spots. But the business of Europe has always been done in its cities, the art and thought of Europe were created there, its political fate was decided in them.

These cities were the result first of politics and religion, second and most importantly of trade, third of crafts and manufacture. The first significant European cities were the city states of Greece, of which Athens was merely the most powerful and the most creative. Attica, originally the apotheosis of the Greek polis – a small self-contained unit of city and surrounding countryside, within the natural boundaries of a river basin – finally grew into the centre of a great trading empire that stretched from one end of the Mediterranean to the other, a model that was borrowed and extended by Rome. On the fall of the Roman empire cities decayed but not, it is now thought, disappeared; they soon grew again with the resumption of European trade, and not only were Roman cities restored and extended, but hundreds of new cities and towns were founded. Invariably their core was a defended fortress of a local prince or bishop, sometimes within the old Roman core, sometimes (in Scandinavia) taking over a pagan sacred site, rarely (as in Andalucia) converting a former Muslim sacred place. So European cities grew up within medieval Christendom and were the living expression of its culture, even after renaissance and reformation and the Enlightenment transformed them.

For that reason, European cities have enjoyed an extraordinary continuity. Many of the great European cities – Rome itself, Milan,

Naples, Paris, London, Manchester, Cologne – are Roman foundations; some – Athens, Marseilles – go back further. Most others were medieval foundations, and can trace nearly a thousand years of history. Only occasionally did a city decline, and then usually for special reasons: the silting of a port, the royal choice of an alternative nearby site. Even in the new industrial districts that came into sudden prominence in the nineteenth century, older places – Birmingham, Newcastle, Essen, Dortmund, Charleroi, St Etienne – provided the nuclei. The map of trade routes in the high Middle Ages is the map of motorways and high-speed train routes at the end of the twentieth century, and the nodal cities are the same in both.

In particular, the great cities of Europe have uniquely been places of human creativity (Hall 1998). Two and a half millennia ago, the Athenian city state effectively gave to the world participatory democracy, naturalistic art, classical architectural orders, comedy and tragedy, and much else besides, all in little over a century. Fifteen hundred years later another city state, Florence, rediscovered the classical tradition in art and architecture, and built upon it to usher in the Renaissance. Between 1570 and 1620 London saw the birth of modern drama; between 1750 and 1850, Vienna's musicians gave us a large part of the classical music repertoire; between 1870 and 1910 Parisian painters carried through a revolutionary pilgrimage, away from naturalism and towards new forms of representation. Into all these cities, as into Berlin during the 1920s, talented people were drawn, as by a magnet. The entire history of European civilization is an urban history.

These cities did not have to be mega-cities. Far from it. Periclean Athens had between 215 000 and 300 000 people at its peak – including citizens, metics and slaves – in the entire city state; less than half of the citizens, all the aliens and perhaps half the slaves lived in the twin cities of Athens and Piraeus. At its peak, around 1300, Florence numbered some 95 000 people. London in Shakespeare's time had 200 000. Later on, creative cities tended to be bigger: over one and a half million in the Vienna of 1900, over 3 million in the Paris of the same time, 4 million in the Berlin of the 1920s. What we can say is that great creative cities were generally the biggest places of their time. But not always even that: renaissance Florence was smaller than Milan or Venice, and reformation Wittenberg, the town where Luther nailed his theses to the cathedral door and his friend Cranach painted, was a minute place.

Big or small they might be; comfortable or grand they often were not. All Athenians lived incredibly squalid lives by modern standards, but at least they were equal. Almost every later great city was marked by huge differences in wealth and living standards between rich and poor. In Florence in 1427, the very height of the Renaissance, 1 per cent of citizens had 27 per cent of total wealth, while 14 per cent were destitute. In Vienna in 1910 only 7 per cent of dwellings had bathrooms and toilets, a mere 22 per cent had indoor toilets. Even the *haute bourgeoisie* in these cities lived extraordinarily squalid lives compared to the average family in Europe or North America at the end of the twentieth century.

They were uncomfortable places in another and associated sense: every one was a city in rapid economic and social transformation, a city that in consequence had grown with dizzy speed. Athens was the true global trading city. London in 1600, Vienna in 1800, Paris in 1900 were capitalist cities with strong precapitalist features: Florence and London were still guild craft cities, Vienna and Paris had strong *atelier* traditions; Berlin was the only true capitalist manufacturing city. They were trading cities, and out of trade came new ways of economic organization and new forms of production. Generally, they were the most advanced places in their respective territories, and they might even have been world leaders. That made them magnets for the immigration of talent, as well as generators of the wealth that could help employ that talent. That wealth might generate individual patronage, but also community patronage, either at the level of the city or, later, the nation state. Community support was always vital, whether in building the Parthenon, creating the Florentine Baptistery, building the court theatres of London, filling the Louvre or supporting the Vienna Rathaus or the great Berlin theatres.

Importantly, viewed by the standards of today, these were all cities of high culture: with the exception of Athens, culture was fostered by an aristocratic or bourgeois minority and catered for the tastes of that minority. But that explains what the economists call the demand side. The supply side was different: often, it was the recent in-migrants, sometimes from the native countryside, often from far-distant parts of the empire, who provided the artistic or philosophic talent, the metics of ancient Athens, the artists who came to Florence from the countryside or further afield, the provincial musicians of Vienna and provincial artists of Paris, the Jews in *fin-de-siècle* Vienna. And sometimes these newcomers, or their children, provided a significant part of the demand too: they might have become bourgeois, but they still felt themselves in important respects outsiders. Almost without exception, the creative cities were cosmopolitan; they drew talent in from everywhere, often from surprisingly far-away places. As an assertion, that stands up well: no city, probably, has ever been creative without continued renewal of the creative bloodstream.

But there had to be something more. Because these cities were in rapid economic transition, they were in course of transformation: in social relationships, in values and in world views. Again and again, we find that they were experiencing uneasy and unstable tension between conservative forces and values – aristocratic, hierarchical, religious, conformist – and radical values which were the exact opposite: bourgeois, open, rational, sceptical. Sometimes this conflict expressed itself as feudalism versus capitalism, but it is more complex than that: an established bourgeoisie could become a brake on the system, as in Paris and Vienna; sometimes creativity was sparked by sudden downthrow of an old regime, as in Berlin after 1918.

The critical point is that for cities to be creative, it seems necessary that this clash, this division, is experienced and then expressed by a group of creative people who feel themselves outsiders: more precisely, they both belong and they do not belong to the existing system of society and authority, because they are young or provincial or foreign, or because they do not belong to the established order. This is true of the metics (non-citizens) of ancient Athens, of the guild craftsmen of renaissance Florence, of the young actor-playwrights of Elizabethan London, of the court musicians and the Jewish intellectuals of Vienna, of the young painters in Paris, and of all the producers and writers who poured into Berlin in the 1920s. Again and again, a creative city is one where outsiders can enter and feel a sense of ambivalence, neither excluded from opportunity, nor too warmly embraced.

But there has to be more than this: they have to communicate, they even have to sell their creativity to a market that patronizes them. That seems to demand a widespread schism in the wider society. Thus some Athenians heeded the revolutionary doctrines of the Sophists and the playwrights who followed them, even though others were outraged enough to want to prosecute them; some rich Florentine bought and even commissioned the new naturalist art; some Parisian bourgeoisie risked their money on Manet and later Picasso, and some of their Berlin equivalents were willing to flock to the theatres to hear their values parodied and subverted. The point is inescapable: great creative cities are uncomfortable, unstable, uncertain about themselves, cities in the course of kicking over the traces.

For this to happen, there must be traces to kick over. These were cities neither so hidebound that they excluded new views, nor so revolutionary that there was nothing left to oppose. They were cities where a long-established order was being challenged or was in course of being overthrown. Political art could help to do this, of course; but so could less explicitly political art, from Shakespeare's plays to Picasso's paintings.

While the great cities, the established places, were making these huge artistic breakthroughs, other humbler and obscurer urban places were undertaking feats of creativity that were equally momentous. Manchester in 1780, Glasgow in 1850, Berlin in 1870 were all the technological leaders of their day. Obscure inventors, who were to become famous, made breakthroughs which resulted in new industries: Hargreaves and Cartwright outside Manchester, Watt and Boulton in Birmingham, Siemens in Berlin. These places, likewise, grew from obscurity into major cities within a few decades.

They started with few advantages: natural resources like coal and iron and navigable water played their role, but it was seldom decisive in explaining why they flourished while competitor cities did not. What was significant was what the economists call human capital, and that was not a matter of accident. Most key innovations came from entrepreneurs in the heroic garret, later garage, tradition. They were outsiders, and so were their cities. But they were not from the bottom of the social heap: most were middle class; though some early ones had little education and many were self-taught, most tended to have a good technical education, and a few were distinguished scientists.

All had learned what they needed to know. And – key point – all were supported by a local network, which supplied specialized skilled labour and services, but also created a very special climate of innovation in which everyone learned from a dozen competitor-cooperators. In such networks, as the Victorian economist Alfred Marshall put it, 'the mysteries of the trade become ... no mysteries'. Every place had its family tree, as successful firms spawned other firms. There are astonishing parallels between the region around Manchester in the 1780s and Silicon Valley in the 1980s.

These places had a special character: they were not the leading cities of their day, even the leading industrial cities, but neither were they on the edge of the world. They had egalitarian social structures. Careers were open to talents. There was a prevailing ethos of hard work, achievement, making money, and also investing that money in new ventures. There was invariably an open, freely available educational system: able children from modest backgrounds could achieve a university or at least a good technical education. The important point was that scientific or theoretical advances could easily be put to practical application. Because another part of the local economy always needed a better widget, there was constant pressure for improvement, for chains of incremental innovation that might extend over decades.

European cities were far from alone in this process. After 1870, the innovative palm passed from the United Kingdom to Germany, but even more so to the United States. After 1945, Japanese cities emerged as significant contenders in the innovation stakes. Europe, it began too often to seem, had lost its innovative edge. Though the great European cities and their surrounding areas – south-east England, the Île-de-France, the Munich region – retained important clusters of innovative high-technology industry, none could remotely claim to compete with California's Silicon Valley. And it increasingly appeared that in the most significant development of all – the marriage of art and technology, as represented in new industries like television broadcasting, the movies, popular music production or the fusion of television, telecommunications and computing into multimedia – American cities were once again taking the lead.

One critical question for the future is whether that is destined to be true, or whether European cities can hold their corner in the innovation stakes. It may be that Europe is still strong in invention, but America is superior at parlaying invention into commercially successful innovation. The World Wide Web was invented by Tim Berners-Lee, a British scientist, at the trans-European CERN scientific centre in Geneva in 1989, but its commercial application in the Mosaic browser came through a young American entrepreneur, Mark Andreesen, four years later. That story unhappily parallels the early history of the motor car from 1885 to 1908, or of computers from 1943 to 1960. It is a question over which European government task forces have been cogitating endlessly for the last decade, but without much practical outcome. Perhaps the explosion of new high-technology companies in the so-called Silicon Fen, around Cambridge, will represent the long-awaited breakthrough. Silicon Fen is not a new phenomenon; it can be traced back to 1969 (Segal Quince Wicksteed 1985), but its growth has been progressive and now seems to have reached a critical mass.

Cambridge is an old European city, though not a large one. But it does form one corner of a European research triangle, London–Oxford–Cambridge, which Danish research has shown to be outstandingly the most scientifically productive in the whole of Europe (Matthiessen and Schwarz 1999). That underlines the important point that the right unit of analysis, the true city at the end of the twentieth century, is no longer a small self-contained place like Wittenberg, nor a small city state like ancient Athens or renaissance Florence, but a huge and complex polycentric region stretching over hundreds or thousands of square kilometres, in which the traditional qualities of urban interaction are now extended over a vast spatial canvas.

That in turn provokes another question: whether the new technologies promise the 'death of distance' (Cairncross 1997) and with it the death of the city. For, if information can now be exchanged freely and almost costlessly anywhere on the earth's surface, the city may effectively lose its traditional advantages of close interaction and agglomeration. But for that there is as yet no evidence. On the contrary: it seems that innovation depends as much as ever on agglomeration, as exemplified in the United States by the San Francisco Bay Area and Greater Los Angeles. And consumption appears likewise to agglomerate, as exemplified by the growth of both leisure and business tourism and by the constant expansion of the convention industry world-wide. The most recent analyses of major global cities (Government Office for London 1996) suggest that they increasingly rely upon, and compete in, a few key advanced service industries – financial and business services, 'power and influence' (government and headquarters), tourism, and creative and cultural industries – all of which effectively involve the generation and exchange and consumption of information, and in all of which the agglomeration principle continues to rule supreme. At most, what can be observed is a short-distance deconcentration of some more routine information processing from core cities to smaller places within the wider metropolitan area, plus the increased importance of specialized concentrations (higher education, research and development) at locations that often have long and complex histories. These concentrations – outstandingly, within Europe, in south-east England, the Île-de-France and the Öresund region of Denmark/southern Sweden – are eloquent testimony to the strength of metropolitan agglomeration and its local diffusion.

Even the most passionate American advocates of the future world of cyberspace, significantly, conclude that the city has not yet had its day (Gates 1995, Mitchell 1995). And one of them, significantly, illustrates his point with European examples.

> Does development of national and international information infra-structures, and the consequent shift of social and economic activity to cyberspace, mean that existing cities will simply fragment and collapse? Or does Paris have something that telepresence cannot match? Does Rome have an answer to *Neuromancer*? Most of us would bet our bottom bits that the reserves of resilience and adaptability that have allowed great cities to survive (in changed form) the challenges

of industrialization and the automobile will similarly enable them to adapt to the bitsphere. (Mitchell 1995, 169)

Exactly. The European city has been a fundamental fact of European life for two and a half millennia, and it will continue to be so for millennia to come. To be sure, in the process it will change its form and its function, as it has ever since the transport and industrial revolutions of the eighteenth and nineteenth centuries. But it will prove equally resilient to the equally momentous transformation that is now taking place: the informational revolution.

## References

Cairncross, F., *The Death of Distance: How the Communications Revolution will Change our Lives* (London: Orion, 1997).

Gates, W., *The Road Ahead* (London: Viking, 1995).

Government Office for London, *Four World Cities: A Comparative Study of London, Paris, New York and Tokyo* (London: Llewelyn Davies Planning, 1996).

Hall, P., *Cities in Civilization* (London: Weidenfeld and Nicolson; New York: Pantheon, 1998).

Mitchell, W.J., *City of Bits: Space, Place, and the Infobahn* (Cambridge, Mass.: MIT Press, 1995).

Matthiessen, C.M. and Schwarz, A.W., 'Scientific Centres in Europe: An Analysis of Research Strength and Patterns of Specialism Based on Bibliometric Indicators', *Urban Studies*, 36 (1999), 453–77.

Segal Quince Wicksteed, *The Cambridge Phenomenon: The Growth of High Technology Industry in a University Town* (Cambridge: Segal Quince Wicksteed, 1985).

# 36
## Football and Europe[1]

*Simon Kuper*

It is often noted that most Britons hold no strong views on the European Union. 'The EU has neither attracted enthusiastic support nor explicit opposition,' says Karlheinz Reif, former head of the EU's polling wing.[2]

Meanwhile – and this too may be a symptom of dumbing down – many Britons appear obsessed with football. The only comprehensive survey on the subject, conducted by Fletcher Research, showed that 18 million people in England and Wales, or 35 per cent of the population, describe themselves as football fans.[3] Even greater numbers than these watch the biggest England matches on television.

The European debate in Britain is conducted partly, subconsciously, through football. The game has helped make many Britons much more pro-European. This is true in Scotland as it is in England, but the Scottish debate is different and where necessary I shall refer in this article to England rather than Britain.

This season, about half the players in the English Premier League are foreigners, most of them from EU nations.

These players are disproportionately prominent. The Football Writers' Association has chosen a continental European as its player of the year for four years running. The latest winner was David Ginola, the Frenchman who also figures in shampoo advertisements on television and is thus known to many people who don't even like football. Ginola has also been voted Britain's best dressed man, as has Ruud Gullit, the former Dutch footballer (Britons and non-footballers are also eligible for the award).

Gullit's former club Chelsea has transformed itself from an outfit featuring second-rate British clodhoppers into one of Europe's best sides with a largely foreign line-up that usually includes just one token Englishman, Dennis Wise. Chelsea are managed by an Italian, Arsenal and Liverpool by Frenchmen, and Wimbledon by a Norwegian former Marxist. That foursome outnumbers the total number of foreign managers in the English top division between 1900 and 1995.

In short, foreigners are taking over English football clubs. That is not happening in many other business sectors. Only if you work in one of a few select offices in central London are you likely to have many continental European colleagues.

Nor do Britons encounter continental Europeans in many other spheres of daily life. They may be served by an Australian in their local pub or by a naturalized Bangladeshi in their local Indian restaurant, but unless they live in central London, probably not by a European. Just 1.6 per cent of EU citizens are permanent residents of another EU country, and few of those live in Birmingham or Aylesbury.

It is true that the British increasingly visit continental Europe, where they meet continental Europeans. However, most of those contacts are probably shallow: with waiters, petrol pump attendants or strangers in nightclubs.

In short, most English people probably have only a casual acquaintance with continental Europeans. In the past the remove was even more extreme. It is no exaggeration to say that even ten years ago, to most Britons the French were people with berets and garlic, while the Dutch wore clogs and smoked drugs. They were all forever caving in to the Germans, and if you went on holiday to poor southern European countries such as Italy or Spain you were likely to be cheated.

And here is the first way in which football has shaped the British European debate: it has put a few living Europeans into the British public mind. Ten years ago, how many Britons could have named a living Frenchman or German? Perhaps Brigitte Bardot, maybe Helmut Kohl, just possibly Franz Beckenbauer. Few Continental film stars or musicians have ever become big in Britain, and ten years ago the tabloids had already given up their foreign coverage. Roger Jowell, director of the National Centre for Social Research, says: 'Even when the *Sun* ran that disgusting headline, "Up Yours, Delors", I think 90 per cent of the British public probably didn't know who Jacques Delors was.'[4] (Delors, needless to say, was President of the European Commission.)

Today, too, few Britons probably know who Gerhard Schröder, Lionel Jospin or Massimo d'Alema are. Jowell knows of no polling on the subject. However, he says: 'Even after Gordon Brown had been chancellor a few months, a poll showed that most people in Britain didn't recognise him. I think it's extremely fanciful to believe that they know foreign politicians.'[5]

Ten years ago, too, British football crowds encountered Continental footballers almost only as opponents in international matches. Narcissistic foreigners who rolled their socks to their ankles or wore their shirt outside their shorts were jeered. Commentators and coaches used to dismiss 'Continentals' as 'lacking bottle' and being inclined to cheat.

By contrast, among the most photographed, written-about figures in England in recent years have been Eric Cantona (French, handsome, charismatic, a brilliant footballer, arrogant), David Ginola (French, handsome, charismatic, a brilliant footballer, arrogant, enemy of Cantona), Ruud Gullit (Dutch, handsome, etc.) and Dennis Bergkamp (Dutch, handsome, deeply uncharismatic). Jowell agrees that these footballers probably enjoy widespread 'male recognition', if not 'female recognition'.[6] Gianluca Vialli, the Chelsea manager, and Gianfranco Zola, one of his best players, are certainly better known in Britain than their compatriots D'Alema and Romano Prodi (who is, needless to say, President of the European Commission).

All this matters. Ginola, Bergkamp and Zola help put faces on those abstract notions 'the French', 'the Dutch', 'the Italians'. It would be hard to design more attractive faces if you were a marketing man for the European Union.

The continental Europeans playing in England are mostly better players than our own. They are also considered more sophisticated. They tend to speak good English, and many of them are well educated. Bergkamp finished school to the equivalent of A-levels, while Slaven Bilic, the Croat who played for Everton and West Ham, has a law degree. By contrast English football, which virtually requires aspiring players to leave school at 16 and become an 'apprentice', has a selection bias favouring the least educated members of the population.

Foreign players also tend to look better than British players. This, in part, is the result of a healthier diet. Until recently, British footballers ate British working-class staples like chips, sausages, bacon and beer. When the foreign players arrived they proclaimed themselves astounded.

Most foreign players have also been clever enough to state frequently how much they like living in England. This tends to come easiest to those who live in London. 'Every day I'm very happy that I am a Chelsea player', Gullit, who lived on Cadogan Square just off the Kings Road, told the *Evening Standard*. However, Bryan Roy, a Dutch winger with Nottingham Forest who found the East Midlands wanting, was astute enough not to tell the British press.

Most of the foreigners also seemed capable of getting on with English people. The young Manchester United players adored Cantona, while Bergkamp and his erstwhile striking partner at Arsenal, the black, rap music loving, loud Ian Wright, struck up an unlikely friendship. The message was that Britons could work with Europeans.

In response, fans even adopted foreign symbols to cheer on their clubs. Manchester United fans at the FA Cup final of 1996 waved French *tricouleurs* in honour of Cantona. Arsenal fans briefly chanted '*Allez les rouges*', while Middlesbrough supporters wore Brazilian team shirts for Juninho. When the German striker Uwe Rösler became a cult hero at Manchester City, fans celebrated the Luftwaffe's wartime bombing of the Manchester United stadium with T-shirts that read: 'Uwe's Granddad Bombed Old Trafford.'

Admittedly there is no desire for a European football team, something occasionally called for by Europhiles. However, there are signs that foreign teams are no longer regarded as entirely foreign. When France won the 1998 World Cup the *Daily Mirror*'s front-page headline was 'Arsenal Win the World Cup', above a photograph of Arsenal's Frenchmen Emmanuel Petit and Patrick Vieira embracing. It was parochial and internationalist at the same time. Similarly in golf's Ryder Cup of 1999 the British tabloids supported the purportedly gentlemanly European team against the supposedly cheating Americans. And in the rugby World Cup later that year, most British fans ended up supporting France.

Had the Conservatives watched sport, and football in particular, more attentively, they might have realized that going into the 1997 and 2001 elections with a Euro-bashing campaign was unlikely to work.

There are, of course, foreigners who offend English sensibilities. Sasa Curcic, a Yugoslav player with Barnsley, reported that the women in the Yorkshire town were ugly. The Italian Paolo di Canio fought dirty with Celtic in order to get more money, won a contract with Sheffield Wednesday, and there pushed over a referee, enhancing perceptions of Latins as greedy, violent, lawless and emotional.

However, none of these sins matches those of English players such as Paul Gascoigne (alcoholic, wife-beater, caught eating a kebab early in the morning in Soho shortly before the last World Cup), Paul Merson (once addicted simultaneously to alcohol, cocaine and gambling) or Robbie Fowler (mimed snorting cocaine and offering his backside to a purportedly homosexual opponent during matches).

So the profile of continental European footballers in England is high, and their image overwhelmingly good.

That the presence of footballers from other EU nations can encourage pro-EU feelings has often been remarked. 'The invasion of European football players is seen by most people as a good thing', says the journalist Martin Jacques. 'Ordinary kids in Britain will follow their favourite players around Europe and say, "My team is Juventus."'[7]

The EU long ago grasped the same point. The Adonino Committee, set up after the European summit at Fontainebleau in 1984, chaired by the Italian MEP Pietro Adonino, recommended various measures to build the public's sense of European identity including a Euro-lottery, the adoption of the blue flag with gold stars as the EC emblem, and the creation of European sports teams. The current Chelsea side can be seen as the epitome of Adoninismo. Oddly enough, the man who did most to make that possible is the Eurosceptic Rupert Murdoch, whose Sky channels provided the money that allowed English clubs to buy the best foreigners. Almost every day of the football season Sky transmits 90 minutes of pro-European propanda.

However, the continental Europeans at English clubs have done more than just stimulate a sort of 'Alle Menschen werden Brüder' integrationism. They have – and this is crucial – spread the notion that the Continent does things better. In politics, Europhiles and Eurosceptics can still argue their corners. But in football, ideologies are tested quickly by results. And in recent times the Europhiles have won almost every match.

Until the early years of Margaret Thatcher the British could still believe that when it came to football they were best. Teams from the English provinces, typically consisting of hard-drinking muscular Britons supplemented by a couple of hard-drinking muscular Irishmen, won the European Cup seven years out of eight between 1977 and 1984. Those were the days when Nottingham Forest were a better team than Juventus of Turin or Real Madrid.

Even then English fans might have agreed that the Continentals played a more sophisticated sort of football – more passing, more brain, less brawn – but this was then seen as a drawback. The simple, British way worked best: long punt to the toothless centre-forward, goal. It was thought to be to the credit of the English that they did not mess about with Continental ideas. Just look at the trophies.

Then, on 29 May 1985 at the European Cup final in the Heysel stadium in Belgium, Liverpool fans ran rampant and 39, mostly Juventus, fans died. From that day on the Eurosceptics have been losing the footballing argument.

For a start, hooliganism became known as 'the English disease'. To the average Italian or German, who probably did not know many English people personally either, the image of the young Englishman became to some degree that of a hooligan. The foreign press explained that these thugs were the products of unimaginable deprivation in places like Liverpool and Manchester. In England, too, there was shame.

In fact, leaving that day at the Heysel aside, hooliganism should never have become such a great law-and-order issue. The violence palled besides violence in pubs and nightclubs that had nothing to do with football. Ten years ago, when hooliganism was at its peak, there were still more arrests on an average Saturday night in Oxford city centre than in the entire second division programme for that weekend.

To Britain, hooliganism mattered chiefly as an image problem. The violence, though usually quite slight, was often broadcast and shown around the world. Thatcher made things worse by raging about it publicly.

The upshot was that English fans came to be seen at home and abroad as worse people than Continental fans. There was much talk of the Italian family men who loved football and had never seen a fight at a game until they died at the Heysel. The English image problem persists, in weaker form, to this day. At recent World Cups and European Championships, almost all violence has been caused by England fans.

After the Heysel, English clubs were banned from European tournaments. When they were allowed back, in 1990, they could no longer win trophies. The consensus was that by losing touch with the Continental game, they had fallen behind. It took until 1999 for an English side to win the Champions League (the successor to the European Cup), and that Manchester United team, playing with the sophistication of the best Continentals, led by a manager who frowned on drinking, featured a Dane, a Dutchman, a Swede, a Trinidadian and two Norwegians, one of whom scored the winner. This was hardly a straightforward British triumph.

For the best English clubs have adopted Continental ways. Watching Cantona go off to train voluntarily in the afternoons, the young Manchester United players of the mid-1990s realized that maybe there were more useful ways of spending their time than playing snooker. At Chelsea, when Gullit became manager, he made the dinner ladies at the training ground serve salads and pasta at lunchtime. Vialli, while still playing for Chelsea, was so careful of his muscles that he did not even drive to training, using a chauffeur instead.

Ten years before that would have been considered a laughable foreign affectation. But in the new era it was held up as an example. Healthy living became the consensus. A book called *The Italian Footballer's Diet* was published in Britain. At Arsenal, the players agreed to ban alcohol from the players' lounge after matches. Recently, the Chelsea chairman Ken Bates publicly attacked Jody Morris, one of his few remaining English players, for eating too many hamburgers. At the top, English football has become a distinctly European game.

Conversely, and significantly, Continental football has not become at all British. As I write Steve McManaman of Real Madrid is the only top-class English footballer playing abroad. Most of the others who have tried have failed to adapt, not learning the language and shocking locals with their beer consumption. Ian Rush came back from two miserable years with Juventus saying it had been like a foreign country. Such failures make the transition of the Continentals – Vialli has even begun speaking Estuary English, dropping his Ts – look all the more impressive.

The Continental Europeans in English football have become poster boys for mobility: they have taken exciting, well-paying jobs in a foreign country and are mostly coping well. This is crucial because mobility of labour is a central EU ideal. Asked in a poll what the EU meant to them, the most common answer among 15- to 24-year-olds was 'the ability to go wherever I want in Europe'.[8] Continental footballers show that it can be done.

When it came to the England team in the 1990s, the Europhile victory was even more complete. The team's manager at the start of the decade, Graham Taylor, favoured a traditional English muscle-based game. 'Football should be honest, open, passionate', he once said. 'Part of a nation's culture is the way it plays its sport. And the British way is with passion and commitment.'

It proved a disaster. Beaten by a more sophisticated Dutch team, England failed even to qualify for the World Cup of 1994. Their defeats, and those of the cricket team, mirrored the simultaneous collapse of the British economy under John Major and seemed to sum up better than John Osborne ever did the sense of British decline. Many people felt this. One day in 1993 the *Independent* ran photographs of Taylor and Major side by side on its front page above almost identical quotes about the need to forget past failures and soldier on.

Taylor resigned, became immortal through his starring role in a hilarious fly-on-the-wall documentary called *Do I Not Like That*, and was succeeded by Terry Venables. Nicknamed 'El Tel' after his years coaching Barcelona, where he had even picked up some Spanish, Venables picked the Dutch as his role model. He created an England team that played Continental football. At Wembley on 18 June 1996, in a European Championship match, his side thrashed the Dutch role models 4–1. That night remains the most vivid enactment yet of the Blairite message that Britain can turn itself into a modern European country.

Significantly, the 4–1 was not greeted with Rule Britannia-style triumphalism. Instead, spontaneously, the Wembley crowd began to sing a chart song called 'Football's Coming Home' written for the England team that year by David Baddiel and Frank Skinner. The lyrics said that after years of failure the fans knew that

> *England's going to*
> *Throw it away*
> *Going to blow it away.*

The refrain was bittersweet:

> *Thirty years of hurt,*
> *Haven't stopped me dreaming,*
> *Football's coming home,*
> *It's coming home.*

The song found a resonance beyond football. It was sung at Ascot and at Wimbledon. Major, Blair and Paddy Ashdown all referred to it in their speeches to their party conferences that autumn. It became the unofficial national anthem. Few people could still keep a straight face for 'God Save the Queen'. But Football's Coming Home seemed to tell the English who they were: a proud nation that had endured much failure but now saw a better future. Had the lyrics been stodgy and free of verbs, they could have been written by Blair.

It is worth inserting a caveat here. So far I have argued exclusively that football has produced pro-European propaganda. However, one of the most enduring tenets of English nationalism is that foreigners cheat at football. There is nothing that so outrages an English crowd as a long-haired foreigner writhing on the ground clutching his head trying to get an English defender sent off for a possibly imaginary foul. English fans consider such behaviour not just dishonest but possibly effeminate. Given their general lack of contact with continental Europeans, these dives make a disproportionate contribution to anti-European feeling.

But the debate is shifting. In recent years some English footballers have adopted the dive just as they have other Continental practices. Michael Owen, the best young English player, has become a leading exponent. It was his dive that won England a crucial penalty against Argentina in the last World Cup.

It is true that the English dive is more goal-oriented than the Continental version: the English player goes to ground but then, in the machismo tradition of English football, quickly stands up instead of feigning near-death. His acting is minimalist. He is not trying to get his opponent sent off, just hoping for a free-kick or a penalty.

Nonetheless, even when it comes to diving – the archetypal continental sin – the Dover–Calais divide is blurring. We are becoming more like them. We have had to.

Many British fans would probably rather watch good British players than good foreigners. But there can be very few now who think that the British style of football is best. The traditional English game is dying out, the victim of a sort of cultural Darwinism. The Continental way has proved more efficient, more modern.

You may ask whether this matters. Football is only a game. Surely its fans are able to see that issues such as the single European currency, the Common Agricultural Policy and the powers of the European Parliament should be assessed on their own merits?

The problem is that most have little idea what these merits are. British tabloid newspapers, radio stations and television channels do not give European issues much of an airing. I fly regularly to the Netherlands and am always struck on returning to Britain how low-brow most British news is. On the aeroplane the Dutch newspapers are full of technocratic debates about interest rates or social security benefit levels for 2004. The front pages of British newspapers, once devoted to Conservative sex scandals and Princess Diana, now feature David Beckham and Posh Spice, Paul Gascoigne or photographs of Ginola. On the airport bus in Luton recently, the first news item I heard on the driver's radio was about the Beckham–Spice wedding.

When the tabloid newspapers do discuss European issues, they do so chiefly by evoking popular narratives such as these:

1. Hitler tried to conquer Europe, and now the Germans are using the EU to do the same. We Britons must stand up to them.
2. The Europeans have always been given to wild theories devoid of common sense, and now their bureaucrats are striving for straight bananas, cucumbers and the like. We Britons must stand up to them.
3. The Europeans cheat: the Italians vote for European Union directives and then never implement them, the French illegally ban British beef, and they all dive when they haven't been fouled. We Britons must stand up to them.

These tabloid narratives obviously have some popular appeal. Yet they have failed to swing the British public decisively against Europe. Even when it comes to an untried and revolutionary idea savaged by the tabloids such as the single currency, most Britons still seem open to persuasion. One reason might be the subliminal messages that so many of them receive from football:

1. Continentals are not bad people. In fact, they drink less, fight less, look better and are better educated than we are. They can work in harmony with Britons.
2. The Continental way is more efficient than the British way. If we don't follow them we will be left behind.

These messages are particularly potent in the most arcane European debates. Nobody, not even economics professors, knows whether joining the euro will end up being good or bad for Britain. This means that the way Britons vote in a referendum will depend chiefly on their gut feelings about Europe. And those gut feelings are shaped, in large part, by football.

## Notes

1. Some of the ideas in this chapter were developed in a conversation with Ian Buruma in 1997. I am indebted to him. This chapter is based in part on an article of mine that appeared in *Prospect* magazine in October 1997.
2. Quoted on p. 31 in Mark Leonard, *Rediscovering Europe* (London: Demos, 1998).
3. Neil Bradford and William Reeve, *Net Profits* (London: Fletcher Research, 1997).
4. Conversation with Roger Jowell, 8 December 1999.
5. Ibid.
6. Ibid.
7. Quoted in Leonard, *Rediscovering Europe*, p. 20.
8. Directorate General XXII, *Young Europeans* (Brussels: European Commission, 1997), quoted in Leonard, *Rediscovering Europe*, p. 51.

# 37
## Islam and Euro-Identity: Muslims, Diversity and Inclusion

*Yasmin Alibhai-Brown*

An estimated 17 million Muslims live within the European Union. What they think and what others think of them will determine in part how the massive project of further European integration develops into the next century. While European leaders worry endlessly about coins, bureaucrats and flags, feelings about this fundamental question of relationships are burning away within the diverse Muslim communities of the EU. They do not yet see themselves as part of the project in any meaningful sense and many of those in the wider community remain unconvinced that this group can ever be incorporated into their ideal vision of the Union. Media reports from around Europe suggest that discrimination against Muslims is growing. Even in the most egalitarian social democratic states (or actually especially in these), such as Sweden and Denmark, Islam is seen as a massive blot on the landscape of the future. On the other side, even the most Westernized Muslims – including myself – feel that post-Bosnia Europe only holds terrors for us.

Such paranoia and mutual mistrust will indeed become a self-fulfilling prophecy unless we can develop a more positive and interactive dynamic between European Muslims and non-Muslims. This cannot be based on 'celebrating diversity' or 'tolerance' or other such anodyne concepts, but on informed conversations about the new identity of Europe in the next century. We must all begin to understand first that Islam is now *an essential and intrinsic part of the West*. Moreover, modern European leaders have failed to inform their populations that this presence goes back a very long way and their so-called 'Christian' places such as Florence and Venice show clearly the long connections and the cultural and commercial exchanges which have taken place over the centuries. Secondly, we need to acknowledge that European Muslims, even in the most conservative communities, have themselves been transformed after generations of living in the West. And there is no going back. Muslim women in Europe, for example, would never submit to the version of Islam propagated by Iran or fanatics in Pakistan and Afghanistan.

It is a pity that the European Union project defined itself at the outset around the definition of Europe as a white Christian entity and around assumptions of a shared culture based on Graeco-Roman roots and Judaeo-Christian ethics and Beethoven's Ninth Symphony. It is a pity too that so many Muslims in Europe have a view of themselves only as outsiders. It is no longer feasible for European Muslims to requisition or request enclaves within states or in the pan-national context of the European Union. As Fuad Nahdi, the editor of *Q News*, a newspaper for young British Muslims, wrote recently: 'Muslims here cannot operate as if they are a majority; they have to rediscover a theology and Islamic jurisprudence suited to a minority living in a multi-faith and multicultural society.'[1] More important than these sensible limitations on aspirations on both sides and beyond the contested spaces and ideas, there are extraordinary possibilities available which European and Muslim leaders have failed to grasp. Unfortunately, even Demos did not adequately address this vital issue in its recent well-received publication, *Making Europe Popular: The Search for European Identity*, although there was a recognition in this document that 'neither a narrative of cultural highlights nor a banal unity based on regulating the noise emissions of European lawn mowers' will provide a meaningful Europe-wide identity which we can all buy into.

What do we need to do in order to nurture the positive aspects of Islam in the West? The first step would be to reject the prejudice which has become dangerously commonplace when one is discussing the subject: that Islam is a new enemy and a threat. White Europeans and Muslims have too easily and lazily accommodated this prejudice, partly because it is so easy to gather evidence to back their views and partly because there is political advantage to be reaped out of these binary conflictual descriptions. We need to believe you see us as a threat in order to heighten our own sense of grievance and separation. The advantages the other way are even greater. Influential Europeans who speak out on this 'threat' have a lot to gain, especially as our more enlightened leaders seem trapped in an embarrassed silence on the issue, which somewhat reflects how they themselves share the anxieties. It is not simply political cowardice which is responsible for this shifty approach, although there is no doubt now that Le Pen and others like him are a force to be brokered with in France, Germany, Denmark and other countries in which 'Islamophobia' is proving a great vote catcher at local elections.

But the problem is more complex than this and the eventual response of the Western allies to the Kosovan crisis shows that politics is not easily imprisoned within 'ethnic' divides. Muslims across Europe were astonished that 'Christians' were prepared to bomb other Christians and protect Muslims. There is no awareness among the ruling elites in European countries and the Commission about what European Muslims are doing, saying or thinking. How many of us (and I speak now as a British Muslim) circulate among those with power and influence? How aware, therefore, can the leadership be of both the real dangers of the self-selected or imposed exclusion of so many people and the extraordinary opportunities that this can throw up? A couple of years ago I was asked to chair a Council of Europe conference on diversity and gender equality. The level of ignorance about Islam among even these well-meaning and highly intelligent European intellectuals was terrifying.

Without intimate, ongoing knowledge, all we are ever likely to get is a tendency towards fear and loathing, which in turn encourages certain vocal sections of European Muslims to promote their own hateful and resentful messages. As Fred Halliday wrote in his thoughtful 'Islam and the Myth of Confrontation', this in the end helps nobody at all:

> regrettably, for politicians, popularizers and demagogues, the reality is far more complex than they normally imply. There are very real issues underlying the rise of Islamic movements, their relationship with Western Europe and the formulation of a European policy in regard to them. These genuine concerns can only be reached by cutting away some of the jungle of misconception that normally surrounds them.[2]

Unfortunately and quite extraordinarily, it is often intellectuals who contribute most to the gathering misapprehension of Islam. People who would never dream of making prejudiced generalizations about black or Jewish people repeatedly express their Islamophobia with impunity. The list is long and includes Fay Weldon and Connor Cruise O'Brien. Others simply misrepresent realities. When the highly regarded defence correspondent Claire Hollingworth writes of 'fundamentalist' Islam 'fast becoming the chief threat to global peace and security... akin to the menace posed by Nazism in the 1930s and then by communism in the 1950s'[3] and Samuel Huntington speaks ominously of 'the clash of civilizations'[4] and the writers who support Rushdie denounce us as dangerous barbarians, what hope is there for enlightenment among ordinary Europeans?

This is not to suggest that the sense of threat which is felt by white Europeans is simply foolish. There are historical reasons why it seems to make sense to many citizens. Not only do traces of the fear of Islam which fuelled Crusades linger on; one of the most potent binding forces in the past for this continent – which excelled at blood letting within its own borders – was the idea of overseas conquest and the innate superiority of Christendom. When she made her powerful speech on Europe at Bruges in 1991, Margaret Thatcher spoke of how Europeans needed to be proud because 'we' conquered and civilized the rest of the world. This speech is revealing for several reasons. There is no attempt made here to pretend that her vision of Europe's cultural identity is anything other than white. Her use of the word 'we' and the assumptions that follow make this clear enough. She epitomized what many across Europe truly believe to be true. The word 'European' conjures up an image of whiteness. 'Multiculturalism' always refers to those who are not white. In a new pamphlet, *After Multiculturalism*, published by the Foreign Policy Centre, this problem of 'multicultural thinking' is discussed in depth.

The great challenge for the European integration project in relation to Islam (and the rest of Europe's non-white 'others') is to turn both these terms around and make them more inclusive. It can be done but the political will needs to be in place and the minorities, especially Muslims, must want it to happen too and not merely on terms of rights and religious privileges.

It should be of concern that young, highly educated Muslims are developing a new sense of superiority through victimhood. Many are attracted to the idea of *intifada* and of an unworkable, though romantic, pan-Islamic identity, and the notion that they can live within their own ideological and religious imaginary territories. The young British-born Muslim men incarcerated in Yemen show that these fantasies materialize among some into action. A few of these men, not all, were indeed influenced by militant Islamic clerics. These militants like nothing better than to be attacked for this so they can develop even stronger mental fortresses for themselves. Unless EU leaders understand this, they will unwittingly engender more than enough xenophobia for this process to escalate. This is why, although it was enormously important to bring out some of the hatred and discrimination targeted at the Muslim community in Britain, the Runnymede Trust report on Islamophobia needed to do more than just that.[5] It needed also to show, just as we now do for the Jewish community or black and other Asian Britons, the strengths and talents of Muslims. We cannot be just victims – and we are not.

Do Muslims want to be a part of Europe or a part within Europe? That is a key question and whatever the answers, there will be a thousand variations. A recent Institute for Public Policy Research seminar provided some information on what young British Muslims are saying about this, although here too there is healthy disagreement. One group of highly vocal, well organized, young Muslims was convinced that their Islamic identities mattered to them rather than the 'ethnic' identities that were foisted on them. They were young mothers, fathers, journalists and so on. They had their own self-help groups, Saturday schools, marriage guidance services and a political agenda which was assertive and well thought through. They were resentful that funding organizations refused to recognize their distinct and separate needs. Integration – even of the most local kind, even with other Asians – was the last thing on their minds. But unlike their parents, who identified themselves in terms of their original countries, they said they were British. The ironies are obvious.

At the other end of the spectrum were young Muslims who saw themselves as part of a wider movement of other disenfranchised groups seeking a place for themselves in society. Dr Yunus Samad from the University of Bradford has carried out extensive research among Muslims in Bradford. He concludes that although rhetoric rather than reflection still formed the basis of much discussion within the young British Muslim communities, there was no doubt that they identified themselves as British and Muslim in ways which were dramatically different from their parents.[6]

This all indicates that modernization is taking place but not in the direction that was once expected. There are other trends emerging. British Muslims have more rights, ease of existence and a degree of cultural autonomy than their counterparts in France and Germany. This is not producing confidence that we might be more able to integrate on our own terms. Instead, many Muslims see an abyss ahead. They reinterpret their lives, settle their descriptions at the lowest common denominator and do not think strategically. For example, the fact that Muslims have won the battle for state funded Muslim schools is creating a queue for more schools. We might use this moment of victory to take stock of what this might mean in terms of our further alienation and demonization.

What, then, can be done to integrate Muslims into the new Europe? Why should they wish this to happen? How can they be persuaded that it is in their interests to join in? And what would they gain by doing this when they see a potential loss of their faith, clarity and self-respect? On the other side, do white European leaders have the capacity, energy and idealism to cast out their Islamophobia and develop something more wholesome in its place? And how might we begin to bring about change?

First, we must enable white Europeans to educate themselves on their Muslim neighbours and to understand how vital this is. The ill thought-out treatment of Turkey by the EU – which may in a short time become another Algeria – proves how superficial and short-sighted awareness still is. Secondly, it would be helpful to establish a Europe-wide Muslim task force which would include Muslim historians, political scientists, scientists and others. This group might formally and informally work with EU institutions as well as national governments. Most university departments in this country, even in the top universities, have Muslim academics and post-graduate students. Many are dynamic women who are prepared to fight for gender equality on their own terms. These individuals could also create an important forum for young Muslims and encourage a sense of a more complex and integrated identity than that which is being asserted at the moment.

It is only through such steps that we will be able to understand how we now have, across Europe, the flowering of a new Muslim intellectual movement which is unique because it is both Islamic as well as self-consciously part of the West. If European Muslims were part of the informed decision-making processes they might have been able to offer political ideas which would have helped our thinking on Bosnia and might still help to avoid the disasters such as we have seen in the Balkans. Western Muslims have produced architectural masterpieces like the mosques in Paris, in Edinburgh or in London (opposite the Victoria and Albert museum). There are impressive Muslim art publications now on offer, as well as poetry, plays and intellectual tracts like the recent book, *Post-modernism and the Other*, by the prolific writer Ziauddin Sardar.[7] In a dreamy mood, I can even imagine a re-creation of the glory of the Islamic and Christian cultural masterpiece of Granada; if only Europe had the imagination to encourage such a thing. Many Europeans fear a future of distrust and conflict with Europe's Muslims and the world of Islam beyond the Continent. Many EU Muslims share this dark anticipation. It need not be so. But to create a truly integrated Europe the talent and energy of Muslim cultures must be properly nurtured and incorporated into the new identity of Europe.

## Notes

1. Paper presented at an IPPR seminar in March 1998, to be published in a forthcoming report.
2. Halliday, F., *Islam and the Myth of Confrontation* (London: IB Taurus, 1996).
3. *International Herald Tribune*, 9 November 1993.
4. *Foreign Affairs*, summer 1993.
5. Runnymede Trust, *Islamophobia* (London: Runnymede Trust, 1997).
6. Paper presented at IPPR seminar.
7. Sardar, Z. *Post-modernism and the Other* (London: Pluto Press, 1998).

# 38
# Britain as Europe

*Linda Colley*

History, we are frequently told, explains why the British are so different from, and have such trouble with, Europe. But it would be far more accurate to say that the problem is not history as such, but rather the truncated and selective view of it that is often purveyed and believed.

A few years ago in 1994, these islands had two major causes for celebration and remembrance. To begin with, 1994 was of course the fiftieth anniversary of the D-Day landings. You will all remember the enormous scale of the commemoration of that event and the massive sponsorship it received from monarch, ministers and media alike. But there was, or there should have been, another major cause for celebration in 1994 – the opening that year of the Channel Tunnel.

Yet as far as the British, as distinct from the French, were concerned, this was a noticeably low-key event. The powers that be here were prepared, absolutely rightly, to pull out all the stops to celebrate the invasion and liberation of continental Europe in 1944. They were conspicuously less willing to devote time, energy or imagination to celebrating the opening of a highway with continental Europe. Instead, the Channel Tunnel was discussed at the time overwhelmingly in terms of its safety or otherwise; or the damage it might do to property values in Kent; or the effect it would have on holidays in France; or the quality of its train service. It was treated, in short, almost exclusively as a late twentieth-century amenity, about which people remained ambivalent, and not as something epic.

In retrospect, how strange this was and how sad. In our history, the idea of a channel tunnel long preceded the Second World War. In Britain, as in France, a tunnel was discussed and debated repeatedly from the early 1800s onwards. Great British engineers and entrepreneurs like Isambard Kingdom Brunel backed the idea. So did Queen Victoria. In the First World War, British and French generals were agreed that a channel tunnel might have shortened the war. And in the 1920s and 1930s, the tunnel was repeatedly advocated by Winston Churchill as 'a notable symbol in the advance of human civilisation'.

By largely ignoring all this, when the Channel Tunnel was finally achieved in 1994, we actually did violence to our history and, in the process, detracted from our present achievements and our future potential. The Tunnel is one of the greatest engineering feats of the twentieth century. British skills were heavily involved in its construction. Yet in 1994 we did not feel able properly to celebrate it. The Tunnel promised a quantum leap in the speed and volume of contact with continental Europe. It changes our lives, but we could not celebrate that either. Instead we chose to focus in 1994, not on our present, not on our future, and not on our long and complicated history, but on D-Day and our comparatively recent past.

I am in no way minimizing the significance either of the Second World War or of Britain's role in it, but the notion that this was 'our finest hour' has since 1945, and in a way that the author of that phrase would never have wanted, cast something of a paralyzing spell. By remembering a certain version of the Second World War too well, we have sometimes neglected and misperceived our longer history, and in the process missed out on possibilities on offer in the present and the future. This has been particularly true with regard to the question of Europe.

In this lecture I want to argue that a longer historical perspective makes the question of Europe more interesting and more amenable. I want, first of all, to say something about Britain as Europe over the *longue durée*. Then I want to sketch out how a particular interpretation of the Second World War has sometimes worked to distort and limit our vision of Europe and of ourselves within Europe. Finally, I want to suggest what a renovated Britain, with a better and more complex sense of itself and its past, might hope to achieve in a better and renovated Europe.

## Britain as Europe

Britain is a set of islands on the western periphery of Europe. Nonetheless, and as a major British politician once observed, our links to the rest of Europe, the continent of Europe, have been the dominant factor in our history. Who said this? Margaret Thatcher in Bruges in 1988. And whatever the tactical intent behind this statement, as a historical judgement it was absolutely correct. In terms of political organization, parts or all of what is now Britain have been repeatedly linked over time with different parts of continental Europe. For almost four centuries, much of what is now Britain was governed from Rome. From 1066 to the sixteenth century, kings of England were also kings of part of France. At the end of the seventeenth century, this country was successfully invaded and subsequently ruled by a Dutch monarch. From 1714 to 1837, the British throne was occupied by successive German kings, who ruled over us in tandem with their home state of Hanover.

The impact of all this went far beyond politics, since these successive invasions and Continental linkages influenced the texture of our society, and still do today. The Romans and the Norman French contributed massively to the vocabulary we use now. Dutch expertise helped to construct the City and the Stock Market. Until recently, the British royal family was overwhelmingly German in terms of blood, and often in terms of preferred language as well.

You might say, granted all this, surely the determining factor in Britain's history is that it is an island, cut off from the Continent by the sea? On some occasions, yes, of course this was vital. For certain minds, it is always vital. But the sea is a highway as well as a barrier. Indeed, before the coming of the railway, transport by water was much faster and more effective than transport by land. Consequently, the most important impact of the sea on parts of Britain was not that it cut them off from the rest of Europe, but rather that it facilitated regular and substantial contacts with it.

Just think of the close maritime, trading and cultural links which have always existed between the Orkneys and Shetlands on the one hand and Scandinavia on the other, or between East Anglia and the Dutch. Even now, Norwich, my own home town, has no direct air link with London, but you can fly directly from Norwich airport to Schiphol, near Amsterdam. These many and variegated regional linkages with the Continent underline the point that historically it makes little sense to generalize about Britain's relations with Europe, as though these two entities ever were or are monoliths. Over the centuries, different parts of what is now Britain have had different relations with different parts of the rest of Europe.

And, of course, different relations as well with each other. One of the many ways in which Britain resembles other parts of Europe is that it has evolved as a composite state, as a multiple kingdom – very like Spain in fact. Wales was only incorporated and given representation at Westminster in the sixteenth century. Scotland, which regained its own Parliament in 1999, also possessed one before 1707. The Irish had their Dublin Parliament until 1800. Without detracting from the importance of the Westminster Parliament, then, it is simply not the case that it represents a thousand years of exceptional *British* constitutional development. To claim this is to confuse and conflate what is English with what is British. For parts of what is now Britain, Westminster's centrality is a more recent phenomenon. Viewed this way, devolution is less an innovation than an overdue recognition of differences within these islands which have always existed.

## War and empire

Yet what of war and empire? In the past, these indisputably helped to knit the rest of Britain together. But did they also drive it apart from continental Europe? As with the sea, it depends which lens you choose to look through. Maritime empire was actually something the British had in common with many other European states. Portugal possessed an overseas empire. So, at different times, did the Dutch and the Danes, the Belgians, the French and, above all, the Spanish. Spain's American Empire, remember, lasted for a greater number of years than Britain's did, a point which has implications for current politics, and to which I will return.

Imperialism, then, was not something which distinguished the British from other European powers, or indeed from many non-European powers. What was exceptional about Britain's empire was rather, for a century or so, its sheer size. Yet those who argue that the Empire on which the sun never set gave Britain a global, rather than a European, vision are implying a choice which the British were never able or willing to make in the past, any more than they can or should make it now.

In the past three centuries, there has only been one major war in which the British have fought without significant Continental allies. In the past three centuries, there has only been one major war in which the bulk of the Royal Navy has been sent outside European waters. And in the past three centuries, there has only been one major war in which the British were defeated. In each case the conflict involved was the same, the lost war with Britain's American colonies.

From that conspicuous defeat, the obvious and correct moral was drawn. Britain, even at its most powerful, could not attempt a global strategy without first consolidating its position in Europe. It had first and foremost to be a European power, because otherwise it could not be powerful anywhere else. From a historian's viewpoint, then, Britain is a set of islands, but it has rarely been able to be insular. It was once imperial, but it has always been European.

Acknowledging these links between Britain and the Continent, whether in terms of imperial experience, or state formation, or trade, or migration, or culture and so on, is not in any way to discount or deny our distinctiveness. Like every other state, Britain has evolved over time as a result of a particular set of geographical, political, military, religious and cultural circumstances. But as a historian, I regard with extreme scepticism the notion that our particularities are somehow bigger, more momentous and more deep-rooted than those of our European neighbours. Is Britain really more different, for instance, from Spain (another composite state and one-time empire) than Spain is from, say, Denmark? I have to tell you that you would have a hard time demonstrating this. Why, then, should it be supposed that Britain's particularities, such as they are, point it away from the rest of Europe, when Denmark's and Spain's respective particularities can, with some effort, flourish within Europe? And why, anyway, should difference in itself, whether within Britain or within Europe as a whole, necessarily dictate separation? Why should it be supposed that a constantly renegotiated and struggled-over union, whether it be the British Union or the European Union, should necessarily imply homogeneity among its participants? We should be mature and learn to accommodate differences, within Britain as within Europe.

As Kenneth Minogue remarks, with his customary sharpness,

> Britain is simply one of the countries of Europe, sharing in varying degrees of European defects and strengths. In some respects Britain is unmistakably superior, in others not so.

In some respects our development was and remains exceptional, in others much less so. It follows that one of the most outrageous invented traditions of post-war political debate is the notion that there are two monolithic and opposing entities called Britain and Europe.

I have already stressed that there are, to paraphrase Roy Foster, 'varieties of Britishness', that different parts of Britain have evolved distinctively and have often developed their own particular connections with other parts of Europe. By the same token, there are varieties of Europeans, including ourselves. Europe is not and never has been a separate collective entity against which Britain can plausibly be contrasted. Earlier generations understood this very well. They referred to Britain and the Continent, or Britain and continental Europe, thereby tacitly conceding that Britain was part of Europe as a whole. The blunt phrase, Britain and Europe, like the familiar and wildly ahistorical assertion that Britain has always been at war with Europe (as distinct from with France, or with Spain), is therefore at best sloppy and at worst partisan semantics – and fairly recent partisan semantics at that.

## Britain as distinct from Europe

Why then have these notions grown up so powerfully in some quarters? There is no sound historical case, as we have seen, for arguing that Britain has evolved invariably in isolation from, or at odds with, the rest of Europe, while there is ample historical evidence of strong and persistent linkages between these islands and the Continent. Why, then, do some believe, often very sincerely and fervently, otherwise? Two reasons, I believe.

First, political debate in these islands, perhaps more so in England than in the rest of Britain, has often included a tradition of isolationism of various kinds. This has never been the only tradition on offer, but it has been a durable one, and historically has been found as much on the Left as on the Right. Sometimes this tradition has taken the form of a suspicion of 'continental entanglements', as the radical William Cobbett called it, a fear that European involvement can only result in expensive wars. Very often, in the eighteenth and nineteenth centuries, it took the form of a belief that our constitution was uniquely free and that the Continent was a pit of despotism in comparison. Sometimes, of course, isolationism has been merely that. Declared Winston Churchill of Stanley Baldwin: 'He knew little of Europe, and disliked what he knew.'

Euroscepticism. then, even Europhobia, have a long pedigree, and it would be foolish not to recognize this. Yet, taking a long view of the past, isolationism has formed only one part of the spectrum of political attitudes in these islands, and often a subordinate and unsuccessful part. As Cobbett frequently complained, however much men like him railed against Britain's Continental entanglements, the British remained persistently entangled. In the late seventeenth century, and in the eighteenth and nineteenth centuries, as in the twentieth, geography and self-interest gave them little choice. In the long past, even those politicians who boasted chauvinistically about the peculiar glories of Britain were often, in practice, cosmopolitan in style and knowledge, because once again they had little choice. Lord Palmerston, that quintessentially Victorian Prime Minister, was called 'the most English Prime Minister', but he still spoke several European languages, was fully at home in the great European capitals, and devoted most of his career to European affairs.

By contrast, post-war Euroscepticism here has not always been well informed about the rest of Europe and has sometimes appeared shrill and anxious. To an extent, as we have seen, it looks back to a long tradition of isolationism in British cultural and political debate. But it has acquired its particular tone, I believe, from more recent history, above all from the

Second World War. To understand why, you only have to remember that famous David Low cartoon of a British soldier standing firmly on his island, raising his fist to a Nazi-dominated Continent and declaring, 'Very well then, alone'. It is a genuinely moving and heroic image. It is just a shame that, as with Churchill's invocation of our finest hour, this image has sometimes had the effect of fixing our attitudes and our view of history in aspic, so that we forget our longer past and find it hard to come to terms with the realities of the present and the possibilities of the future.

Of course, those who fought in the Second World War, or lost family and friends in it, were marked by it for life. That is understandable, but as far as these islands are concerned, it is often those too young to have been directly involved in the war whose vision has apparently been rendered most rigid by the image of it. With regard to attitudes towards Germany, attitudes towards the United States and our alliance with it, and attitudes towards parliamentary democracy in these islands, events which happened some 50 years ago have fostered, in some minds, amnesia about the longer past and compromised clear thinking and adaptability in the face of the present and the future.

One need only remember Nicholas Ridley's singularly honest and indiscreet comment that what is now the EU was 'a German racket designed to take over the whole of Europe', to realize how deep suspicion of German ambition rankles in some British Eurosceptic souls. On one level, this may seem understandable. The two World Wars destroyed millions of lives and permanently undermined Europe's global primacy. But then, this is true not just for us, but also for France, Belgium, the Netherlands, Italy, Denmark and Germany itself. Most suffered greater demographic and economic losses in these conflicts than Britain did, but they nonetheless manage, most of the time, to subdue their respective wartime grievances and work together.

I suspect, therefore, that behind British Eurosceptic Germanophobia is often something other than the wars, terrible though they were. Some individuals, it is clear, cling to the old and, among reputable historians, discredited view, that Germany after its unification in 1870 was characterized by a kind of original sin, which makes it inevitably the hammer of the Continent. In addition, some British Eurosceptics, I suspect, harbour resentment and envy. Since 1945, Germany has frequently been more economically buoyant than Britain. It has played a leading part in pushing European projects, while we have often held back. But then, whose fault is that?

Whatever the cause, excessive suspicions of German ambition can get in the way of British self interest and in the way of a balanced historical perspective. As Paul Kennedy showed, the history of British/German antagonism exists side by side with a longer history of considerable collaboration and mutual understanding. Indeed, before 1914 many British politicians and pundits argued that Germany was our natural ally in continental Europe, a position for which there is much to be said.

## Britain, Europe and the United States

It will be important for Britain and the rest of Europe in the twenty-first century that we remember that historically our relations with Germany have been mixed and sometimes excellent, that we look beyond what happened between 1939 and 1945 to a broader, longer view. It will be vital, too, that we keep our close alliance with the United States in perspective and understand what kind of society this superpower has become.

I have spent the last 18 years of my life working in the United States. I owe its people a great deal and remain deeply attached to it. While there, I sometimes came across articles and speeches by British Eurosceptics to the effect that the close alliance between Britain and the United States, which was so crucial in the Second World War, represents the only viable model for the future. They argue that Europe is an alien distraction and that we should instead accept the logic of our history and forge an ever closer union with our English-speaking cousins across the Atlantic. Only recently, Paul Johnson has suggested in *Forbes Magazine* that Britain should actually become a part of the United States. We can, apparently, hope to make up at least five states, and possibly these shores may even in the future breed up an American President.

I confess that I find it strange that individuals who claim to be worried about Brussels' infringements on Britain's autonomy are apparently eager to surrender its independence entirely to a country three thousand miles away, which does not remotely want it. I find it even stranger that these same individuals, whose affection for the United States I do not doubt, and indeed share, seem nonetheless to have such a restricted knowledge of what sort of country it now is.

The United States is a very great country, but it is not overwhelmingly made up of or led by our English-speaking cousins any more. I come back to my earlier point, that Britain was never the only European power with an overseas empire. The Dutch had settlements in America, so did the French, and so, above all, did the Spanish. The rapid growth of the Hispanic population in the United States in recent decades, as well as its Asian and black population, is something which many Britons still do not appreciate. As anyone resident in the States will tell you, the Spanish language and Spanish culture are increasingly important there. This is not just the case in states historically linked with the Spanish empire, places like Texas and California, but elsewhere as well. Even my own former base, Connecticut, an east coast state which was once a British colony, now issues all its public notices in Spanish as well as English.

This is something which British foreign policy in the future is going to have to take ever more into account. For all sorts of reasons, the twenty-first century American governing elite will be much less European in background, outlook and style than earlier generations. Even those Americans who continue to value their European heritage will, in many cases, feel closer cultural and emotional ties with Spain than they do with this country. These ongoing and accelerating changes inside America do not necessarily mean that Britain's close alliance with it will contract, but they do make it imperative that we approach this alliance in a hard-headed, observant and flexible fashion. They should make us wary of putting all our eggs in one transatlantic basket, for why on earth should we seek to do so?

True, it is sometimes implied that Britain's historic links with the United States, plus our receptivity to all kinds of American popular culture, mark us out from the rest of Europe, and that we occupy a peculiarly midway position between the United States and the Continent. Yet these claims rest more on wishful thinking than on solid evidence. A glance at a map demonstrates very quickly that we are not midway between America and the Continent. The Atlantic is over 3000 miles wide; the Channel is 20 miles wide at its narrowest. Equally, in many respects Britain is not like America at all. In terms of its National Health Service and many of its assumptions about welfare, in terms of its attitude to capital punishment and gun control, in terms of its treatment of the environment, in terms of the sports it plays most (rugby and soccer, not baseball or basketball), and in many other matters, Britain resembles its European partners far more than it does the Americans. Naturally so. Since European states are geographically adjacent and have impacted upon each other for centuries, their developmental patterns are bound in many areas to be similar.

Of course, Britain also has features in common with the United States, particularly in the realm of law and politics, and I do not mean to underrate those at all. Of course, Britain is drenched in American popular culture, but this does not distinguish us from other parts of Europe as much as some imagine. I have already spoken of Spain's close and dynamic links with the modern United States, but I could equally well have cited the important links between France and America. It was, after all, France which enabled the Americans to win their independence from Britain in the first place. It was France which helped to design Washington. It was France which gave New York the Statue of Liberty. America and France are sister republics, their histories and politics inevitably intertwined by the fact that the revolutions which created them occurred so close together. France, like virtually every other Western European state, is as fond of American popular culture as Britain is. Jacques Delors himself, once the *Sun*'s favourite hate figure, loves US jazz, US films, US baseball. He even works with a poster of Citizen Kane behind his desk. None of this, to put it mildly, prevents him from being European.

What I am suggesting, therefore, is that for reasons of history, but also because of current American trends, there can be no one special relationship between a European power and the United States. There are, rather, several close relationships, each of them different. The close but different relationships with the United States possessed by Spain, by France, and indeed by Ireland do not prevent those three countries from also seeing themselves as European, any more than being European prevents them from also being assertive nation states.

## Democracy and Europe

Britain, too, needs to develop a similar, confident, political ambidexterity. We are not mid-Atlantic, but why shouldn't we look positively and creatively across the Atlantic at America from a secure position within Europe? Because, some would argue, Britain, like America, holds fast to certain democratic values and practices, which cannot flourish within the European Union. Our constitutional values, according to this view, naturally make us far more comfortable in an American alliance than in Europe, which has different political traditions. These arguments arouse strong emotions, and are too large and complex to deal with in a brief lecture like this, but let me make some points as a historian.

Clearly it is the case that the Westminster Parliament has a distinctive and distinguished history, a point which has frequently been conceded by continental Europeans from Voltaire to Delors. And, as recent events have made all too clear, the European Commission and the European Parliament undoubtedly need reform. It was understandable that the Second World War should at one time have conflated the Continent in British minds with Nazi tyranny, while allowing us to view ourselves as defenders of freedom, and ultimately as liberators. There is nothing wrong and a lot right in cherishing a cult of freedom. But, once again, a selective memory of the Second World War should not obstruct our understanding of our own long history, or of conditions in the present.

Historically, it is simply not the case that Britain has invariably been more democratic than continental Europe. Quite the reverse, in fact. In 1914, it is estimated that only 18 per cent of adults in the UK were enfranchized. Most of the men and all of the women who struggled for our freedom in the First World War had themselves no freedom to vote. This was not only unimpressive in itself, it was unimpressive by European standards. In 1914, Switzerland, Sweden, Serbia, Norway, Italy, Greece, Germany, France, Finland, Bulgaria, Belgium and Austria all had wider franchises than Britain did. Indeed, the only European state which was even less democratic than Britain in 1914 was Hungary. The significance of this goes beyond the historical. It has implications for politics now. Traditionally, Britain has been precocious in evolving stable and effective representative institutions. It has also been strident in celebrating its free constitution. But this very stridency has sometimes concealed the fact, not least from the British themselves, that their governing institutions have not always been matched by an equal precocity in extending citizen rights.

With regard to other European democracies, therefore, both balance and modesty are in order. It may be the case that, as Jacques Delors generously remarked,

> You have to keep the British in Europe for their democratic tradition, if nothing else. They have the best journalistic debates, the best parliamentary committees, the best quizzing of Prime Ministers.

In these respects, we have much to contribute towards Europe's better governance. But in terms of safeguarding citizen rights, and in broadening democracy at every level, we may actually have quite a lot to learn from other European states.

Thus far in this lecture I have been concerned to deploy a battery of historical facts against some of the myths, complacencies and anachronisms that can get in the way of reasoned discussion about Britain as Europe. The claim that Britain was always disjoined from the Continent by factors other than geography, and frequently at odds with Europe, I have argued, is a massive oversimplification of the past. Even at the height of its empire, Britain viewed itself as a European power, and its fortunes and developments have always been closely linked with the Continent. Like virtually every other European state, Britain has sporadically warred with European rivals, but only in alliance with other

European states. I repeat, Europe is not, and never has been, a monolith against which Britain can plausibly or usefully be contrasted.

## Surviving Britain's mid-life crisis

Acknowledging this and all that it implies is not just essential if we are to engage positively and clear-headedly with the rest of Europe, it is also indispensable if we are to renovate Britain successfully. As Timothy Garton Ash has pointed out, much of the so-called European debate has in fact been a debate about Britain itself. Uncertainty over Europe in these islands has often stemmed, perhaps particularly in England, from a protracted and tortured uncertainty as well about our own identity. That was probably inevitable, since the massive internal and external changes which Britain has experienced since 1945 have provoked a gigantic mid-life crisis, as it were. Mid-life crises can be cathartic and can aid necessary change, but too prolonged a process of introspection and agonized self-doubt leads to paralysis and loss of nerve. It is time we snapped out of it. The empire is lost, we still need a role, and we will not carve out or inhabit a new role successfully unless we come to terms with the complexities of who we are.

I persist in remaining optimistic. It may well be that the current changes in Britain's governance, far from leading to break-up, will help in all sorts of ways to break through the impasse. Whoever wins the forthcoming elections in Wales and Scotland, it seems clear that a new Scottish Parliament, like the new Welsh Assembly, is going to support a more proactive role within Europe. In the past, there is a good case for arguing that the so-called peripheries of these islands played a major part in forging Britain. So now Wales and Scotland may play leading parts in persuading some of their English neighbours to come to terms with Britain as Europe.

And perhaps the English won't be as hard to persuade as some people imagine. Englishness is very important, but Englishness is not monolithic and the English are not monolithic. Recent issues of the survey *British Social Attitudes* suggest, for example, that London, as one would expect from such a cosmopolitan centre, is far more positive about the EU than the south of England generally. In the near future, London will acquire its own Mayor and a more independent voice, so it may be that here too we will see shifts in the governance of Britain contributing to stronger and more frequent arguments being made for Europe's possibilities and for our possibilities as Europe. What I am suggesting, in short, is that just as our long paralysis over Europe derived in part from uncertainty over

Britain itself, so now tackling and coming to terms with Britain's internal diversity may also help to resolve this broader paralysis.

Just how important it is that we play a leading part in defining and sustaining a new Europe is clear from recent events in Yugoslavia. Like most people, I suspect I have mixed feelings about that crisis, but of one thing I am certain. The argument that some have advanced that it demonstrates the efficacy of an American-led NATO, whilst simultaneously proving the inutility of the European Union, is wrong and short-sighted. War and defence are one thing, and NATO is indispensable for both. However, making and maintaining peace, and coming to terms more broadly with the new, ill-defined Europe which has emerged with the end of the Cold War, will require pan-European institutions other than NATO, and will require, too, leadership and resolve from within Europe itself.

I believe that a renovated Britain can both contribute a great deal to a new Europe and get a great deal back in return. But in the end the fundamental case for an effective and renovated European Union is very simple and, like so much I have talked about today, looks back to our long past. Precisely 120 years ago, the great Liberal Prime Minister, William Gladstone, described what he saw as being Britain's abiding interest. He said it was

> to strive to cultivate and maintain to the very Utmost what is called the concert of Europe, to keep the powers of Europe in union together. And why? Because by keeping all in union together, you neutralise and bind up the selfish aims of each.

New Britain, old Britain, in this case, the same point holds true.

*This is a revised version of a lecture which Linda Colley originally gave to the Smith Institute in 1999*

# 39
# European Film

*David Puttnam*

It is 30 years since the French media entrepreneur Jean-Jacques Servan Schreiber published his seminal text *The American Challenge*, in which he brilliantly anticipated Europe's relative economic decline in the face of the overwhelming penetration of American goods, ideas and services. As he put it, '[T]he confrontation of civilisations will now take place in the battlefield of technology, science and management.' He concluded that: 'The war we face, will be an industrial one.' That war has in my view barely begun.

Certainly this is a phrase that struck a particular chord with me as I first came across it in 1995 when I was spending a great deal of my time drafting the text for a book entitled *The Undeclared War: The Struggle for Control of the World's Film Industry*. In the book, the principle adversaries are France and the US; countries that seem to me to most dramatically represent fundamentally opposed conceptions of cinema, in fact of the arts generally, conceptions which, in one way or another, have been at the core of a cultural and trade war which has effectively waged for the last 100 years.

It's a battle that the Americans have long since won, with American movies now dominating the world's cinema screens. Walk through the downtown streets of just about any city in the world and the paraphernalia of advertising is dominated by giant ads for 'Event' movies, *Star Wars*, *Matrix* and the *Austin Powers* sequel. The ubiquity of these movies – and the marketing campaigns which support them – is surely the ultimate testimony to the maxim that Hollywood is 'not a place, but a state of mind'.

International sales of American software and entertainment products now total over $60bn a year – more than any other US industry, according to figures from the US Commerce Department. Since 1991, exports of intellectual property from the United States have almost doubled in value.

To give you some idea of the specific importance of the movie industry to the American economy – American distributors took in almost $6bn at the foreign box office last year, and experts estimate that growth will continue to climb at a rate of about 6 per cent to 7 per cent annually – about three times as fast as the country's gross domestic product.

It wasn't always like this of course. The cinema was invented in Europe, by the Lumière brothers, and throughout its early years the global film business was dominated by European companies and by European films. Yet while the Europeans largely concentrated on creative and technical innovations, it was the Americans who really set out to systematically market and profit from the economic value of film. In fact, the American studios have been operating as globalized businesses ever since the end of the First World War – in the 80 years since they have built up vast distribution networks through which they pump an endless stream of movies to cinema screens in every corner of the globe.

Now, as we enter a new millennium, a new battle between the Americans and the Europeans is emerging in the field of digital technologies. Thanks to these technologies we are witnessing a new era of convergence between the printed word and the technologies of television, computers and the Internet. This is resulting in a 'blurring' between many of the distinctions we have traditionally taken for granted; such as those between 'printed' and 'electronic' information. As a result, we are rapidly moving from a society in which the principal characteristic of information was 'scarcity,' to one in which its chief characteristic will be its ability to multiply, seemingly without limit.

So just how does Europe sustain its cultural identity in an era dominated by an ever increasing proliferation of images and information, much of it emanating from the United States?

I'll try to begin sketching out an answer by giving an example from my own experience. As a boy I would sit in the darkness and soak up the influence of films like Fred Zinneman's *The Search*, Elia Kazan's *On the Waterfront* and Stanley Kramer's *Inherit the Wind*. Those films which were made in America, with what today would be seen as a very European sensibility, were to all intents and purposes, my education. It was from films like these that every tenet by which I and many of my post-war generation have attempted to steer our lives, somehow evolved. Many of these films were sharply critical of American society, but they also demonstrated that capacity of the Americans for a kind of infinite hopefulness, that 'pursuit of happiness' so very usefully enshrined in the American constitution.

Consider just one of those films, Stanley Kramer's *Inherit the Wind*. This, the story of the 'Scopes/Monkey trial', concerns itself with the right of a teacher to discuss, in the early 1920s, in his own classroom, Darwin's theory of evolution, in opposition to the then accepted community belief. In a very moving courtroom scene, the somewhat cynical lawyer Clarence Darrow (played by Spencer Tracy) is confronted by the presidential candidate William Jennings Byran who demands of Darrow whether he believes in *anything* that's sacred. Darrow retorts emphatically 'Yes!' and continues by saying:

> I believe in the individual mind. In a child's power to master the multiplication table there is more sanctity than in all your shouted 'Amens!' An idea, is a greater monument than a cathedral ... Why did God plague us with the power to think? Why do you deny the one faculty which lifts man above *all* other creatures on earth; the power of his brain to reason?

*Inherit the Wind* reminds us (if we need reminding) of the value of the individual and the right to think and express oneself, even in opposition to all received wisdom. It offers a vision, one that reminds us that a just society has to be built around beliefs which bind its members together, beliefs which are themselves built on the pursuit of happiness, liberty, justice and truth. Just as importantly, it provides its audience with an understanding of a debate which had (and still has) huge social, moral and cultural consequences. It's a film that offers us what every film should aspire to; it offers both dreams and knowledge.

The vast majority of films now made by Hollywood have no such similar ambition. Although France remains something of an honourable exception, Hollywood effectively dominates the world's cinema screens – whilst itself remaining dominated by the tyranny of the so-called 'bottom line'. Dreams, maybe, but 'knowledge', the advancement of what it means to be a complex human being, these issues seldom if ever enter the equation.

The impact of Hollywood has become even greater in recent years because 'the movies' are no longer just about what's playing at the local multiplex next Saturday night. Their impact is now far, far greater than that. Today's movies are really 'brand names'. Every single film put out by the Hollywood studios is, in a way, its own brand which, when successful, becomes a locomotive dragging behind it many, many other sectors of the economy, everything from fashion to fast food chains, books and video games. An entire panoply of other products and services latch on to the back of a successful movie. For instance, *Titanic* generated over $1bn around the globe from box offices outside of North America, and has sold a staggering 24 million units on video, 40 per cent more than the previous record-holder, *Jurassic Park*. As a consequence, *Titanic* has probably generated several billion dollars more on the back of all those other commercial activities drawn along in its wake. *Godzilla* is possibly an even better example, in that this relatively unsuccessful movie has been driven to profitability by apparently spectacular merchandizing results. The posters got it right, size does matter after all!

In these circumstances, it should be a matter of the greatest concern that America's extraordinary dominance in the field of films, television and the moving image just goes on intensifying.

This concern is only heightened by the fact that they're *already* 'light years' ahead of us in terms of Internet-based entertainment and information. The development of the Information Society and its potential to further increase the commercial and cultural domination of the United States raises the real prospect of a fundamental dislocation between the world of the imagination, created and stimulated by the moving image, and the everyday lives of ordinary people in Europe, or for that matter anywhere around the globe.

And we have no idea what the consequences of such a dislocation might be, for it's genuinely without any form of social precedent. But it is surely no exaggeration to say that it has the potential to be one of the social and cultural time-bombs of the twenty-first century.

In January 1998, at the World Economic Forum in Davos, Hillary Clinton proclaimed that 'American culture is America's biggest export', citing the examples of fashion, music and movies. Surely that represents a challenge that the rest of the world, and particularly the nations of Western Europe, should be rising to, rather than truculently acknowledging as some form of permanent 'force of nature'.

But this is not *just* an economic and industrial challenge. It's also about rising to an intellectual challenge, albeit one that's rather different in nature: the need to find a way of understanding and communicating relatively complex ideas is itself becoming ever more urgent; not just within our educational system, but across the whole of our society. European integration and enlargement is an excellent example of this.

One of the most extraordinary by-products of our potentially information-rich society is the creation of a kind of 'unknowing', even ignorance, that is strangely at odds with these ever increasing means of communication which, in theory at least, are widely available to all of us.

Perhaps there is something about this sheer 'plethora' of information that creates, not illumination and clarity, but rather, incoherence and meaninglessness. Out of the babble of voices only the simplest and most shrill are heard; out of the swift succession of images only the most showy and compelling seem to be noticed.

The media, certainly in the UK, have become far more interested in the 'sensationalized story' than in the truth; for the simple reason that 'fear' sells newspapers. It's back to that 'tyranny of the bottom line!' Institutionalized and wilful disregard for rational analysis cannot be healthy for any democracy – and, in my judgement, it ultimately leads to an increasingly misinformed society.

To return to that movie, *Inherit the Wind*, as Clarence Darrow says 'progress has never been a bargain. There's always a price to pay.' As he puts it, 'Mister, you may have conquered the air, but the birds will lose their wonder, and the clouds will smell of gasoline.'

What we as Europeans need to grasp quickly is how to harness all of the cultural forms available to us as a means of helping us to understand ourselves – our hopes, our fears, and most importantly, our European potential.

In his recent book, *Business at the Speed of Thought*, Bill Gates argues that 'if the 1980s were about quality and the 1990s were about reengineering, then the next decade will be about "velocity"' – there's that word again. He believes that 'Business is going to change more in the next ten years than it has in the last fifty.' I suspect he'll be proved right.

But above all, these new digital technologies, in all their cultural forms can be an invaluable *learning* tool. For perhaps the most significant development of this new Information Society is its likely impact on our formal educational systems. As information technology becomes more and more essential to the functioning of those systems, the need for world-class software and support materials is going to grow, and at a prodigious rate. Yet there's very little evidence to suggest that anyone has even begun to optimize the teaching and learning potential offered by these technologies. In my view, this is where the real opportunity for Europe lies. For even in those places, like the United States, which appear to be educationally advanced, it's still likely that there are 30 children in the class, sitting in front of a blackboard – as if the traditional 'chalk and talk' model of teaching remained the only model for imparting knowledge.

In truth, the human race has barely begun to get to grips with the way in which information and communications have the power to revolutionize the face of learning, and, by extension, to change the way we think, communicate and create. We must not come to see the impact of the computer on education as merely akin to the impact of the calculator on arithmetic; speeding up and simplifying the process, without offering any significant change to the process itself. If these technologies are sensitively and intelligently used, they have, as I've said, the potential to change the whole development of the educational process – and with it, our European future.

And it's as Europeans that I believe we must seize the opportunity this presents. For if control of the largest and most influential component of our 'entertainment' business has inexorably shifted abroad (and believe me it has), and then we allow the same to happen with our educational and information resources, what can possibly remain of our capacity to sustain, let alone develop, our respective cultural identities?

European filmmakers, along with all of those working in the media, can help us develop that cultural identity; not by defensively clinging to the glories of the past, but by helping us understand exactly where we've come from, and, just as importantly, where we might be going. Creative artists, and those who work with them, have, in my judgement an unavoidable moral responsibility to challenge, inspire, question and affirm, as well as to entertain. Movies, television programmes, the new electronic media; they are all much more than fun, and far more than just so many new 'business opportunities'; they serve to reinforce or undermine most of the wider values of society.

Of one thing I am certain; if we fail to use these media responsibly and creatively, if we treat them simply as so many 'consumer industries' rather than as the complex 'cultural' phenomena they really are, then we are likely to damage possibly, irreversibly, the health and the vitality of our own society. Trash, trivia and sensation can be brought to the marketplace at a surprisingly low cost. Truth, responsibility and quality have always taken longer, and for the most part carry a far higher price – and thereby, necessarily, a far higher social value.

I have always believed that there are two great errors into which filmmakers, in fact artists in general, can fall; the first is the belief that they can achieve everything; the second is the belief that they can achieve nothing. The former is arrogant in the extreme. But the latter is plainly irresponsible and unacceptable. I remain entirely convinced of the law of cause and effect, that we will eventually inherit the society we deserve.

To illustrate all of this allow me to cite a passage from the autobiography of the great Russian film director Andrei Tarkovsky. Shortly before he died, Tarkovsky wrote this:

> The connection between man's behaviour and his destiny has been destroyed; and this tragic breach is the cause of his sense of instability in the modern world ... because he has been conditioned into the belief that nothing depends on him, and that his personal experience will not affect the future, he has arrived at the false and deadly assumption

that he has no part to play in the shaping of even his own fate … I am convinced that any attempt to restore harmony in the world can only rest on the renewal of personal responsibility.

We are now at the end of a century which has witnessed tremendous success in entrenching the rights of individuals in confrontation with the power of the modern state. Sadly, no such similar improvements have been made in matching individual responsibilities to these new and important rights. Without question this will be one of the great social challenges of the early part of the next century. It's vital that we, and by 'we' I specifically include the media, come to treat each other as individuals – offering and entitled to respect and consideration. That we *actively* promote a civil society.

For the sake of all of us, let's hope beyond hope that Andrei Tarkovsky's implied belief in us proves to have been justified. Surely it must be possible, through education, for us to turn a renewed sense of personal responsibility into an intelligent energetic and sustainable belief in *collective* responsibility. So that working together across the Continent we can help create the type of coherent, inclusive and civil European society which will enable us to reap the social and cultural benefits of the digital era.

*This text is a revised version of a speech given to the Friends of the London School of Economics in France delivered in Paris in June 1998*

# 40
# Why I'm Glad to be European[1]

*Hugo Young*

*Will we ever warm to the euro, which starts its working life on Monday? Hugo Young confesses his conversion from the sort of Euro-agnostic who only got a glow when Britain won something.*

As a boy, I was entirely English. There was nothing else to be. This was true even though an education by Catholic monks offered alternative possibilities. Henry VIII, we learned, was a very bad man, and the heretics burned at the stake by Mary Tudor deserved their fate, whereas the victims of Elizabeth were martyrs and saints. The arrival from Holland of William of Orange, displacing the Catholic Stuarts in 1688, far from inaugurating the Glorious Revolution from which, as I now believe, most British constitutional freedom flowed, was a disaster for the one true faith.

This bias in the teaching of history didn't touch our real allegiances in everything that mattered, cricket, soccer, rugby, the ubiquitous redness of the map, the naturally British order of things. Allegiance, with victory as its quest, was the habit that school instilled in me: gangs, cliques, houses, teams, Sheffield Utd FC, the Yorkshire County Cricket Club and all who played in it. There had to be something to support, and on the international plane Britain, or England, had to win.

This tendency stayed with me for many years. It has never really gone. When Brits do well, it still gives me a warm glow. Cricket continues to matter, especially when Darren Gough plays a blinder, and partisanship defeated all temptations (those swilling lager louts, the Union Jack as offensive weapon) to forget the World Cup was going on. I'm obscurely glad that Simon Rattle is British. When a great British movie, like *Secrets and Lies*, captures the world, its national origin matters. When the SAS took the first Serbian war criminals, I remember feeling quietly pleased it was us.

My esteem for Britishness also stretches into professional fields. We do some governmental things better than other people, and should want to keep it that way. Our public life is relatively honest, our judges are

240

straight, almost all our politicians selflessly industrious. Our Parliament is a living thing. As for our history, it's a wonderment, reaching out from this tiny island, producer of a language and a literature and a record of power that the people of pretty well every other nation must regard with awe.

So I can confess to being disgracefully congruent with a typical reader of the *Daily Telegraph*. And in the early days of 'Europe', this collection of awarenesses sheltered me from the new cause. Voting Yes in the 1975 referendum was a routine orthodoxy, shared with two-thirds of the British people, including quite a number who now seem to have changed their minds. For years, I never felt zeal for either side. But now I do, and I wonder why. What has happened, while the majority allegiance appears to have gone into reverse, to push me effortlessly the other way? The initiation began with a book I wrote about the history of these matters. I started work on *This Blessed Plot* as a Euro-agnostic, but completed it a few years later in a state of struggling incredulity at the demons and panics I had uncovered: the British exceptionalism that has seduced generations of our politicians into believing that 'Europe' is somewhere to escape from: the hallucinations, both positive and negative, that have driven so much of the British debate for so long. Having begun with the idea of writing a history that might call itself detached, I found myself in a process of self-instruction that now concludes, as the new currency gets under way, with the great simplicity of describing why I am a European.

The most obvious but least relevant part of this is cultural. It's easy to say how keenly I adore Schubert, and wallow in Proust, and am anticipating my next journey to consort with the shades of Virgil in the Roman Forum. But this is almost completely beside the point. European culture is the world's inheritance, absorbed on every continent, and the ability to appreciate the works of Johann Sebastian Bach, or even to speak his language, says nothing important about anyone's sense of 'being' a European.

Even Peter Lilley loves Michelangelo, as he and his colleagues never cease to explain, by way of proving that they are not anti-Europe, merely anti-'Europe': the European Union, the artefact of federalists, the dismal construct that has illicitly purloined the received identity of what Europe is held to mean these days. Lilley has a house in France, and Michael Portillo has roots in Spain, and there's a cross-party agreement that Umbro-Tuscany is where the British political classes most like to take their holidays. Does this not show their un-insular engagement with the Continent, and expose the calumny that they might be Europhobic? But the test cannot be who has heard more versions of The Ring between

Bayreuth and Covent Garden. As the boy becomes a man, the discovery that Shakespeare has a peer-group who write in different tongues may begin to broaden the mind. It is helpful to learn that these are not rival cultures, a zero-sum game of allegiance, but that they mingled and grew together. This discovery makes no demand on anyone's sense of belonging. Though the Conservative government proposed a ban on Beethoven's Ninth as the theme music for Euro 96, a football competition staged in England, it's safest to say that a taste for the Renaissance and Enlightenment is too universal to be significant. Like the travel, it proves nothing.

Very soon, therefore, what raises itself is the political question. About the culture, there is no issue. It may be important to many Eurosceptics to be able to say that because they love Mozart, they love Europe, but this isn't what the argument is about. The division between the pro- and anti-Europeans is, in the real world, about nothing more or less than the European Union. Everything else is sand in your eyes, an evasion. The EU, enlarged, or not: reformed, or not: with or without all its multiple imperfections, is the only item on the agenda.

It is not possible to be a European, in any meaningful sense, while opposing the EU. And it is not possible to support the EU without also supporting the success of the euro, and the belonging to the euro of every country that wants to call itself European.

I can think of many points which, added together, make a formidable critique of the EU. Its bureaucracy is strong, its democracy is weak, its accountability is seriously underdeveloped. The complexity of its tasks is always in danger of overwhelming the consensus needed to carry them out. Getting it to act demands formidable energy and patience and willpower from national leaders. Ensuring the singleness of the market it purports to be is work that is far from completed. Equally, I can make the case against the euro, a project which fills those who support it with almost as much anxiety as it does excitement. Will this risk, which includes a repudiation of nationhood as traditionally understood, pay off? Will its hazards be sustainable? Is the closer political integration, which it undoubtedly foretells, something that the members, with or without Britain, have the wit, will and wisdom to express in acceptable forms? These questions don't fill me with horror. Their terrain awaits a long unfolding. They assume a process not voluntarily attempted anywhere in history: tampering, by common agreement, with aspects of national identity, and working to create, in limited but significant aspects, a new kind of consciousness. To modify the nation state throughout Europe is an extraordinary ambition, full of risks and difficulties. Yet if I'm ever tempted to despair of it, I need only remind myself of the alternative world summoned up by those, most ferociously in Britain, who devote passion to dismantling it.

They've had a long time to describe this non-European Britain, and the picture, where it is clear, is not persuasive. I conclude it is not meant to be. Portillo wrote not long ago that even to ask the question was 'extraordinary'. All the future has to satisfy, in the minds of many Eurosceptics, is the need not to be 'European'. As long as it meets that test, the details hardly matter.

Thus, Little England (Scotland will be long gone from this) is, incorrigibly, a straitened place. Striving to define it, David Willetts, a Tory front-bencher, wrote a pamphlet, 'Who Do We Think We Are?', which, as well as saying our politics and economics were different from Europe, made much of the Changing of the Guard and Wensleydale cheese, calling in support some ancient paragraphs from T.S. Eliot and George Orwell to exalt the eternal time-warp in which England must be lodged. In all these tracts, the mystic chords of memory echo. Betraying history is most unimaginable, while predicting the future is subsumed into fantasy: the dream of an independent Britain, freed to assert her famous sovereignty, throwing herself on the mercy and markets of the non-European world. So the anti-Europe cave is claustrophobic. It is also being refilled (for we've been here before) with futile arrogance, making it obligatory not merely to criticize Brussels but abominate the Germans, laugh about the French, find nothing good to say about another European country, lest this betray our beleaguered sense of Britishness. A smart-ass headline writer in the *Sun* can get attention when the BBC finds an item of punning xenophobia so funny as to be worth a mention in the news.

At the heart of this is an impenetrable contradiction in the anti-Europe British mind. It cannot decide between terror and disdain. Britain is apparently so great, as well as so different, a place that she can afford to do without her Continental hinterland. But she is so puny, so endangered, so destined to lose every argument with the Continentals that she must fear for her identity if and when she makes the final commitment to belong among them. Studying the movements of sceptic thought, I see in their inability to provide a clear answer on this fundamental point a mirror of the vacillations, pro- and anti-Europe, that mark the personal histories of so many of the characters in the story. Either way, the conclusion points in the anti-Europe direction.

The same axiomatic outcome has penetrated every stage of Conservative Party thinking about the euro. While often purporting to be technical, the discussion has in fact been wholly political. First they said the euro wouldn't happen: 'a rain-dance', Major called it. Then they said it wouldn't work. Then they said it might well work. Now they say that even if it does work, it cannot work for Britain, as they edge into a position that bets their entire political future on its failure. As each prediction is falsified the threshold for the euro's acceptance is raised. Shamelessly, the playing field is tilted to make the game unwinnable, though most Tories still shrink from saying what they so plainly believe: that, as far as they're concerned, the British national identity as we know it can never co-exist with membership of the European single currency. Thus the party that took Britain into Europe prepares to fight to the last in favour of excluding Britain from what 'Europe' any longer means.

My own odyssey has been quite different. The euro presents massive political challenges, but there seems no point in being outside it, since our future – the only future anyone has been able, with any respect for realism, to describe – is entirely bound up with its success or failure. Far from the development of 'Europe' being a conceptual barrier to belonging, it's the very reason why belonging ought soon to be seen as essential. I know the snags, and will argue for some radical political reform, but the European-ness of the euro is what makes it an exciting and benign adventure. We need to be a part. It should be Britain's own millennial leap, away from the century of nation statehood, into a new time. All our neighbours are seeking a different way of bringing a better life to the Continent and its regions.

What is so strange about Britain – so particular, so fearful, so other-worldly – that she should decide to withhold her unique wisdom from the enterprise? I can reject the premise of the question because I've grown up. Allegiance, to me, no longer has to be so exclusive. I still need it, as a psychic prop, a way of belonging. But the threat to the national identity now strikes me as bogus. This categorizing is what anti-Europe people insist on, but the best evidence of its falsity is to be found in the places that have been part of the new Europe for 40 years, as against our 25. Would anyone claim that Germany is less German as a result of the experience? We are all invaded by America. If cultural defences are needed, it's against transatlantic domination. But do I hear a single soul, on either side of the Channel, contend that France is less French than it ever was because of the EU? So it will be with Britain. This reality won't come easy. Decades of propaganda defining national identity in the language of scorn for other nations can't be wiped out at a stroke. Persuading the British that they are allowed to be European should be the simplest task, yet the accretions of history, manipulated by frightened politicians, make it difficult. Though the Queen in Parliament already looks like a bejewelled dot on the ocean of the global economy, there are voices that insist the only way of being British is by proclaiming her supremacy. Redefining identity is not a task for the furtive. It cannot be done by the back door: another lesson of history. Nor will it be easily done by political leaders who still feel obliged to stand aside from the project they think they eventually want to join. But neither should the work be too alarming. In the twenty-first century, it will be exciting to escape from history into geography: from the prison of the past into a future that permits us at last the luxury of having it both ways: British and European.

## Note

1. This chapter is taken from an article in the *Guardian*, 2 January 1999.

# 41
## Jeruasalem Address:
## Europe and the Novel[1]

*Milan Kundera*

That Israel's most important prize is awarded to international literature is not, to my mind, a matter of chance but of a long tradition. Indeed, exiled from their land of origin and thus lifted above nationalist passions, the great Jewish figures have always shown an exceptional feeling for a supranational Europe – a Europe conceived not as territory but as culture. If the Jews, even after Europe so tragically failed them, nonetheless kept faith with that European cosmopolitanism, Israel, their little homeland finally regained, strikes me as the true heart of Europe – a peculiar heart located outside the body.

It is with profound emotion that I receive today the prize that bears the name of Jerusalem and the mark of that great cosmopolitan Jewish spirit. It is as a novelist that I accept it. I say *novelist*, not writer. The novelist is one who, according to Flaubert, seeks to disappear behind his work. To disappear behind his work, that is, to renounce the role of public figure. This is not easy these days, when anything of the slightest importance must step into the intolerable glare of the mass media, which, contrary to Flaubert's precept, cause the work to disappear behind the image of its author. In such a situation, which no one can entirely escape, Flaubert's remark seems to me a kind of warning: in lending himself to the role of public figure, the novelist endangers his work; it risks being considered a mere appendage to his actions, to his declarations, to his statements of position. Now, not only is the novelist nobody's spokesman, but I would go so far as to say he is not even the spokesman for his own ideas. When Tolstoy sketched the first draft of *Anna Karenina*, Anna was a most unsympathetic woman, and her tragic end was entirely deserved and justified. The final version of the novel is very different, but I do not believe that Tolstoy had revised his moral ideas in the meantime; I would say, rather, that in the course of writing, he was listening to another voice than that of his personal moral conviction. He was listening to what I would like to call the wisdom of the novel. Every true novelist listens for that suprapersonal wisdom, which explains why great novels are always a little more intelligent than their authors. Novelists who are more intelligent than their books should go into another line of work.

But what is that wisdom, what is the novel? There is a fine Jewish proverb: Man thinks, God laughs. Inspired by that adage, I like to imagine that François Rabelais heard God's laughter one day, and thus was born the idea of the first great European novel. It pleases me to think that the art of the novel came into the world as the echo of God's laughter.

But why does God laugh at the sight of man thinking? Because man thinks and the truth escapes him. Because the more men think, the more one man's thought diverges from another's. And finally, because man is never what he thinks he is. The dawn of the Modern Era revealed this fundamental situation of man as he emerged from the Middle Ages: Don Quixote thinks, Sancho thinks, and not only the world's truth but also the truth of their own selves slips away from them. The first European novelists saw, and grasped, that new situation of man, and on it they built the new art, the art of the novel.

François Rabelais invented a number of neologisms that have since entered the French and other languages, but one of his words has been forgotten, and this is regrettable. It is the word *agélaste*; it comes from the Greek and it means a man who does not laugh, who has no sense of humour. Rabelais detested the *agélastes*. He feared them. He complained that the *agélastes* treated him so atrociously that he nearly stopped writing forever.

No peace is possible between the novelist and the *agélaste*. Never having heard God's laughter, the *agélastes* are convinced that the truth is obvious, that all men necessarily think the same thing, and that they themselves are exactly what they think they are. But it is precisely in losing the certainty of truth and the unanimous agreement of others that man becomes an individual. The novel is the imaginary paradise of individuals. It is the territory where no one possesses the truth, neither Anna nor Karenin, but where everyone has the right to be understood, both Anna and Karenin.

In the third book of *Gargantua and Pantagruel*, Panurge, the first great novelistic character that Europe beheld, is tormented by the question: Should he marry or not? He consults doctors, seers, professors, poets, philosophers, who each in turn quote Hippocrates, Aristotle, Homer, Heraclitus, Plato. But after all this enormous, erudite research, which takes up the whole book, Panurge still does not know whether he should marry or not. And we, the readers, do not know either – but on the other hand, we have explored from every possible angle the situation, as comical as it is elemental, of the person who does not know whether he should marry or not.

Rabelais' erudition, great as it is, has another meaning than Descartes'. The novel's wisdom is different from that of philosophy. The novel is born not of the theoretical spirit but of the spirit of humor. One of Europe's major failures is that it never understood the most European of the arts – the novel; neither its spirit, nor its great knowledge and discoveries, nor the autonomy of its history. The art inspired by God's laughter does not by nature serve ideological certitudes, it contradicts them. Like Penelope, it undoes each night the tapestry that the theologians, philosophers, and learned men have woven the day before.

Lately, it has become a habit to speak ill of the eighteenth century, to the point that we hear this cliché: The misery that is Russian totalitarianism comes straight out of Europe, particularly out of the atheist rationalism of the Enlightenment, its belief in all-powerful reason. I do not feel qualified to debate those who blame Voltaire for the gulag. But I do feel qualified to say: The eighteenth century is not only the century of Rousseau, of Voltaire, of Holbach; it is also (perhaps above all!) the age of Fielding, Sterne, Goethe, Laclos.

Of all that period's novels, it is Laurence Sterne's *Tristram Shandy* I love best. A curious novel. Sterne starts it by describing the night when Tristram was conceived, but he has barely begun to talk about that when another idea suddenly attracts him, and by free association that idea spurs him to some other thought, then a further anecdote, with one digression leading to another – and Tristram, the book's hero, is forgotten for a good hundred pages. This extravagant way of composing the novel might seem no more than a formal game. But in art, the form is always more than a form. Every novel, like it or not, offers some answer to the question: What is human existence, and wherein does its poetry lie? Sterne's contemporaries – Fielding, for instance – particularly savoured the extraordinary charm of action and adventure. The answer we sense in Sterne's novel is a very different one: for him, the poetry lies not in the action but in the *interruption* of the action.

It may be that, indirectly, a grand dialogue took shape here between the novel and philosophy. Eighteenth-century rationalism is based on Leibniz's famous declaration: *Nihil est sine ratione* – there is nothing without its reason. Stimulated by that conviction, science energetically explores the *why* of everything, such that whatever exists seems explainable, thus predictable, calculable. The man who wants his life to have a meaning forgoes any action that hasn't its cause and its purpose. All biographies are written this way. Life is shown as a luminous trajectory of causes, effects, failures, and successes, and man, setting his impatient gaze on the causal chain of his actions, further accelerates his mad race toward death.

Against that reduction of the world to the causal succession of events, Sterne's novel, by its very form, affirms that poetry lies not in action but there where action stops; there where the bridge between a cause and an effect has collapsed and thought wanders off in sweet lazy liberty. The poetry of existence, says Sterne's novel, is in digression. It is in the incalculable. It is on the other side of causality. It is *sine ratione*, without reason. It is on the other side of Leibniz's statement.

Thus the spirit of an age cannot be judged exclusively by its ideas, its theoretical concepts, without considering its art, and particularly the novel. The nineteenth century invented the locomotive, and Hegel was convinced he had grasped the very spirit of universal history. But Flaubert discovered stupidity. I daresay that is the greatest discovery of a century so proud of its scientific thought.

Of course, even before Flaubert, people knew stupidity existed, but they understood it somewhat differently: it was considered a simple absence of knowledge, a defect correctable by education. In Flaubert's novels, stupidity is an inseparable dimension of human existence. It accompanies poor Emma throughout her days, to her bed of love and to her deathbed, over which two deadly *agélastes*, Homais and Bournisien, go on endlessly trading their inanities like a kind of funeral oration. But the most shocking, the most scandalous thing about Flaubert's vision of stupidity is this: Stupidity does not give way to science, technology, modernity, progress; on the contrary, it progresses right along with progress!

With a wicked passion, Flaubert used to collect the stereotyped formulations that people around him enunciated in order to seem intelligent and up-to-date. He put them into a celebrated *Dictionnaire des idées reçues*. We can use this title to declare: Modern stupidity means not ignorance but the *nonthought of received ideas*. Flaubert's discovery is more important for the future of the world than the most startling ideas of Marx or Freud. For we could imagine the world without the class struggle or without psychoanalysis, but not without the irresistible flood of received ideas that – programmed into computers, propagated by the mass media – threaten soon to become a force that will crush all original and individual thought and thus will smother the very essence of the European culture of the Modern Era.

Some eighty years after Flaubert imagined his Emma Bovary, during the thirties of our own century, another great novelist, Hermann Broch, wrote that however heroically the modern novel may struggle against the tide of kitsch, it ends up being overwhelmed by it. The word 'kitsch' describes the attitude of those who want to please the greatest number, at any cost. To please, one must confirm what everyone wants to hear, put oneself at the service of received ideas. Kitsch is the translation of the stupidity of received ideas into the language of beauty and feeling. It moves us to tears of compassion for ourselves, for the banality of what we think and feel. Today, fifty years later, Broch's remark is becoming truer still. Given the imperative necessity to please and thereby to gain the attention of the greatest number, the aesthetic of the mass media is inevitably that of kitsch; and as the mass media come to embrace and to infiltrate more and more of our life, kitsch becomes our everyday aesthetic and moral code. Up until recent times, modernism meant a nonconformist revolt against received ideas and kitsch. Today, modernity is fused with the enormous vitality of the mass media, and to be modern means a strenuous effort to be up-to-date, to conform, to conform even more thoroughly than the most conformist of all. Modernity has put on kitsch's clothing.

The *agélastes*, the nonthought of received ideas, and kitsch are one and the same, the three-headed enemy of the art born as the echo of God's laughter, the art that created the fascinating imaginative realm where no one owns the truth and everyone has the right to be understood. That imaginative realm of tolerance was born with modern Europe, it is the very image of Europe – or at least our dream of Europe, a dream many times betrayed but nonetheless strong enough to unite us all in the fraternity that stretches far beyond the little European continent. But we know that the world where the individual is respected (the imaginative world of the novel, and the real one of Europe) is fragile and perishable. On the horizon stand armies of *agélastes* watching our every move. And precisely in this time of undeclared and permanent war, and in this city with its dramatic and cruel destiny, I have determined to speak only of the novel. You may have understood that this is not some attempt on my part to avoid the questions considered grave. For if European culture seems under threat today, if the threat from within and without hangs over what is most precious about it – its respect for the individual, for his original thought, and for his right to an inviolable private life – then, I believe, that precious essence of the European spirit is being held safe as in a treasure chest inside the history of the novel, the wisdom of the novel. It is that wisdom of the novel I wanted to honor in this speech of thanks. But it is time for me to stop. I was forgetting that God laughs when he sees me thinking.

## Note

1. Speech delivered on the receipt of the Jerusalem Prize at the Hebrew University of Jerusalem, in the spring of 1985. Reprinted, unchanged, with permission from Milan Kundera, *The Art of the Novel* (London: Faber & Faber, 1988).

# Index

**Note**: Certain terms, to which reference is continually made, such as the Commission, Council of Ministers, European Parliament, and, of course, the European Union itself, have been excluded from the index.